GULFPORT

GULFPORT
A DEFINITIVE HISTORY

VOLUME I

LYNNE BROWN

THE History PRESS

Published by The History Press
An imprint of Arcadia Publishing
Charleston, SC
www.historypress.com

Cover Image
Front cover: Trolley #104, one of the first to be used on the streetcar line.
Back cover: "After the hunt" people gather near to admire a trophy. Courtesy Webb family.

All illustrations courtesy of the Gulfport Hisotrical Society, unless otherwise noted.

First published 2004

Manufactured in the United States

ISBN 9781596290181

Library of Congress CIP data applied for.

Notice: The information in this book is true and complete to the best of our knowledge. It is offered without guarantee on the part of the author or The History Press. The author and The History Press disclaim all liability in connection with the use of this book.

CONTENTS

Foreword

RESEARCHING THE HISTORY OF GULFPORT creates many more questions than answers. This was not a literate society; no one kept definitive journals or wrote informative letters. Instead, stories were told and retold over generations, adding here, subtracting there, until a kind of legendary mythic evolved, in which fact and fiction blend with a terrible charm. Even after incorporation as a town in 1910, no one bothered much with record keeping of any kind. When everyone knew everyone else, why write it down? Consequently some of the great gaps in the provable history can only be filled by speculation, based on as many knowns as is possible to locate at this remove.

As the late Claudette Renney Dean, a descendant of the first family, once said, "Gulfport is a city with a past, and I mean, some of it we can tell, and some of it we can't, but what we can tell, we can be proud of."

This is an attempt to tell it all.

Acknowledgements

THIS BOOK WOULD NOT HAVE been possible without the many families of Gulfport who have shared with me their ancestors' lives, photos, documents and stories. I am indebted to them all. To the officers and volunteers of the Gulfport Historical Society, much appreciation for the use of materials and resources of the Museum and for your unflagging support throughout these long years of research.

Special thanks go to several people who have generously helped in that research: Donna Boyd of the City of Gulfport, Tom Bourke of the Gulfport Public Library, and Mary Stull of Stetson University College of Law. My deepest gratitude goes to my "designated reader" Emmett Walsh, for all his invaluable comments; to Mark Epstein for technical advice; to my fellow history writer Scott Taylor Hartzell for our many long gossips over ancient events; to Jan Dutton of Small Adventures Bookstore for endless encouragement; and above all to Sherrie Lynn Shamo, Rebecca's great-great-great-granddaughter, for letting me be part of her family for a little while.

Note on Spellings

CORRECT SPELLING OF NAMES AND places was not much of a priority until rather recently. Even official documents such as tax rolls, census registers and city directories were never in agreement over how to spell the following names. In most cases I have simply made a choice and used it throughout. The following is a list of more problematic names:

Aldermen HAYNES or HAINES; McGEE or MAGEE or McGHEE.

The LEONARDY or LEONARDI family; the spellings were used interchangeably early on, though later most adopted the "Y" ending.

Hotel manager McCLAIN or McCLANE.

Farmer Charles PURRINGTON, PERRINGTON, or several other variations.

ALMERON or ALMIRON Renney.

RHOADS/RHODES/RHOADES were used interchangeably for that family.

The Steinwinder girls had names often written in familiar form; thus AURORA became ORA and RUSHA MAE, RUCHA.

The THOMES family often found their name written THOMAS, TOMES or even THUMB.

Henry Elisha (or Elisha Henry) WEATHERS or WETHERS.

The young teacher Miss Ethel DAUM suffered many various spellings of her name, the worst of which was DUMB.

The locals applied phonetic spellings to many names, thus RENNEY was pronounced RAINEY, and so often appears as such in writing. The same applies to MEASEY/MEEZIE and CUSSON/CUZZIN.

Henry SLAUGHTER chose to spell his name SLAUTER and some members of the family also used that version, but there was no uniformity to the usage, even by individuals.

Men were almost always identified by initials only, making it difficult to differentiate between members of large families with similar given names, such as the Nashes, the Renneys and the Robertses.

The BAY VIEW HOTEL was also often written BAYVIEW.

The body of water at Gulfport's front door is known today as BOCA CIEGA BAY. However, until officially changed by the United States Geographic Board in 1924, it was always written BOCA CEIGA and pronounced "CEEGA" rather than "CEE-AY-GA." I have used the earlier spelling where appropriate.

Gulfport: Essential Facts

THE CITY OF GULFPORT IS located in west central Florida, in the southwest corner of peninsular Pinellas County on the shores of Boca Ciega Bay, which is an estuarine system of the Gulf of Mexico. Incorporated in 1910, Gulfport takes in an area of approximately three square miles, and is primarily an urban residential community with a population of about thirteen thousand. Elevation varies from sea level to a height of approximately forty feet at the extreme northeast corner of the city. The climate is classified as subtropical, with mild winters and hot humid summers.

Chapter I
Rebecca's Family

1. The Arnolds and the Slaughters

When the Eve of Gulfport sailed across the Bay and took the first step onto the land that would become her home, she had already endured thirty-two years of a seemingly endless journey south along savage trails, through war and terror, births and deaths, flight and starvation. The second half of her life would be devoted to tearing a home out of this wilderness of sand and palmetto scrub, and like so many people to come after her, she would never leave again.

Rebecca Arnold had begun life in 1836 in Georgia, a stop on her family's long southern migration. From a starting point in the Carolinas, the Arnolds had followed this gradual movement, this familiar mid-nineteenth-century pattern, a few years spent digging out subsistence crops from one holding and then on to another, driven by a combination of poverty and the urge to explore new frontiers. Families were large and the small farms could not support their many sons. Younger boys were faced with few options; find another livelihood or move on.

By the early 1850s the Arnolds had arrived in north Florida, where in the spring of 1854 at Shady Grove in Madison County, a crossroads town east-southeast of Tallahassee, Rebecca married Sam Slaughter.

Samuel Butler Slaughter was the son of a man with the same name. The elder Slaughter, born in Georgia at the end of the eighteenth century, was reputed to be of a Kentucky family. Some speculation exists among his descendants that there was a connection to Daniel Boone, which may well be true. Boone did, in the 1770s, cross paths with a Colonel Thomas Slaughter, and given the sparse population of the southern frontier at that period, these Slaughters could be of the same family.

Though the Slaughters were still in Georgia when Sam was born around 1833, he and at least some of his sixteen or seventeen brothers and sisters would eventually end up, like the Arnolds, in north Florida. In 1845 the territory of Florida had become a state, still a vast and empty place with a total population of fewer than thirty-five thousand, about equally divided between black and white and almost all living in the far north. Pensacola, Tallahassee and St. Augustine were the only towns to speak of, though there were some notable county seats in the area, such as Quincy, Monticello and Madison, and it is near the latter that we find our founding families.

Rebecca's mother seems to have died during this period and her father, Herman, remarried and moved on once again. He appears to have reached Pinellas County, then known as Point Pinellas (from the Spanish, *Punta Pinal,* "point of pines"), in the spring of 1856. Some memoirs indicate he lived first near Largo and then in the Lealman area until the Civil War, during which he died. No doubt Rebecca had a number of siblings, for the name Arnold appears frequently in records of the time. Some of her brothers and sisters may have stayed in north Florida, but certainly some also traveled on with their father.

The young Slaughters were soon parents of a family of their own. Their firstborn was a girl named Martha Jane, followed by Henry Lacey and Sarah Melissa. Dates for the children's births vary greatly in recollections, but they are probably 1855, 1857 and 1860 (a granddaughter, Gladys Sawyer Girard, gave them as 1854, 1858 and 1861).

The time of conflict was perilously approaching, and despite the responsibilities of a wife and children, Sam Slaughter enlisted at the very beginning of the Civil War, avoiding conscription, which was only three months away. There may be many good reasons for this, not least of which was that service in the military could lead to an opportunity to receive land rights in the territories. Perhaps it was a matter of the money; there was a bounty given for joining and a regular stipend to those who served, a powerful incentive to a poor dirt farmer. Less charitably, it could have been a desire to exchange a life of drudgery for one of adventure and excitement. Or, of course, it may have been fervent patriotism and a commitment to the cause of the South.

Whatever his reasons, Sam became a private in Company A, 5th Regiment, Florida Infantry, on January 5, 1862. He is shown as present on just two muster rolls of that company. On the third, this note follows his name: "died at Winder Hospital, Richmond, Va., on August 18, 1862." The cause of his death was said to be pneumonia, though whether as a result of complications from a battle wound or not is unknown.

Sam Slaughter had a very short war.

2. Rebecca

It was going to be a lot longer for his widow and three children, left in what circumstances we can only imagine. What brought Rebecca south? It may have been the Civil War itself, since Union attacks on the area caused many people to withdraw to the interior or move on along that eternal southern trail.

Other than actual danger to her family and her life, it is hard to imagine a great enough reason for Rebecca to leave her familiar and settled world. But at some point she decided, as the story goes, to hire an oxcart and driver to bring her family from Madison County to the Pinellas peninsula. In this adventure she may have been along primarily as a companion to her sister Hilda, who wished to join her husband, a Major Sheffield, sometimes referred to as Ira, who was stationed at Fort Brooke in Tampa.

Often in the old recollections, which are a main source of information, ranks have been elevated over time. Privates have turned into captains with astonishing regularity. There may have been an Ira Sheffield connected with the Arnold family, but if so, he is never heard from again.

What became of the Sheffields after the war is also unclear. In one map showing the Disston Land Purchases of 1884, a large portion of Gulfport is shown as belonging to Sheffield; however, this designation appears nowhere else, though John Bethell in his history of Point Pinellas refers to Sheffield settlers without further elaboration, and Jay Starkey's memoirs also mention Sheffield cattlemen someplace along the Disston ridge.

The oxcart trip took over a month, and was an epic in itself, as the two women confronted wild animals, renegade Indians and deserters. A photograph of a very similar group—two women and three children, with an oxcart—appears in Page Jackson's book, *An Informal History of St. Petersburg*. These travelers, along with their dog, have stopped in an area of palmetto scrub and pose beside the high-wheeled cart wearing many layers of clothing and towel-like head coverings. Their luggage seems to consist of a trunk, some boxes and a couple of wooden tubs. No doubt many other people traveled in this manner at this time, but the small, stern and determined woman holding her youngest child in the foreground is just the image of the twenty-eight-year-old Rebecca one would expect.

Apparently they came first to Clearwater. Rebecca's father or some other family members may have been in the area, with Bethell's report of Herman in Clearwater in 1856, and two Arnolds, H.G. (Herman? Homer?) and M.E., mustering into Captain James McMullen's volunteer infantry company at Clear Water Harbor (as it was written then), on July 20, 1861. The company drilled for a month or two, but were never paid or formally accepted into the Confederate Army. They disbanded in October, at the expiration of their promised three months' of service.

At any rate, Rebecca's father was apparently not in Clearwater, and Clearwater was not to her liking. With twelve families already settled there, she felt it was "too crowded," according to her descendants. However, by this time she was quite destitute and in need of some means to feed her children, so she moved again, to Fort Brooke, where she found work as a cook or hospital attendant or perhaps some of both.

Fort Brooke had been established in 1823 as a military post in the middle of the huge Indian reservation formed by the Treaty of Moultrie Creek. Lieutenant Colonel George Mercer Brooke chose the site on the east bank of the Hillsborough River where it enters the bay and stationed four companies of militia there to "protect" the Seminoles. It had seen its best days before the great hurricane of 1848, which destroyed most of the buildings, but was reactivated as an outpost at the onset of the Civil War.

It seems possible to place Rebecca at Fort Brooke in May 1864, when the fort fell briefly to the Yankees. She had expected to find her father and brother (or brother-in-law) at the fort, but they were not there. A number of Confederate troops had formed a sort of cowboy detail, keeping cattle available for provisions, quite likely the type of work in which the Arnolds may have had experience. This "Cow Cavalry" was away on a cattle drive when the Union ship *Adele* came into the bay, captured Fort Brooke, spiked the large cannons, took away the smaller one and destroyed many of the fort's facilities. Again the place changed hands, when the Confederates returned and reoccupied the fort for a few days, until the Union troops got the upper hand once more and were in charge for another month.

Rebecca and Hilda and the children survived this turmoil by fleeing into the woods, a time during which Rebecca reached perhaps the low point of all her adventures, for starvation became more than an idle threat. How could she have come to such a predicament? Not so long ago she had had a husband, a nice little farm and well-fed babies. Unless she was a remarkably altruistic woman, she probably blamed Sam Slaughter for a lot of it.

3. James Barnett

James Barnett was about the same age as Sam Slaughter, but from an entirely different part of the world and way of life. Born in the Bahamas it is said, to a long line of Irish clergymen, he chose a remarkably uncharitable career. He became a wrecker, which was a rather polite name for pirate. In many ways, Barnett and Slaughter, who would combine with Rebecca Arnold to settle and populate Gulfport, represent the two sides of the future citizenry. The Slaughters were land people, solid and tied to the earth, hardworking, honest and maybe a little bit drab, while the Barnetts were sea folk, mercurial and adventurous, full of humor and daring.

The early wreckers were nautical experts, sailors, shipbuilders and travelers throughout the world. They came to America from the Bahamas by way of Key West, Florida, after their vocation was legitimatized in an 1828 superior court decision. Before 1828, it was officially ruled that cargo belonged to the first salvage crew reaching a doomed ship; however, the United States, a growing naval power, would not condone the removal of the cargo to a foreign port. The easiest way for these wildcat Bahamians to avoid trouble was to take up American citizenship and to establish homes and warehouses in Key West, which was a world of its own and a strange one at that, sometimes called the beginning and the end of civilization.

Key West was a foremost source of that much-needed commodity, salt, and so Union forces occupied it during the Civil War. This required that an escape route be plotted for those who did not support Federalism, which the people of Key West, in general, did not. They were fishermen, smugglers, wreckers and traders, whose ties were to Havana and Key West itself. The United States Government, with its many rules and regulations, was actively disliked. Getting out was easy for people whose very home was more sea than land, so they easily evaded the blockades and made their way to Tampa and Fort Brooke.

James Barnett was one of those Key Westers, called "Conchs," who, along with the Bethells and the Mirandas, the Currys and the Lowes, the Robertses, Sawyers and Renneys, would end up as Pinellas founders. When the Civil War began, they joined as much for the adventure as for any philosophical or political position.

Barnett had first become involved in the Civil War when Brigadier General J.M. Taylor called into service a detachment of coast guard in the summer of 1861. In charge of this unit was Second Lieutenant Abel Miranda (here spelled "Able Merander"), the "swashbucklin', fiery Florida Spaniard" who would play a foremost role in the settlement of Gulfport. John Bethell and five others made up the rest of the detachment, which was disbanded early in September. Barnett then joined Captain Henry Mulrennan's Florida Volunteer Coast Guards, which was organized and called into service by Special Order No. 2 issued from the Adjutant General's office in Tallahassee in November, enlisting on the first of December.

After the disbandment of this unit he apparently stayed around the Tampa area, for in April 1862, he appears on the roll of Captain Robert B. Smith's Company K, 7th Florida Infantry, in Tampa. Bethell was a lieutenant of this troop and there are other familiar names in its ranks, including two men who married sisters of William Roberts, another Key Wester whose descendants would merge with Rebecca's to become one of Gulfport's early families.

On January 28, 1864, seventeen members of Company K wrote to the secretary of the Confederate Navy from their camp near Dalton, Georgia, with the following request: "[We] being seamen by profession and having followed a sea-faring life up to the commencement of the war, do respectfully petition that we may be transferred from the above mentioned company and regiment, to the Navy of the Confederate States, and further that if transferred we may be assigned to the C.S.S. Savannah." James Barnett was the second to sign.

On February 15, the commander in charge, with the approval of the secretary of the navy, forwarded the request to James Seddons, Secretary of War, and the seventeen petitioners were sent to Flag Officer Hunter, Commanding Naval Forces at Savannah. On June 3, the Ram *Savannah* engaged the United States War Ship *Water Witch* and James suffered a serious wound, variously reported as in the side or in a leg, which would cause him a lifetime of pain and an early death some twenty-two years later.

According to the *Service Records of Confederate Enlisted Marines* by Ralph W. Donnelly, a James "Barrett" (Private, Company E) of the CSS *Savannah* was captured at Fort Fisher, North Carolina, on January 15, 1865, and sent as a prisoner of war to Point Lookout, Maryland, where he was immediately placed on the roll of sick prisoners. One James "Barnett," listed only as a seaman in the C.S.N., is described as of fair complexion, with light brown hair and blue eyes, five feet eight and a quarter inches tall. All prisoners were released in June 1865, after swearing an oath of allegiance to the United States.

Our James was sent to Fort Brooke to recuperate.

4. James and Rebecca

In April 1866, while still in Tampa, James Barnett married the widow Rebecca Arnold Slaughter, who had been introduced to him by John Bethell's sister Eliza Miranda. He was then about thirty-three years old, and apparently had never married before, while she, at thirty, was the mother of three young children. It is probably pointless to speculate on the reasons for this union; wounded soldiers are not unlikely to fall for their caretakers, and perhaps Rebecca was that to James during his recuperation. From her viewpoint, another marriage was next to necessity, and the match a distinct improvement in her status. However, for James, as a man so badly wounded that he never quite recovered, it is a somewhat surprising venture. Children could, of course, be helpful in homesteading, especially boys. However, Henry was only about eight, and Sarah Melissa may have been as young as five or six. James was taking on a large new responsibility.

The first two years of their marriage are another matter for speculation. There is some indication in one family recollection that they traveled first to Bradenton, or at least the Manatee area, though another source places them on the Alafia River in Hillsborough County. Whatever they tried to do and wherever they tried to do it, whether fishing or farming, life was not satisfactory. The story goes that James had seen the bluff at the center of Gulfport's waterfront during his days patrolling the coast as a blockade runner, possibly even camped there, using it as a lookout point in his surveillance of the Union Navy, and the pleasant, isolated site had remained at the back of his mind.

Carl Norberg, in *Our Story of Gulfport*, wrote the following imaginary version of the Barnetts' landing:

A small sailing craft cautiously worked its way toward a wild coastline showing no visible signs of habitation. Frequently the captain thrust a long pole into the water, testing its depth. Finally he brought his sloop into the breeze, flapping sails rustled down to the deck, and an anchor was heaved over the side. The date was 1868, the year that Florida returned to the Union. Captain James Barnett, recent Confederate officer, was feeling his wounds of battle as he relaxed a moment to scan a worn piece of brown wrapping paper that was his chart and map. This was the area he was determined to explore in order to stake out the first parcel of land to be settled in what was to become the City of Gulfport.

After two futile years at Manatee, Barnett was impatient to make a home here for his wife and family and to start a farm for their livelihood. By good fortune, he had anchored off what is now 52nd Street, at a point where depth of water was favorable and a series of bluffs promised safety from heavy storms. Eagerly he boarded his small boat, leaving his wife Rebecca and her young ones safe on board the larger craft and with a few supplies, rowed toward the sandy beach to set foot upon his new domain. In the days that followed he explored the interior and was happy with what he found—that is, high level ground, rich soil, and wild game aplenty. Not a single person was in sight. Determined now, he staked out his claim, returned to his family and set sail for Tampa, the County seat and U.S. Land Office, where he made his purchase and filed for record. This done, he replenished supplies and returned to his new home site with his wife.

A perhaps more accurate report has the Barnetts arriving on the boat of a "Mr. Tompkins," which may indeed have been the case, since there was an English sailor, Ambrose George Tompkins, born in 1832, who lived with the Barnetts until his death. Tompkins had been put off his ship in Miami during the Civil War, and according to the tale, crossed the Everglades on foot to Fort Myers, where he joined the Union Navy and took charge of a supply boat. How this brought him to the Barnetts' acquaintance is not known, but he did drift back to stay around 1870, and remained for several years.

The palmetto hut they constructed must have been extremely primitive, even by standards of the era. Still, the bay was pristine and clear and teeming with fish, game roamed the woods and fruits and berries abounded. For people used to drawing sustenance from the land, they might well have been in worse locations.

They were, however, very much alone.

5. Point Pinellas

The land that would become Pinellas County was almost uninhabited. The part of that land to become Gulfport was completely uninhabited. One outstanding difference between pioneer Pinellas and the western American frontier was the virtual absence of a native population.

The Native Americans had once been here, of course, and in large numbers. Centuries ago, the ocean level was much lower, and since settlement tends to follow shorelines, remnants of the earliest human habitation have long been lost to the rising waters of the gulf and Tampa Bay. In more recent times, Point Pinellas was home to a rather large community of latecomers, Native Americans variously called Timucuan, Calusa, Tocobaga, who lived by the bounty of the shallow bays.

These people were quite primitive, without the methods and materials of farming beyond some corn cultivation, without a written language, without even simple technologies such as metalworking or the wheel. They built mounds, some forty or fifty of which survived around the Point until the coming of the white settlers. These mounds served three quite separate purposes; some were burial sites, some were of a religious nature and some were simply kitchen middens, scrap heaps of discarded shells and other refuse. Few have lasted to the present, having long since been leveled unceremoniously, without a thought to their historic or archaeological value.

As far as has been ascertained, no mounds ever existed in the three square miles that have become Gulfport, although some have suggested there was originally one on Barnett's bluff. Neither were there any Native Americans since the early eighteenth century, the Tocobaga having died of white men's diseases, succumbed to capture, or simply left after decades of attack and destruction by European invaders.

Since the days of Spanish exploration and conquest, there had been a Hispanic presence in Florida. Missions were established across the northern part of the state, and simple fish camps at the southern end, on both east and west coasts. The Native Americans, who were peaceful unless brutalized (which often happened), provided workers for these fish *ranchos*, as they were called, and came to be known by the English as "Spanish Indians." These folk were by no means entirely of the original stock, having blended over the years with Cubans, free blacks and escaped slaves, and the southward-migrating Creeks known as Seminoles.

The Treaty of Fort Moultrie in September of 1823 forced the Native Americans to agree to move south of Ocala and stay inland, which brought up another complication for men like Antonio Maximo Hernandez, who had operated since the mid-1810s a *rancho* approximately where Eckerd College and Maximo Park are now located, and William Bunce, running a *rancho* on the islands with some thirty or so workers, twenty of them Spanish Indians. By the 1830s, Bunce was held in violation of the treaty's terms and ordered to remove his Indian workers from the coast. He petitioned the Indian Agent, stating that his workers had lived all their lives together at the camp, had intermarried, spoke Spanish and knew no other way of life except fishing. The petition was in vain. In 1840, the commander of Fort Brooke sent off a detail to burn him out of business.

There were no more Spanish Indians around Point Pinellas.

6. The Bethells and the Spaniards

On August 4, 1842, the Homestead Act was passed. Better known as the "armed occupation" act, it provided that any United States citizen over the age of eighteen and willing and able to bear arms, who could clear five acres, build a home and live there five years, would be granted the land. It was designed to eliminate what few pockets of Native American resistance remained, and fill the empty peninsula with permanent settlers. Perhaps it was this law that brought the Slaughters and the Arnolds to Florida.

There was a much greater response to the offer in the northern part of the state, which is quite understandable, as farming becomes more difficult with the approach to the sub-tropics. In the entire area of the future Pinellas County there were only twenty-four applicants, and these were almost all at the northern end, from Clearwater and beyond. The southern part of Pinellas was not attractive to farmers, as this lack of response to the Homestead Act demonstrates. It was, and would remain for quite some time, the place where fishermen lived.

The few early settlers were deeply affected by the great hurricane of 1848, which reportedly left most of Pinellas under water for a time and changed the face of the barrier islands. Maximo Hernandez, for instance, lost everything, gave up and went back to Cuba, never to return. There was almost no one left living in the southern area, except those who passed by to fish and hunt turtles. One of these was John A. Bethell, who, like so many in Pinellas at the mid-point of the nineteenth century, was a Key Wester with family antecedents in the Bahamas, and before that, England. In 1859, John and his brother William put up a fish *rancho* just about where Maximo had sited his.

Another was Abel "Cat" Miranda, a descendant of Minorcan immigrants to St. Augustine. He had served in the first volunteer company of Captain Richard Turner as an Army scout during the Indian wars, arriving on the peninsula perhaps as early as 1857. He claimed some land along Big Bayou, a large inlet just north of today's Coquina Key, and there established a fish *rancho*. His wife Eliza, whom he had married in 1850, was an older sister of John Bethell.

In 1862, Miranda was blamed for the murder of Scott Whitehurst, who had been shot and killed from ambush while apparently delivering cattle to the Unionists. No doubt Bethell was involved as well, but it was only Miranda who suffered, when his homestead was raided and burned, his crops, animals and boats destroyed. He and Bethell made their way to Tampa in an old rowboat, and returned to take their families to safety. For the rest of the war, Miranda was a rabid blockade-runner, causing considerable consternation to the Union forces. When he returned to Point Pinellas in 1866, he moved inland to a more protected site, and John and Sarah Bethell took over his old place at Big Bayou. Thus the Mirandas and the Bethells were the entire population of southern Pinellas when the Civil War came to an end and the Barnetts arrived to homestead five miles to the west, separated by an impenetrable wilderness marked only by dim cattle trails, or a day's sail in good weather.

The population increased by one when Sarah's cousin, fifteen-year-old Alex Leonardi, came to live with the Bethells. Alex's and Sarah's ancestors, like Miranda's, had migrated to America from Minorca in 1768, when East Florida was under the sovereignty of England, as was the small Mediterranean island of Minorca, where Dr. Andrew Turnbull, a London physician, sought colonists to populate his new world land grant. The Leonardis arrived with some fifteen hundred other settlers and were taken to Las Mesquites, today's New Smyrna Beach. In a few years, disease and crop failure had driven them away from their settlement and to the gates of St. Augustine, where they appear as a farm family on that city's 1786 census.

Around 1808 Bartolome Leonardi married Antonia Bonelli, a young woman who had survived capture by the Miccosukees in her early teens. Among their own nine children, all born in St. Augustine, were Alex's father Vincent (born

1820) and Florencia (born 1810), the mother of Sarah Bethell. These two, along with some sisters and brothers, moved to Tampa shortly after Vincent's 1849 marriage to Venancia Andreu.

The youngest of Florencia's daughters, Mary Eliza, then sixteen, left a memoir of the trip. "[We] came by stage coach from St. Augustine to Picolotta on the St. Johns river, thence by boat to Palatka, traveling afterwards in a canvas-covered wagon drawn by two horses, down to Tampa, which [we] reached without molestation from the dreaded Indians." When they arrived in the "gay, sociable little village" of Tampa, they found "only a handful of people" living there, besides a small detachment of soldiers at Fort Brooke.

Alexander Florenz Leonardi was the second of Vincent's eight children. He arrived here from Key West in a schooner purchased after the accidental drowning of its previous captain, a man named Roberts. His partner in this venture was Frank Futch, who, like Alex, would some years later marry a Slaughter daughter. Alex stayed with John and Sarah Bethell until his father moved here later in 1868 to homestead forty acres along the trail that ran westward from Big Bayou. Vincent was a skilled carpenter and master builder, known to have worked on some fine houses in Tampa before the Civil War. The little cabin he built for himself, though, was far from a model home. Fifty years afterward, a fellow pioneer recalled that between the logs were cracks big enough to let in skunks and other nighttime marauders who thumped around cleaning out cans, their toenails scratching across the floor.

Two grapefruit trees at either end of Vincent's porch were grafted to produce a grove, which developed fruit of an unusually attractive flavor and appearance that became known as "Leonardi grapefruit." As the story goes, Abel Miranda had given Vincent a basket of particularly heavy, large and sweet oranges, from a tree that grew from budded grapefruit stock. Vincent saved and planted the seeds of these oranges; they grew rapidly and within five years produced small, orange-like grapefruit, which became for a time quite popular. The variety did not reproduce well, however, and eventually died out, though at least one of the original trees survived to the mid-twentieth century, by then growing bent and gnarled, and almost parallel to the ground.

The 1870s saw the arrival of the final settlers to have an immediate effect on the population and growth of Gulfport. First to come, in September 1874, were the New Orleans contingent, true homesteaders who brought with them their families and intended to stay, establishing a community they called "New Cadiz."

One such was Richard (or Ricardo) Strada, who traveled here by boat to Cedar Key, then onward to Clearwater and Point Pinellas. He was about thirty-one, Spanish-born and carried with him a good reputation as a sculptor. Unfortunately not much more is known about his work as an artist, except that he may have carved some cemetery stones. Strada had a daughter, Sophie, age three, and two stepchildren, John and Virginia, from his marriage to a widow named Mary Young. He bought some eighty acres in the Maximo area, in the general vicinity of today's 38th Avenue and 37th Street South, a site discovered more than a century later to have contained a series of Indian mounds. (Strada himself would live nearly a century to the age of ninety-seven.)

Ricardo Strada (1843?-1940) with two youngsters he adopted in later life.

Virginia Young, only fourteen at the time of their arrival, soon met and married William John Roberts, one of the Bahamian/Key West seamen with connections to the local settlers. The July 1877 wedding was held in Tampa, after a sail across the Bay on one of Roberts' regular bi-monthly trips for mail and provisions.

Also on the *Angelina* with the Stradas were some members of the Puig and Kimball families, a clan of brothers and sisters, who settled across Clam Bayou from the Barnetts. Their friend Joseph (or Jose) Torres was another New Orleans import critical to Gulfport's history. Like the Puigs (whose name was pronounced, locally at least, "Pooch"), Torres was of Spanish origin. Reputedly a former soldier in Maximilian's Mexican campaign, he arrived here with the reputation of a carpetbagger due to his activities in Reconstruction-era New Orleans, but also with the two most important qualities a fledgling community could ask: money and enthusiasm.

Eighteen eighty-two map of West Hillsborough County showing location of Bonifacio (Gulfport) and Big Bayou, as well as homesteads of Tim Kimball and Ricardo Strada.

7. Barnetts' Bluff

Life in Pinellas was, to say the least, fitted only for the hardy. The first arrivals got wet, they got bitten by a variety of creatures and they ate whatever they could find. The ecology of Gulfport was not particularly inviting. Virgin forest of closely spaced pine trees was literally impenetrable in places, as were the stands of palmettos, patches of saw grass and coastal growth of mangroves. There were a variety of deciduous oaks and a small scrubby brush called willow oak. A good part of the land surrounding the bayou had been built by the mangrove stands themselves, for as they grow, they send down roots toward the sea floor, which then put up new plants. This complex maze of roots traps whatever mud and debris happens by, and eventually it accumulates, dries out and becomes new land. The bluff where the Barnetts alit, then, was probably about the only place along the entire shoreline where they could have done so.

The immediate area was served by a few small streams, providing fresh water, a necessity until wells could be dug. In general, east-running creeks were long and sluggish, and those flowing west short and few. One such ran southward across 28th Avenue somewhere in the vicinity of 51st Street, and swung slightly west to emerge into the Bay at about 52nd Street. This no doubt also encouraged the establishment of a settlement there, for if too far from a source of potable water, one had to carry it by the barrelful in an oxcart, not an enviable chore.

Game was still plentiful in the 1870s, some of it edible and some of it extremely inhospitable. There were large animals such as deer, bear and panthers, and smaller creatures like bobcats, foxes, skunks, rabbits and gophers. There were plenty of birds around, although none of the large rookeries found elsewhere in Pinellas existed in the immediate Gulfport area. Still, wild turkeys, ducks and coveys of small birds were always evident. If the larder got low enough, there were always squirrels and possums. On the down side, there were alligators, snakes, mosquitoes, gnats, sand-flies, spiders and scorpions, fleas and roaches, all in abundant quantities.

Seafood was the dependable constant. Mullet were so plentiful in the Bay that they could be caught with a pitchfork, or so it was said. No pioneer home existed without a barrel of mullet salted in brine sitting outside the back door. But there were also shark, devil fish, jewfish, tarpon, kingfish, grouper, amberjack, bonito, sea trout, snapper, channel bass and others, plus oysters, stone crabs, scallops, coquinas and clams. For this reason and this alone, nobody starved to death in the early days of settlement. Everybody subsisted by fishing.

This area was not really suitable for farming. Despite later developers' ravings over a lush tropical setting in which crops flourished, the soil here was by no means fertile. In the flat woods of the southern peninsula, only grass and palmetto grew in inhospitable salt marsh or beach sand lacking organic content. One pessimist who was disappointed in his attempts claimed the "soil" would grow nothing but pine needles.

Wild cattle (hogs, too) still roamed freely throughout Pinellas. Descendants of long-ago Spanish imports, they had been collected primarily by Tampa stockmen and gathered into herds, periodically rounded up and sold to beef-hungry military and Cuban markets. Individual homesteaders caught them for a source of milk and meat, but each person was responsible for fencing in his own land to keep the free-range herds away from his personal livestock and crops. Areas where the cattle had been rounded up did provide local farmers with the best ready-made planting sites, thoroughly plowed and fertilized. Neither the cattle nor the hogs were as we picture them today, for they too lived on subsistence food. Without the lush grassy plains that supported them in the Midwest, for example, the cows remained small and scrawny, and the thin wild hogs provided only meat that was "dark and tough." The smart settler would pen them in for awhile and fatten them up as much as possible, then improve them still further by cooking over a slow hickory fire in a smokehouse. Many of the early folks of Hispanic descent made a sort of stew from hog heart, liver and lungs called *gudinga.*

Agriculture was complicated by the fact that these pioneers were not very familiar with a sub-tropical climate. It took some time and some experimentation to discover what would survive here. Without question, it was difficult. Cold spells did happen, and could wipe out an entire planting. Wild animals and birds ate the produce before it could be harvested. Moles could destroy a whole vegetable patch in very little time.

Citrus became the most dependable crop. Oranges, which originated in southern China, had been brought in seed form to the New World with the Spanish explorers and spread through cultivation by both white and Native American populations. In the nineteenth century, the cash potential of citrus was recognized, and many acres were set with the small native orange trees. These withstood about everything the ecosystem could throw at them until the great freezes of the 1890s, when the trees themselves were destroyed along with the current crop of fruit. With the industry in the northern part of the state wiped out, growers moved south, bringing serious orange cultivation to the Pinellas peninsula, where until then citrus had been a private venture, every homeowner planting and nourishing a few oranges or lemons in his own backyard.

At other times, there were attempts at growing limes, strawberries, citrons, figs, wild guavas ("so sour they would make a pig squeal"), bananas, coconuts, dates, loquat, grapes, avocados or alligator pears, pomegranates and pecans. Sea grapes grew naturally in wild profusion and made fine jelly when they turned purple; Clam Bayou had among its many names over the years the appellation Seagrape Point. Pawpaws (some locals used the term pawpaw and papaya interchangeably, though these are two completely different kinds of fruit) were another small wild fruit, which grew in patches of sandy soil throughout the area. These strange little members of the custard apple family, native only to Florida, were just barely edible to some people, though by no means to everyone. A particularly good stand of them was found well into the twentieth century in the block known today as Chase Park.

The staple of the vegetable garden was the sweet potato. People recall that they were served at every meal, sometimes in more than one form—baked, fried, roasted in the coals, grated into a pone or made into a variety of pies and puddings. "They feed you sweet potatoes three times a day," one disgruntled visitor wrote. Mary Emma Leonardi shot so many marauding deer in her sweet potato patch it was said her muzzle loader split on the end and had to be sawed off to a mere eighteen inches.

Turnips and their greens were another common food, as well as cabbage, pumpkins, black-eyed peas and corn. Even the bud of the cabbage palm was used; it could be ground into a base for bread making.

Life in a pine forest had another drawback. The smell of turpentine pervaded everything, including the chickens whose diet was mostly pine nuts, and the eggs they produced. There were some small turpentine stills here, but it was further north that processing pine byproducts had become a major industry. Building a small wood fire distillery was not complicated and the raw gum was easily gathered by notching a cavity into the trees. Heating the gum created a solid residue of rosin, which was used in adhesives and soaps, and the vapors were distilled into turpentine, an extremely handy substance that was the basis for everything from liniments to toothpaste. Other byproducts were pine tar and pitch used to caulk ships' hulls and waterproof riggings. Many physicians of the time felt that breathing turpentine was healthy, and moreover that application of it to almost any kind of wound—sting, puncture, cut, bite, etc.—was a sure cure. A spoonful of sugar with a few drops of turpentine was an almost universal remedy for colds and other minor illnesses.

So while some settlers came here expecting a tropical paradise of beautiful flowers, white sandy beaches and glorious sunsets, what they got was snakes, mosquitoes, smudgepots of cow dung and the overwhelming reek of turpentine and fish, not to mention the hostile climate, which could wipe out a lifetime's work with one touch of a hurricane. A lot of them left.

8. The Family

Why those who did remain chose such a difficult life is a profound and unanswerable question. The Barnetts, for example, must have stood upon that small bluff in the middle of a mangrove marsh and tidal flats and taken some very swift actions simply to survive. First came the erection of some kind of shelter. A primitive camp could be made by driving some posts into the ground and laying out an elevated bed. Palmetto fronds provided some protection when woven into a kind of hut.

Cooking was over an open fire with the one thing they almost certainly had brought with them, an iron pot. A piece of cast iron cookware was a precious possession. It was handed down between generations, it accompanied settlers wherever they traveled; it was the one indispensable item that could not be fabricated or simulated in any way. An iron wash pot was very necessary to survival, said Julia Howell Dowling in her recollections. "Clothes were boiled once a week and certain meats were cooked off at hog killing time and soap was made—all with the same pot." Making a stove was easy. Logs were built up in a frame filled with sand to hold the fire. Sleeping and cooking could thus be managed. Fighting off the insects, snakes and alligators was left to individual invention.

At first, the Barnetts probably built a cabin of one room only. Lumber was certainly plentiful enough, and the land would have to be cleared anyway if any kind of crop was to be planted. So down came the pine trees, cut with crude axes, the tops and brush trimmed off and burned. A simple drawknife was used to peel the bark, eliminating as many insects as possible. Then the logs were sized and stacked, notching each to fit as the walls rose in a basic foursquare format, with a roof of palmetto thatch. These homes were not unlike the simplest form of living accommodation known to man since prehistoric times.

But the log cabin had some serious difficulties. There were almost more chinks and gaps than solid wall surface. These were stuffed with anything that came to hand: mud, Spanish moss, more palmetto fronds or a kind of homemade lime made from crushed oyster shells. But nothing really kept out any of the biting, stinging natural denizens. A nightly ritual involved burning something in every room just before extinguishing the lights in order to discourage as many mosquitoes as possible. This, then, was life on the immediate Pinellas frontier of hammock, swamp and salt marsh. Days cutting and clearing the scrub brush and pine forest, hunting, fishing and foraging for food, nights trying to sleep in a shelter that offered little protection from the elements and the predators.

There were no neighbors, and no roads. Some rough cattle trails did exist, thanks to the Tampa stockmen and their cowboys. There was a sort of path

A typical log cabin of the period set amid pines and palmettos. *Courtesy Cloe Dance*

across the peninsula, the old way west from Big Bayou, skirting the northern shore of Salt Lake (now Lake Maggiore). Still called Lakeview by many older residents, this route has become 22nd Avenue South, or, within Gulfport's borders, Gulfport Boulevard. Another trail ran north and south; it would become first Disston Avenue and then 49th Street. But in early days these were only clearings in the vegetation, grubbed or worn down in some places to the sand, with no improvements at all, and no bridges across the many little creeks and streams.

We hope the Barnetts had a sailboat, but even that is not certain, for if they did indeed come with Mr. Tompkins, he and his boat were no doubt not always at their disposal. Even with a boat, of course, the Bay was occasionally too rough to be navigable. When they could sail round to do so, they could have gone to Tampa or Bradenton for supplies or to visit the Bethells, Mirandas and Leonardis. Otherwise, though not far in miles, the overland trip to these homesteads would have been a fairly challenging undertaking.

They had by now some children of their own. Julia (some family stories indicate the possibility that Julia was illegitimate) was born in 1867, either at Tampa or during the Manatee stay. James, Jr., born in 1873, is often called the first white child to be born in Gulfport, but that should perhaps be amended to "first white boy," as his older sister Mary Elizabeth was born in May of 1872 and there is nothing to suggest that her birth occurred anywhere else. Of course it may very well be possible that Rebecca chose to deliver this child in some slightly more civilized area. The Barnetts' final child was another girl, Laura Inez, born in 1877. While these four survived, some two or three more were lost at birth or shortly thereafter.

In 1873, Martha Slaughter was about eighteen and during that year married Alex Leonardi. Melissa was in her early teens when the Barnett babies started to appear; she would later marry Alex's old partner Frank Futch. Young Henry Slaughter left home at the age of fifteen to strike out on his own. The reason for this departure can only be a matter of guesswork. Did he have an unfortunate relationship with his mother's new husband? Was he tired of his incessant chores in this household, one of which was the cooking-off of salt for his family? Or was it a more usual occurrence than we can today imagine for a boy so young to leave home and make his own way in the world? Whatever the reason, Henry moved a few miles eastward and chose a plot of land neighboring the homesteads of Mirandas, Puigs, Kimballs, Bethells and Leonardis. It would take him five years of hard work as both farmer and boatman to save up the $40 required to buy this section from the state, but that he would do.

Henry's land contained in a corner one of the great old shell mounds, a particularly peaceful place, naturally protected by oaks and magnolias. For that reason, as well as its elevation above the often-flooded lowlands, it was an obviously perfect site for a graveyard, and may have been used as such by some of the early fish *rancho* folk far back in the century. While Emma Kimball, who survived her arrival in Pinellas by only a month, was probably the first settler to rest in the mound, she was soon joined by William and Virginia Roberts' first daughter. After the Roberts' request for the interment of their baby in this safe, dry spot, Henry gave permission for a small segment, perhaps two-and-one-half acres, to be set aside for the community's burials.

It would not be long, though, before Henry would have to give up his dream of being a landowner. In November of 1879 he sold his hard-earned property, including the little cemetery, to William Roberts for $31. Henry then returned home, to help Rebecca, who was laboring ever more alone as Jim Barnett's condition worsened.

"Henry's Cemetery" would become known by many names over time—the Disston City Cemetery, Glen Oak Cemetery—and it was for years the only burying ground in that part of the Point. It also became more than just a cemetery; it was a meeting place that united the sparsely spread settlers for picnics, gatherings and outdoor worship, until some years later a church would be built on the site. Glen Oak would grow to contain many graves, as one by one the pioneers came to rest there, including James Barnett, and then Rebecca. The burial ground still exists, though in complete disrepair, at 20th Avenue South and Auburn Street, just west of 26th Street South.

In 1876 Joseph Torres bought out the Barnetts' land and improvements and settled down on the bluff, while James and Rebecca moved north of their original holding, adding another 120 acres purchased from the state. The reason for the Barnetts sale of their waterfront acreage has been given as the fact that James was "ailing." Each year, apparently, the disabilities he had incurred in the war grew more bothersome. The question remains, however, why would it have been better to move and start all over again, building a new home, planting a new garden, setting out new citrus trees?

There is the possibility that the Barnetts' eight or nine years of work had brought them enough profit, so that, along with Torres' payment, they may have been able to afford help in establishing their new homestead. This area, covering several blocks today, was located along what is now 49th Street South, westward to about 51st Street and from 24th to 26th Avenues South.

Here the Barnetts more than likely had a larger and more comfortable cabin, crops in the ground and the beginnings of a citrus grove. The better of these cabins were elevated above the ground, offering some protection against the elements and the animals and may indeed have kept out some of the dampness but few of the snakes and bugs. Roofs developed large overhangs, to protect porches, which ran around two or three sides of the structure (many homes had a screened box called a shakedown just inside the door, where one brushed off mosquitoes with a palm frond before entering the living space). More sophisticated carpentry provided handmade shingles for the roof and pine planks for the floors. Some families, such as the Leonardis, had brought in lumber from Key West and built extremely sturdy little houses, constructed like boats, with wooden pegs instead of nails. Whittling these pegs was a nightly chore, as all family members worked together to have a supply ready for the next day.

Real beds were built, with frames of wood strung with rope, and mattresses were made, stuffed with palm fronds, Spanish moss or pine needles, or if very elegant, feathers. Chairs and tables were not difficult to put together. Soon a level of comfort, perhaps only of the most basic kind, but still an improvement over the early camps, began to exist.

Cloth was very precious and difficult to come by. Muslin for bed hangings to protect against mosquitoes was the first need, and after that came clothing, which here was far more utilitarian than fashionable. Hoops and bustles, hats and bonnets and Victorian styles and colors reigned elsewhere. In the pioneer south, women wore long skirts and blouses of homespun or gingham. They might have had one gown of calico or alpaca for dressing up, though that couldn't have been much of a priority. Men had rough shirts and trousers and heavy shoes, sometimes one black suit. The one indispensable accessory was a hat of straw or palmetto.

Evelena Leonardi, one of Vincent's daughters, was credited by her daughter Bertha Strauss with introducing to the area the art of making such hats. "The palmetto buds must be picked at just the right time . . . opened by hand and placed in the sun to bleach," she said. "This requires about three days according to the brightness of the sun. Next, the palmettos are placed for two or three nights in the dew and are brought indoors during the daytime. The straws then are stripped fine or coarse according to the weave desired." It is not only for fishing that these hats are made. Mrs. Strauss remembered the Sunday-go-to-meeting hats she wore as a little girl. "They were fancy braided with colored cloth linings under the brim . . . flowers made from palmettos at the crown or a band to match the lining. I'd dash around in a hat like that feeling right kipper," she said.

Children wore a kind of overall of some sturdy cloth, and usually didn't bother with shoes during the years of rapidly growing feet. People in later life almost invariably recalled how they earned their first store-bought shoes, a purchase that came at a considerable price for these families. One told of days spent feeding cane stalks into the juicing rollers of a mill. Another caught and sold skunk hides: "She had to live in the smoke house for a few days, but she got her shoes and they were good ones."

There were a few other things that simply had to be purchased. Flour was one, and at the price of $25 a barrel, it was not bought very often. Biscuits were an extremely rare treat. Coffee was another, and while not the staple that flour is, settlers did want it and sometimes sacrificed to buy it, generally in the form of green beans, which they baked and ground. When that was impossible, black-eyed peas or parched corn kernels could be substituted to make a kind of drink that would have to do. Other things that inevitably cost money rather than effort were nails, matches and gunpowder. Everything else was homemade. Grease and ashes were saved to make lye soap; an unpleasant process if ever there was one. Salt was distilled and candles dipped. Dolls, medicines, seesaws and jump ropes, bed linens, wagons, washing tubs and water barrels—you made it or you did without.

9. The Centennial

Eighteen seventy-six was the Centennial Year, which heralded an era of renewed optimism about the future of the Union. The country was recovering from a period of depression earlier in the 1870s, and political changes were evident not only in the South but throughout the United States. So what incentive could bring folks from the threshold of the modern world to this backwater? It's possible there were some remnants of the earlier "lure of the wilderness" ethic that so profoundly affected early-nineteenth-century Americans, but by now there was an additional and even more potent dream, and that was to make money. This was the age during which vast fortunes were being built, and the ways of accumulating great wealth were many, not least of which was the acquisition and development of land.

Though still the rawest of frontiers, Pinellas was growing rapidly, benefiting like the rest of Florida from an active and organized effort to attract homesteaders. From a population of some one hundred and eighty-eight thousand in 1870, the state had come to include almost two hundred and seventy thousand people by the 1880 census. The Pinellas peninsula had tripled in size to over eleven hundred people (most of them located in the northern half of the territory) but there were still none of the refinements of a settled area.

Connection to the outside world was slim and chancy. There was a weekly mail packet, whose scheduled run was from the railhead at Cedar Key to Tampa to Manatee to Key West, with stops elsewhere if demanded. Supposedly it called in at the bluff once in awhile, but even its official schedule was never very dependable; any extra excursion must have been a rare thing, indeed. Nor were there any of the amenities of a local government. The state had passed legislation mandating the establishment of schools in the late 1860s, and over six hundred had come into being by 1876, but not here. As far as can be ascertained none of the Slaughter or Barnett children had even the least suggestion of a formal education. They may or may not have been literate; nothing exists to prove the supposition either way. We do know that Rebecca could not write as witnessed by her mark, an X, on her application for James's pension in 1899. And it is important to remember that even a pencil, much less a pen and ink, would have been a rare possession for such a family.

There were no doctors or dentists, and the fatality rate from the simplest of maladies was astronomical. People died from spoiled or contaminated food, from poorly set bones and infections. They died from measles. The one and only medication (always excepting the universal turpentine) was alcohol. A concoction called "bitters" was reputed to cure anything, and at about one hundred ninety proof, it probably did.

During cattle round-up times, an able-bodied man who owned a horse could sign on and make some decent money, fifty cents or even a dollar a day, for the experienced hand. Pinellas cowboys sometimes carried six-shooters, if they had them, but not to engage in gun duels as in the west. Here, they were needed for snakes. Settlers learned early not to walk incautiously through palmetto scrub or wade through swampy ground. Rattlesnakes, cottonmouth moccasin, coral snakes and their many cousins ranged from the downright deadly to the merely annoying, but shooting on sight was the best plan for dealing with any of them.

The turpentine still and the sawmill would before long provide some small jobs, but for now there were few opportunities to earn a living. Certainly, crops could be raised and fish could be caught in abundance; however, there was nothing to do with them after that. With no dependable means of transportation, there was no way to get produce to markets in saleable condition. Yet Joseph Torres, even before the appearance of Hamilton Disston, had an idea that this land could be very profitable, if not at the moment, certainly in the near future. He hired Vincent Leonardi to build him a house (3102 52nd Street South), and after the death of his first wife Louise in 1884, would marry into the Nash family, gaining both Leonardi and Slaughter in-laws.

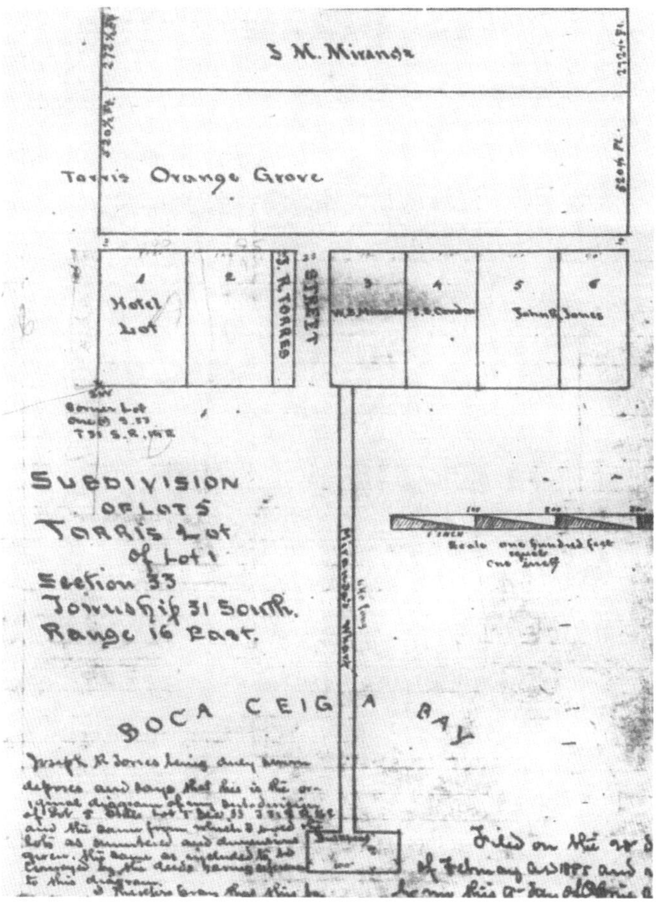

Joseph Torres' lots on the waterfront, showing the proposed hotel, Torres' own property and Miranda's wharf.

Torres now controlled the entire waterfront of the settlement from the mangrove marshes of Clam Bayou to the western tidal flats. He was here to stay, and it was his presence, more than any other, that marked the beginning of the end of the pioneer era, the last gasp of the clan society of sea-wise conches and wood-wise crackers, and the start of the entrepreneurial period. Barnett's bluff gave way to Torres' town, and there he was joined by the final newcomer of importance to the story of Gulfport during this era. William Bonifacio Miranda, a nephew of Abel, turned up in 1876 with the law as only one of his many vocations. He soon earned or gave himself the title justice of the peace, and his seal and signature appear on contemporary official documents, wedding certificates, deeds and wills. When together Torres and Miranda began planning just how the tiny town might make their fortunes, one thought was uppermost in their minds, as in the minds of all the other potential land barons: the railroad.

Chapter II
The Dream

1. Hamilton Disston

William Bonifacio Miranda was one of the first people in the area to get wind of a new player in the Florida game. He was always looking for "opportunity" and when he heard about Hamilton Disston, he must have felt that fate had dished him up that opportunity on a golden plate indeed.

Disston was a rich young easterner who had inherited his family's Philadelphia saw, tool and file business in 1878, at the death of his English immigrant father. With four brothers, he was apparently not much needed in the daily affairs of the company, so, at thirty-four and something of a playboy, he came to Florida to try the tarpon fishing. While here he got the idea of building a new fortune—his own—from the open emptiness of a region just waiting for the right man and the right plan.

As it happened, the state of Florida was waiting for that man, too. Florida was broke, destitute, bankrupt and willing to sell four million acres of probably worthless swampland for almost nothing to compensate for huge debts accumulated in railroad building schemes. Even at twenty-five cents an acre, Hamilton had to put together a consortium of his English contacts to raise the required one million dollars. The sale was made, Florida was solvent again, and Hamilton Disston became the largest single landowner in the entire country.

In an era of risk-taking venture capitalists, he certainly held his own.

Disston's purchase started a new boomlet in Florida, and particularly in Point Pinellas, for in his 1881 deal he had acquired one hundred ten thousand acres of the future Pinellas County, about three-quarters of all the acreage in what is now St. Petersburg and just about everything that is now Gulfport, excluding only Barnett's and Torres' holdings.

He immediately set out on a tour of his new empire, and started at once to dig canals, reclaim wetlands, build sugar refineries and establish little towns. But he soon recognized a lack: he needed a center, a capital where he could reign in style over that empire. His first choice was Tarpon Springs, or what would become Tarpon Springs. Disston had fetched up there on a boating excursion south from Cedar Key and immediately set about platting and planning a new community. Never mind the settlement had only three families, and there were virtually no facilities. Strange little railroads went here and there without much design or connection and no dependability. Hotels were non-existent. And the natives still didn't like Yankees much.

Disston's fateful first encounter with Miranda occurred during an 1883 tour of his holdings in the lower peninsula. Miranda put himself forward as Disston's guide, much as uncle Abel had done with the earlier military explorers, and pointed out the many advantages Pinellas could offer over the Tarpon Springs area. Disston bit, whether through Miranda's reputedly effective salesmanship or simple recognition that the attractive setting would, in fact, make a good town site.

Miranda became Disston's agent—a dream come true—and Torres plotted out his holding into lots that included segments for himself, Miranda and a proposed hotel. Locals, foremost among them Henry Slaughter, were hired to survey the land. The town was platted into five and ten acre lots, with one hundred-foot wide streets and a broad boulevard along the waterfront.

Now at last, the dream had a name. The Disston City Land Company was born on August 21, 1884, with capital stock of $100,000, and plans for a town of fifty thousand inhabitants covering its twelve thousand acres. (In actuality, money was so scarce that a five-dollar bill could have been traced through the entire peninsula with little difficulty.)

2. Bonifacio

In fact, the settlement had had a name of sorts since May 10, 1880, when the ever-modest Bill Miranda had been granted a post office at "Bonifacio." Considering that by best estimates there were only some six to nine families in the area, this was a considerable achievement, for the establishment of a post office franchise was the most significant mark of "arrival" in pioneer Florida.

Miranda had seen to it that Joseph Torres was appointed postmaster, a position he held until the discontinuance of the franchise in April 1883. This may have been the point at which Hamilton Disston decided the town should have his name, not Miranda's, but that proposition was turned down by the postal authorities due to the similarity in name of another Hillsborough County town, Diston. We find "Bonifacio" reinstated in early 1885, with Torres once again postmaster.

Letter with a Bonifacio postmark, September 1888.

The mail was carried by Cedar Key steamboats, which ran all during the period, including the 1883-1885 hiatus, though they were far from reliable. Disston purchased four steamers to keep his settlements in contact with the outside world. The best known of these locally were the *Mistletoe* and the *Mary Disston*, the latter named after his mother. Discounting the simple sailboats that came and went as they pleased, the *Mary Disston* was Bonifacio's only means of communication.

Local steamboats were necessarily limited to paddle wheelers with less than seven feet of draft, considerably smaller in size than the famous Mississippi riverboats. Designed to navigate the sandbars and shallows of Florida waterways, they usually featured a paddlewheel about a quarter of the vessel's width, recessed and enclosed to protect it from overhanging branches along rivers. A rudder extended behind the boat and gave it good maneuverability.

Designed by a Captain Topliff and built in the early 1880s in Cincinnati or Pittsburgh—accounts vary—the *Mary Disston* was specified to be 71.12 tons, 83 feet long and 18-and-a-half feet wide, with a 3.8-foot draft. She was originally used at Tarpon Springs as a link connecting the heavier steamboats that carried freight and passengers down from Cedar Key to the settlement around the city wharf, since the Anclote River between these two points was navigable only by such shallow-draft vessels. Once the railroad reached Tarpon Springs, the boat was no longer needed for this purpose and was enlisted to help carry personnel and supplies for the further building of the rail line. That completed, she was assigned to "utility chores" around the Bay. Registered in Cedar Key, the first stop on the southward mail and passenger run, her route was supposed to, and sometimes actually did, include Disston City.

Some claim that the "*Dirty Mary*," as the wood-burning steamer became known for her plumes of black smoke, eventually broke up near Key West. Here, the story is that she came to her eventual end around 1892, when a fire destroyed the Disston City dock to which she was moored. While everyone in town ran to help, it was too late to save the boat, which burned right down to the water. The 1998 archaeological survey of the Gulfport shore seems to support this account, as the long-rumored remains of the boat were discovered in just the location old timers had predicted.

3. Disston's English Friends

The few newcomers to town in the early 1880s were a very different sort of folk indeed from the first settlers. They were Hamilton Disston's followers, a group of Englishmen who had come "out" to this remote part of the world to see what they could see.

As soon as Disston had established his company, he (or Miranda, in his name) set about developing the town, and his first move in this direction was to start building a hotel, to be known as the Waldorf. The genesis of this structure is lost in the mists of time and creates for us once again more questions than answers.

Many sources credit the building of the hotel to Herman E. Baumeister, an interestingly eponymous choice given that his very name is German for master builder, or architect. In any case, he couldn't have done all the work alone, and the project may indeed have brought jobs, not only in the construction but also in the staffing of the hotel, to the families of the Slaughter/Barnett clan. The Waldorf's exact location is not known for sure, beyond the fact that it overlooked the Bay and probably stood near the foot of York Street.

Lumber for the project was brought by schooner from Apalachicola. The vast forests of Southern longleaf pine were even then in the process of being clear-cut into extinction. While we recognize this despoliation as a major social crime from a twenty-first century standpoint, the impoverished post-

Civil War South saw lumbering as a means of survival, if not profit, in an area with few enough potential industries. Logs were floated down rivers to Panhandle ports for shipment to eager builders of ships, houses and barrels. Local maritime men made gains as well, sailing back and forth along the west coast with cargoes of timber to build new homes and businesses in this area.

The hotel, the first in lower Pinellas, went up rather quickly and opened with a grand show on Christmas Eve 1884. Whether this was in the configuration sometimes described as "four rooms up and four down" or the more unlikely "26 rooms in an L-shape," is never made clear. There is also the possibility that there was an original building, with the eight rooms built by Baumeister for Miranda even before Disston's arrival, and he, Disston, only ordered its enlargement.

The hotel's manager was an English import, William A. Wood, who oversaw the festivities that evening and entertained a number of prominent guests as well as the developer himself (probably the locals were not invited). The dignitaries who did attend gave it great reviews ("unbelievable luxury"), although it is incredibly difficult to imagine how any kind of first-class structure could have been built, furnished, stocked and staffed in what was still a very inaccessible and sparsely populated part of the world. No photographs of any kind exist to help us visualize what it might have been like. From the 1998 archaeological survey, we do have a few tantalizing shards of Japanese blue-and-white china which were unearthed in the general vicinity and may well have been part of the hotel's decor. One of the Slaughter descendants, himself too young to have seen the place, claimed there wasn't even a dining room, but that seems as unlikely as the other extreme.

With a vigorous advertising campaign in the Northeast and England, the hotel found itself fully booked throughout most of 1885, its guests marveling over their views of the wild unspoiled forests and the pristine Bay. That is the last we hear of such successes, for after the railroad bypassed Disston City in the late 1880s, the venture failed and came to one or another fate, variously described as having been abandoned after the loss of the *Mary Disston* in 1892, washed away in a gale in 1901, sold to a "Mr. Thomas" (probably Charles W. Thomes, newly arrived from Maine) in 1896 or torn down by locals and the lumber scavenged for other buildings. One account even credits its destruction to a "tidal wave."

The truth may be an amalgam of all these possibilities. The *St. Petersburg Times* of April 25, 1901, in its regular column "Disston City Items" states: "The old hotel building here recently started off seaward, but stranded soon after leaving its blocks and was badly wrecked. Mr. Thomb [sic] has bought the main building and taken it down to use in repairing his house. Mrs. A. Leonardy has bought the 'L' part and expects to put it up at Bear Creek."

Irving Slaughter, Henry's youngest son, who was born in 1901, once said he could recall his father helping to haul off the remains of the hotel to use in building a home of his own in what is today the 2400 block of 49th Street. He also mentioned that between the hotel's abandonment and its eventual destruction, it was used as a temporary shelter by a number of families who "just moved in and out whenever they wanted to—different people lived there over a period of several years."

In July 1901, the newspaper reported that Mr. "Thoms" had taken away the last of the old hotel building, making it impossible that Irving could have recalled this particular instance of lumber recycling. Perhaps he was thinking of the salvage of several waterfront structures following the hurricane of 1921.

Another Disston attempt to turn his town into a real settlement involved building a wharf adjacent to the hotel for the berthing of his steamships. Both 1885 plat maps show the wharf as 640 feet long, though more general tradition has it that the pier was only about 300 feet. The water was not terribly deep here, sounding at about eleven feet on the approach, and as little as five feet at low tide at the end of the 300-foot-pier. The boats, even with their shallow drafts, were quite frequently stuck on sandbars during their comings and goings.

The town was certainly growing, as a resort and a fishing port, boasting a post office and a few stores. One of the latter was the two-story 1886 building (the old house was demolished in the early 1950s and its exact site is difficult to locate today, though it must have been near the foot of 51st Street) housing the post office, manned by Torres until 1888 and then by an Englishman, R.L. Locke. Locke in turn sold both building and franchise to William Woodworth, then about thirty-five, a gentleman whose shadow would reach far into the future of the town. Woodworth was often incorrectly identified as another of the English incomers but was actually from Maine, and his other business ventures included collecting and shipping shells, to what market is unclear, and breeding "Plymouth Rock fowls." He paid about $400 for the establishment, quite a remarkable sum, and one that indicates things may indeed have been booming in Bonifacio.

But the post office often went days without a single cancellation despite the advertisements touting the "great new city" on colored maps and flyers depicting the theoretical broad boulevard elegantly placed between the harbor and business section. These astonishingly optimistic brochures also touted the wonderful fertility of the soil, and the citrus and vegetable crops that could be grown almost without effort in the bucolic paradise surrounding the city. Unfettered hyperbole or not, they had an effect. People began to buy up lots. Quite often this was done by mail order, and the folks themselves never actually materialized to settle here, or if and when they did, soon changed their minds and didn't stay for long.

Some of the Englishmen did put in a few years before moving on; Wood and Locke were two, and among others were the Harrison, Richardson, Stanton and Watt families. Arthur Norwood, the town's first schoolteacher, and his brother Urban were soon to follow.

Arthur Norwood was born in Margate, England, in 1860, and received some basic education there, followed by a stint in a men's clothing store. He and Urban came here with the other English emigrants, and set about building a little cabin on their ten-acre holding north of town, near Tangerine Avenue and 46th Street, which they had purchased for $250. It was hard work clearing palmetto, pine and saw grass, the young Londoners soon discovered, but far worse lay ahead.

Not long after their arrival they were joined by a third brother, Ernest, who came across from Tampa on Bill Neeld's cat-boat, at the moment the mail carrier for the wilderness settlement. Ernest's vivid remembrance of his trip in a *Times* interview stated: "My heart beat high as I stepped ashore, bid goodbye to Bill Neeld and was directed by Joe Bethel how to find my way over the dim trail in the rapidly falling dusk to my brother's place some seven miles to the west."

In November 1886, while the Norwoods were in Disston City, their pine shanty home and all its contents burned to the ground. They lost everything except the clothes they were wearing. The townspeople came to the assistance of the popular young men with donations of money and labor, bedding, utensils and clothing. Arthur's published note of thanks said, "Some will tell you that friends are most plentiful when one is prosperous, but our experience at Point Pinellas is just the opposite, for it was not until we felt the sharp blast of adversity that we found out how many kind friends we had in this locality."

The Norwoods went right back to work and built another cottage, this somewhat more permanent than the earlier shack. Farming efforts didn't go very well, and the boys found themselves forced to "indulge in primitive hunting" for raccoons, selling pelts for forty cents apiece. This life held little appeal for the young British adventurers, and first Urban then Ernest returned to England. Arthur, however, stayed on and found something else to do. He had been working off and on for Disston, at any job that came to hand, and when it was decided that the town needed a school, the developer himself appointed Arthur to be its first teacher.

There had been many attempts to start some kind of a school, all brief and unsuccessful. Finally, in late 1886 one was built at Disston (49th Street and 28th Avenue); Arthur Norwood probably did a lot of the erecting, as well as the teaching. We hear he "whitewashed the school building, dug a well, and built desks and blackboards," though other stories say students brought their own desks, and took them home with them as well, when they didn't feel like staying in class.

This school, known in local legend as "Prop College," was said to be so rickety that three pine saplings were propped against either side to keep it from disintegrating in a strong wind. Other lore has gathered around the history of the little school. Henry Slaughter was supposed to have been its first superintendent. If so, this may have been the first time he had ever encountered formal education (though his 1929 obituary states that he spent some time boarding in Largo, where he attended a "little country school"). Henry's daughters Minnie Clara and Margaret Aurelia, five and four years old in 1886, did both attend class at Prop College.

Norwood was likely the first paid teacher in the area, receiving $25 a month during the first two years (1886–1887) and $30 a month during his third and final term (1888). Schools, of course, were not in session any great length of time in those days, three or four months at the most, so the salary, which seems astoundingly large, was not multiplied many times to arrive at a year's pay. There was almost certainly no grading system and no formal curriculum. Teachers simply taught whatever they knew from whatever books they had, and quite often were not very far advanced of their pupils. Arthur was probably a bit ahead of most, with his good British education, however short his own school days may have been. He is supposed to have offered reading, writing, arithmetic, Latin and Greek, although the latter two subjects could not have found much practical use among the Point folk.

One interesting fact has come to light; the school was integrated. The children of black farmer John Donaldson, who had arrived here after the Civil War with the Key West contingent and stayed on to raise a family, attended right along with their neighbors and no one ever thought to have it any other way.

4. The Van Bibber Report

One of the greatest incentives to settlement occurred in 1885 when the famous Van Bibber report was issued. Dr. Washington C. Van Bibber was a Baltimore physician whose paper before the American Medical Association's annual conference unhesitatingly declared that Point Pinellas was the "healthiest spot in the world." No doubt he was personally convinced of this fact, but it is often overlooked that he had also acquired a considerable piece of acreage in the general location of Maximo's ancient fish *rancho*.

Van Bibber's proposal, in answer to an earlier challenge to find a location for an ideal community, was essentially that "a great Health City should be built here due to the pre-eminent peninsula climate . . . with the broad waters of a beautiful bay nearly surrounding it, with little now upon its soil but the primal forest." In his speech, he quoted a colleague as saying, "Were I sent abroad to search for a haven for tired men, where new life would come with every sun, and slumber full of sleep with every moon, I would select Point Pinellas, Florida." He followed up that presentation by writing an article entitled, "The Frostless Pinellas," which wasn't entirely true, but brought people anyway, who would have an enormous effect on the growth of the area.

Hamilton Disston, of course, welcomed the recommendation warmly and included Dr. Van Bibber's words of praise in some of his lavish lithographic advertisements. All this served to help counteract the more widespread image of Florida as an extremely unhealthy place, full of disease-bearing mosquitoes, yellow fever, malaria and a range of other maladies. Tuberculosis, known then as consumption, was not an uncommon illness in those times, and medical authorities actually recognized this area as a good spot for recuperation. Certainly the death rate from the "white plague" was lower here, and there was some truth to the description of the ameliorative powers of a mild climate and fresh air.

But then yellow fever broke out in the late 1880s, running up through the state from Key West, and causing some serious problems for the Pinellas Peninsula, and particularly Disston's little village. This disease, which had originated in Africa and been brought to the new world on slave ships, was first identified in the 1600s, from which time onward it periodically spread terror and death throughout settlements in the Americas. The following symptoms were quick and violent: headache, backache, fever, nausea, vomiting, then hemorrhage and degeneration of the major organs, then—all too often—death. Eventually it was discovered that mosquitoes (in which this area abounded) were the carriers, but it was not until much later, 1939, that an effective vaccine was formulated.

Bonifacio quarantined itself. Many communities did so, mounting armed guards at their borders and turning away all those frightened refugees from Tampa and points south where the disease was raging and taking its toll. Outsiders were sent instead to Long Key (today's St. Petersburg Beach), or the settlement that would become St. Petersburg. Armed men with yellow flags did not project exactly the picture of "health," and the final death knell to this image came during the Spanish-American War when a large number of soldiers were posted to the Tampa area; soldiers who suffered greatly from the fever, malaria and other tropical ills. This, then was a factor in the final demise of Disston's dream, one more negative effect on the town's growth, as many of those who sought refuge in the area ended up staying and establishing homes—but not here.

No one at all was going to last long unless there was some means of connecting the settlement with the outside world, some means, that is, more reliable than the erratic steamboats and sailboats that were the only way for people, mail, produce and goods to arrive or depart. Disston knew this, and when he built his hotel here, he envisioned it as a connecting point between the railroad terminus and the sea transportation to the south and west.

5. The Sea Breeze

From out of the vagueness of speculation, remembrances and tattered documents, a picture of the town's early inhabitants and life in the spring of 1886 emerges brilliantly, thanks to the efforts of a young man with a desire to become a newspaper publisher.

The Sea Breeze.

VOL. I. No. 11. DISSTON CITY, FLA., NOV. 5, 1886. PRICE, 5 CENTS.

J. R. TORRES & SON,

STAPLE AND FANCY GROCERIES.

DISSTON CITY, FLORIDA.

STOP AT THE

TAMPA HOUSE,

Tampa, Florida.

SPECIAL RATES TO PEOPLE FROM POINT PINELLAS.

THE

CASH STORE,

R. L. LOCKE, Prop'r.

Corner of Baltimore St. and Virginia Avenue.

DISSTON CITY, FLORIDA.

DISSTON MILL!

G. L. KING, Prop'r.

PREPARED TO FILL BILLS AT SHORT NOTICE. LUMBER AT MILL,

$12.00 per Thousand

GENERAL

BUSINESS AGENCY

—OF—

E. B. MACPHERSON & SON,

DISSTON CITY.

FLORIDA.

SPECIAL ATTENTION.

JOSEPH R. TORRES,

General Insurance Agent.

Representing Life, Accident & Fire Insurance.

DISSTON CITY, FLORIDA.

McPHERSON & SONS,

CONTRACTORS & BUILDERS.

Plans and Specifications drawn.

DISSTON CITY, FLORIDA.

Disston City Doings.

Dry.

We need a rain.

Disston has been the scene of some lively political discussions, lately.

Politics in these parts is very much like the eyes of a flounder; all on one side.

The schooner Delia, of Tampa, touched at our wharf Wednesday, enroute to New Orleans.

Mrs. H. Baumeister went to Tampa, to-day, on Capt. Brown's sloop, to attend to some business.

We have had a chilly blast from the north during the past week. Thermometer marked as low as 50°.

Until further notice be given the Sunday School will be held at Mr. Locke's hall, over the Cash Store, at 3 P. M.

Mr. King is preparing to move his saw mill down to the bay, so that the steam whistle will soon be heard near our doors.

We are drawing on our bay now for some very fine fish, clams, scallops, crabs, etc, and with good success, as the supply is unlimited.

Just in! Granite iron ware, glass sugar and butter bowls, lanteros, lamps, anb many other little things useful to a housekeeper at Baumeister's.

Eugene Leonardy moved to Sara Sota the first of this week, where he and his new wife will commence housekeeping. They were accompanied by Mrs. Fripp.

Now is the time of the year to build cheaply in Florida. Those contemplating building this winter should not wait until January and until the rush begins.

The work of grubbing out the streets of the Disston Company's addition to our town is being pushed, and will add much towards showing up the beauties of our situation.

Capt. James McMahan and wife left for Tampa this morning where they expect to remain during the winter. They leave their house in charge of Mr. G. W. Bennett, who moved in to-day and will occupy it during their absence.

While passing down to the wharf last Friday morning, we heard a tremendous racket on the hotel veranda which on investigation we found to be nothing more than the manager, Mr. Wood, turning back summersaults; all on account of a new arrival, the evening before, which he said was a seven pound girl.

WANTED.

Information concerning the best method of manufacturing palmetto fiber into mattress filling and where to market the same. We have many hundred tons of the cabbage palmetto on our Key, that we wish to get rid of, and as we know that the leaves make the finest of mattresses, we propose to start a factory for that business as soon as we can so arrange matters. Would give a man who understands the business a good chance to make some money with us, or would take a partner who has some money to invest in the business, only a few hundred will be required to start it. Address the SEA BREEZE.

Front page of *The Sea Breeze* of November 5,1886. *Gift of the Emily Rautman Memorial Fund*

William J. McPherson first found his way to lower Pinellas during a camping trip to Long Key in the fall of 1885. The McPherson men, Will's father Elias and brothers Edward and Charles, had left Deland in August, with a wagon and camping kit, and spent about a month on their trip here, looking out all along the way for a likely place to settle. They alit first at Big Bayou, where one of the Neelds gave them some "nice fat mullet out of the smoke house when they were warm." After a few days, they pushed on to Bonifacio, where they met Long Key's one and only pioneer settler, Zephaniah Phillips, who introduced them to Torres, "the city merchant and owner of most of the town-site," from whom they bought some property. When they returned the next year, they got to work putting up a house. By winter it was ready to receive the female members of the family, Mrs. McPherson and her daughters Ella and Babbette.

Elias McPherson and his family were typical entrepreneurs of the period; they tried their hands at many things, including a lumberyard, contracting, a general business agency and the famous, though short-lived *Sea Breeze*. In this venture, the youngest son, William, just twenty years old, performed a great service to future historians during the year he spent trying to make a go of his little newssheet. Theoretically it was to appear twice a month, on the first and the fifteenth, but that rarely happened, due to Will's life intruding on his work. He was sick, he had a chance to go on a sailing trip, he just didn't have enough news. The paper got out when it got out. The price grew from one cent to two cents to five cents per issue, then fifty cents for six months, and the editor gave a lot of his space to begging for subscribers; it could not have been at all a successful financial venture. However, it was the first newspaper in lower Pinellas (The *St. Petersburg Times* had an earlier origin in the north county, beginning in 1884 as the *West Hillsborough Times* in Dunedin and Clear Water).

John Bethell called Will's paper "a simple kind of hand-bill affair," though the young editor promised, at the end of the first one-page issue: "We expect to publish a larger sheet about May 1st, giving brief descriptions of the various points of interest on our coast." Here is Will McPherson's description of Disston City:

This rapidly growing town, one of prospective termini of the O.S.S. & G.R.R., is beautifully situated on the west side of Point Pinellas, on Boca Ceiga bay, about 3 miles from and in full view of Tampa bay and two miles from the gulf, from which the bay is there seperated [sic] by Long Key. It contains three stores, a good hotel, a large boarding house, P.O., and the Sea Breeze printing office; also a fish canning factory in embryo, and a neat schoolhouse.

For health and beauty of location this town is unsurpassed by any on the western coast of Florida, and is destined in the near future to become a favorite resort for pleasure and health seekers.

When all the out-flung homesteads were considered, Disston's town had become quite a sizeable settlement, covering a broad area much greater than the boundaries of today's Gulfport and with a population of perhaps one hundred to one hundred fifty people.

In the very first issue, we meet the man who was probably more responsible for the actual publication of the newssheet than Will. "Our friend Admiral G.W. Bennett of St. Paul, Minn., has been looking over the peninsula and keys during the past week, expresses himself as well satisfied . . . We hope that he may decide to locate in our midst. We are indebted to him for assistance in our office." George Washington Bennett, then about forty years old, came here first on a visit in late 1885, on advice to seek a better climate for his health. He returned with his wife Mary and young son Harold the next May, to settle at Disston, where, with his reputed newspaper experience, he set to work helping Will get out the "newsy little sheet." He seems to have been a man of some financial resources and a generally insouciant outlook on life.

By the second issue, Will's advertising blocks included the following local companies: Baumeister's Drygoods, Wm. B. Miranda's Land Company, E.B. McPherson's General Business Agency and J.R. Torres & Son's "staple and fancy" grocery store (though he also offered his services as a "General Insurance Agent"). Not far behind were Locke's "Cash Store," George King's sawmill and a butcher shop run by men named Anderson and Hamilton.

Baumeister, the *Sea Breeze* announced, was planning to open a fish canning business, ordered several cases of cans and began to experiment with the process. But there was an unexpected hitch; he couldn't get enough fish to make it worthwhile. This was a bit before the time when Disston, or its successor, Gulfport, would become home to commercial fishermen. In the 1880s, though there were certainly plenty of fish in the bays, the locals caught only what they needed for their own use. Will addressed the problem: "Our bay is now full of fine mullet. Why don't somebody bring more of them in to sell? Most of us have neither the time or then nets with which to catch them." And so Disston City's embryonic canning industry failed.

Miranda, proclaiming himself a notary public, offered "business lots in the new and prosperous town of Disston for sale. Improved and wild lands for sale. Groves set out, improved and taken care of. Interests of non-residents cared for. Abstracts of title a speciality. Titles examined. Collections made."

Torres' store was at the foot of the Disston City Wharf, where in addition to selling potatoes and onions, he lived and cared for his three children. In August he lost one of them, fourteen-year-old Joseph, called "Muggins," to a "disease of the bowels." The *Sea Breeze* eulogized the child as "one of the best of boys [who] certainly will wear a bright star in that world beyond for his faithful and constant care of his two little sisters, since the death of their mother." A month later Torres married Georgia Ann Nash, Henry Slaughter's twenty-year-old sister-in-law.

George King (born 1835) was an engineer, sometimes said to be from Canada, though more reliable sources place his origin in St. Louis. With his wife Frances and little son Lewis, he brought his sawmill down the Mississippi and across the Gulf of Mexico in 1884, and set up shop along a stream called Mule Branch, which family histories place near 52nd Street. Two years later he moved across the Bayou to where the Puigs were trying to build New Cadiz. Even there he ran into some difficulties. The tides were so low that he could not get his rafts of logs down from Long Bayou, a large inlet in the Bay Pines area, which, now blocked off, has become Lake Seminole. "But he has his men at work near the mill cutting and hauling and can now supply all demands." In the 1890s King would buy a hotel in St. Petersburg and live out his life there, active in politics and civic affairs.

The Andersons had arrived from Dallas in a little two-master schooner to take up residence in the wilderness that was Disston City. "There was hardly a track through it," Mrs. Anderson recalled far in the distant future, adding an interesting glimpse of Rebecca Barnett's character. When George Anderson (1837-1912) nearly shot one of Rebecca's calves, thinking it a deer loose in his garden, Mrs. Anderson rushed to stop him, fearing serious repercussions from her "fighting neighbor." Like all the others, their business failed after the railroad debacle, and Anderson ended up his career in St. Petersburg, where he became the city's first fire chief.

Atop the third issue, June 15, there is a bold new masthead. As the story goes, the largest type available wasn't prominent enough to make a very effective header, and so someone, probably Bennett, carved the letters spelling out "The Sea Breeze," from a piece of black mangrove. The price now had risen to five cents, and the paper began to take on the look of a real publication.

His longest story of the issue was an interesting little tale of an adventure with Bennett, written as follows:

Through the kindness of Mr. G.W. Bennett we, in company with him on his sloop Lottie, took a cruise down the coast to Charlotte Harbor, taking in the various points of interest on the route, and spending two weeks very pleasantly. Our first stop was at Sarasota, a thriving town on Sarasota Bay. It contains one of the finest hotels in South Florida. We then ran out into the Gulf, when Mr. Bennett advised ye editor to take off his shoes; a wise precaution, as everything else came up, (please say nothing about seasickness in our presence.) We stopped next at St. James, a town on the south end of Pine Island. The situation is very good, and it is destined to become a favorite seaside resort. Punta Rassa, the next place that we saw, is a telegraph station on the line running to Cuba.

We ran up the Caloosahatchee river as far as Ft. Myers, a pretty place of about 1000 inhabitants. Mr. T.A. Edison, the electrician, has two fine residences and a laboratory here. Among other curiosities we saw bearing cocoanut trees, and a large date palm. We spent part of an afternoon on Sanibel Island, celebrated for the fine shells picked up on its beach.

The next place visited was the town of Charlotte Harbor at the mouth of Peace Creek. Punta Gorda, just opposite, is the southern terminus of the South Florida R.R.

Our leave of absence having expired, we started for home where we arrived safe and sound. We carried some SEA BREEZES along with us, but when the wind failed, or we ran on a bar (which we did regularly every night) we found that the trustiest breezes that we had were two long poles. I will close by saying we had a very pleasant time.

Now and then the McPherson & Sons Construction Co. got some work. They built the first church on the lower peninsula, St. Bartholomew's Episcopal on Lakeview Avenue, now located further south on 34th Street. A bazaar, including musical and theatrical entertainment, was held to raise money for this venture, primarily by the English settlers, who were more used to that sort of thing. The natives were scandalized. The result, however, was a net profit of $40 toward construction of the 18-by 40-foot board and batten edifice.

In the sixth issue of August 1, Will's father tells of another sailing trip with Mr. Bennett.

With our friend, Mr. Bennett, on the stanch schooner Delia, we left this port on Monday, July 5th and arrived at Apalachicola Thursday, being delayed by calms. We found this town somewhat excited over a gale that had visited them a few days previous. Several vessels having been driven ashore, some with masts gone and some high on land; one fine brigantine [stranded] over a mile from land. Several lives were lost but the heaviest loss to the city was caused by the burning of the planing mills of Messrs. Coombs & Co., which occurred on the Friday following the gale. The Cypress Lumber Co. not having their planing machinery in operation, we decided to go on to Pensacola, a distance of 150 miles and were two days and nights struggling with calms, squalls and head winds, but our schooner rode the waves nicely, and Monday morning we ran up the beautiful bay, between forts Pickens and Barancas and anchored off the thriving city which now contains 10,000 inhabitants. Pensacola is one of the great lumber marts of the world. It has a very beautiful situation, extending up the high bluffs which command a fine view of the bay and gulf. Returning, we headed direct for Tampa bay, arriving Thursday the 22nd. We took our trick at the helm, halyards, etc, and Mr. B. proved to us that he could cook onion and garlic soup, on a one-legged stove, when the coffee pot had to be tied to the mast to keep it from tumbling. We tried fishing with good success, and caught grouper, snapper, dolphin, and barriconter, and speared a porpoise. We returned to our beautiful bay with a feeling of pride that nature had done much towards making our location one that would compare favorably with any other on the gulf coast. E.B.M.

In the meantime, Mr. Bennett has apparently decided to stay:

We are glad to state that Mr. G.W. Bennett, of St. Paul, Minnesota, who with his family has been stopping here during the summer, has invested in a lot in J. Puig's suberb [suburb or superb?] New Cadiz. He stays here because he enjoys our balmy breezes, sweet potatoes, fish, oysters, etc, and is free from the terrible neuralgia and rheumatic pains that made his life almost unbearable while in the North, besides he likes our delightful coast for its natural beauties."

Bennett did indeed stay, first at Disston, and later on the Puig lot, where his cottage, we find many years into the future, was at the eastern edge of a large serpentine mound near what was to become Maximo Road and later 31st Street South. He remained in his Maximo homestead, and held on to his undeveloped Long Key property throughout a long and "eccentric" (Hurley) life. He was still going strong when Bethell penned his 1912 memoir, saying Bennett "credits the climate of the Pinellas Peninsula with the last 25 years of his life.

Items of real news, however, were still very few and far between. In the next issue, November 15, Will complains: "We have attempted tasks frequently that called for tact and ingenuity, but we think none more brain-racking than the effort, to comply with the demands of our devil, to furnish a page of Disston City locals. Things dont [sic] sometimes most always happen."

So he went on to talk about himself. "Ye junior editor has invested in a cast net, and has been experimenting in winding it around his neck, jerking out his front teeth, etc., and has succeeded in frightening a few mullet, but it would make you smile a smole to see the knowing finny chaps come up and nose around the net while we are drawing in our solitary little shiner or leather fish."

Unfortunately the *Breeze* was not blowing that well in Pinellas. "We wish to say to those of our readers who have so kindly given us their patronage and encouragement in various ways, that we will not for a while, or until matters assume a more encouraging aspect, issue our little sheet but once each month, making the first of the month our publishing day. The out lay and tax upon our time to do more than this, merely for amusement and for the small benefit we can be to the public, we think not justifying us in trying to do more at present."

So Will resorts to humor. "The editor of the Live Oak Bulletin offers a cat to each new subscriber. Now we do not intend to let him get ahead of us in this way, so we propose to make a present to every new subscriber added to our list, and to all old subscribers, renewing, as well, of a genuine full grown coon, and we further agree to keep said coons in good condition upon our homestead on the Key until called for by said subscribers, when he or they can have their choice from the whole lot. Send in your subscriptions, but dont [sic] all call for premiums the same day."

By now the end is near, and Will has pretty much given up. In the March 1 issue, most of his news is about himself. "Ye editor had a dish of strawberries on the 17th . . . We were unavoidably detained at Tampa last week, which is our excuse for being late with this issue . . . Another voter added to the list in this precinct on February 17th; Ye editor having attained his majority on that day. Congratulations and subscriptions are now in order." So he has reached the age of twenty-one at the end of a long hard year of trying to make a go of a newspaper in the wilds of Point Pinellas. One has to give Will a lot of credit.

6. Public Transportation and the Mails

The regular delivery of the mails was a subject of paramount interest to the Disston City settlers. Early on, Hamilton Disston himself had arranged for some steamers to perform this duty, but with their erratic and undependable schedules, the results were obviously less than satisfactory.

The *Sea Breeze* followed the saga of the search for regular mail service, and reported each new hopeful, but ultimately unsuccessful venture. In June 1886, the postmaster general ordered that "a contract be made with Wm. C. Chase, of Baltimore, Md., for carrying the mail in safe and suitable steamboats, from Tampa to Ellenton, six times per week and return, with side supply to Pinellas and Bonifacio three times per week and return, from July 1st, 1886, to June 30th, 1887."

Despite the tone of that edict, we hear that "Mr. Chase has thrown up his contract for carrying the mail by steamboat, so that we shall only get two mails a week as at present, instead of three, as expected, and will have to depend upon a sail-boat to bring it." By July 15, Will was moaning, "Oh where! oh where! has our steamboat gone? Oh where! oh where! can she be?"

Months later they are still trying. "Steps have been taken to induce the Plant System [which had brought the railroad to Tampa] to have the steamer 'Margaret' touch at our wharf, on her way from Tampa to Manatee with some prospects of success." A meeting was held at the hotel "to see what could be done to improve our transportation facilities."

Miranda, at least, was losing patience. He said, "Tell the Plant Company, for me, that if they will bring their railroad down to Point Pinellas I will guarantee them plenty of water and sea room, and no rocks or snags to play hob with the bottom of their steamers." Will adds, "So say we all of us. It is no secret that the Plant Company design pushing on, from Tampa to deep water, somewhere, and why not to the Point? Where can it do better? It would not surprise many if the South Florida should be the first railroad to reach the Point after all. 'Change cars for Point Pinellas and Havana.'"

Finally, in December: "We are glad to announce that the staunch steamer 'Relief' has started on a temporary arrangement to make regular trips from Pinellas to Tampa three times a week, and thus far has met with fair encouragement. We trust that those most interested will not fail to see that the arrangement will be perfected to keep the steamer on the route during the coming season."

Then, in the January 1, 1887, issue: "We have now something more tangible to say. The morning star appears above the horizon. We are certainly going to get a steamer to make regular trips on our bays. Mr. Sterling, of Pinellas, who has been vigorously striving in this direction for some time, has induced a Mr. Rouff, an experienced engineer and machinest [sic], from Chattanooga, to unite with him in building a light draft steamer. The lumber has been ordered for the hull, and negotiations pending for the machinery. The boat is to be built on Big Bayou, and is to be pushed forward as soon as the material arrives. The estimated cost of the vessel is $2,500 and one third interest will be offered to the citizens of this locality. Now will be a good opportunity for some of our people to show their faith, by investing small sums in this enterprise. Shares will be given at from $25 to $100, or several parties can unite and buy the whole amount offered. We wish the enterprise complete success."

In February, "Our citizens have perfected arrangements with Capt. Whitehurst, of the schooner 'Cherub,' to make regular trips, twice a week, between this place and Tampa, carrying the mail. The boat leaves the wharf at Disston, Mondays and Thursdays at eight o'clock A.M." But no sooner was that written, than "The 'Cherub' was compelled to remain at Tampa to get her papers renewed and had to send the mail down, last Friday, by the sloop 'Reindeer'. The 'Cherub' is expected down to-day with the mail."

In March, this venture had another turn for the worst. "The 'Cherub' after making a few trips to Tampa with the mail, drew off, and the sloop 'Sneezer', Captain Brown, has been making regular trips ever since. We think that Capt. Whitehurst did not treat the people here quite right in this matter." And, even worse: "Mr. Rouff seems to be weakening on the steamboat business, and is talking of starting another saw mill on the Point. While we believe there will soon be plenty of work for two saw mills here, we do not like to have the steamboat fail." In the last issue, there is a turn-around on this point, perhaps due to some comment from that gentleman, which prompted this: "I take it all back! I was only in fun! Just let me go this time and I wont say so any more! is the way our fighting editor talked when our steamboat man, Mr. Rouff came around and threatened to demolish him and the rest of the establishment if he ever dared to 'stretch the truth' again about him and his steamer."

The steamboat business was obviously a treacherous one, Sterling, Rouff and Whitehurst all falling by the wayside as so many had before and would again. While these ventures staggered through alternately pessimistic and optimistic forecasts, there was another avenue (literally) the settlers were perhaps better equipped to challenge and actually affect: the state of the local roads.

Their condition was well described in a memoir written by David Watt, another English visitor, of a trip from Disston City to St. Petersburg, as follows: "They jogged along slowly behind the sleepy old horse for mile after mile through the unbroken forest, without seeing a clearing or a house . . . He noticed . . . that the soil was all sand—nothing but sand everywhere. The horse went along over the road silently, his hoofs making no noise, and the wheels rolled silently too in the loose material, except when they bumped over a palmetto or a tree root. He had never seen a road just like it . . . It wound to and fro like a snake so as to avoid the trees and the clumps of palmettoes, and if a tree had fallen the road simply took a new course around it and left it undisturbed. The forest looked very attractive to him, with the tall southern pine trees with their red-brown trunks and the crown of dark-green pine needles growing all at the top, just like a canopy, and with a carpet of wild grass or of tropical-looking palmettoes underneath. He had always thought of a forest as dark and leafy, but this one was open and sunny and parklike, with thick clumps of oaks or of swamp growth only at long intervals."

The roads improved only very slowly. "The so called avenue, extending from bay to bay between this place and Pinellas, is a disgrace to the Point." Will expounded at length on this matter, which he called "suicidal to neglect," if "the country people who come to our villages to trade," don't have decent roads to travel on and if, "those who have land to sell," don't provide, "broad clean roads, streets, and avenues," for their potential buyers. He then goes on to interject a rare political comment, criticizing "commissioners" for failing in their duty. He suggests a public meeting, and if all else fails, to do the work by volunteer labor. What particularly was needed, apparently, was "grubbing out the palmettoes."

But it had been a very wet summer, which slowed down the work and "made some serious cuts and washouts that will have to be repaired." All the residents were encouraged to help out in the "many places that should be ditched," and where "those terrible roots should be grubbed out," so that there would be "at least one good drive on the point, and we would think it should be from Tampa Bay to Boca Ceiga Bay." Will promised to keep at the matter "until some substantial results are accomplished worthy of our beautiful point . . . If we expect [people] to locate with us, we must do all we can to encourage them by making them see that we are alive to our interests. Large prices for lands alone are very poor incentives for imigration [sic]."

7. Disston, Demens and Williams

The town that called itself Disston City, except to the post office where it was known as Bonifacio, was beginning to care about its identity, apart from the other settlements on the Point. The *Sea Breeze* said:

We think it is well to have a settled, well established, indisputable name for most things, and especially for towns of the large dimensions, prospectively, of our beautiful bay girt city. Bonifacio, the present name of our post office and the only one that the Post Master General will recognize, is not at all satisfactory to most of our citizens. It does not have the right jingle to the ears of a native born American; Slab Town or Gopher Knoll would be considered an improvement . . . we would not care so much about the name if we had only one name, but as it now is, the annoyance is very great. Our mail gets all mixed up, some is sent to Diston P.O., some to Bonifay [another post office] and we think some of it goes to Cuba or some other place, some letters reaching us two or three weeks after passing through the Tampa office the first time.

Ironically, the right to use the Disston City name would finally be granted on October 15, 1889, just about the time the town began folding up, for Disston City effectively died in 1888 when the railroad reached St. Petersburg. The long story of this demise is a tale involving even more than the usual cast of strange characters and unlikely occurrences.

Railroad building began in Florida in the 1830s, though the first really useful line to this area, from Jacksonville to Cedar Key, was not finished until 1853. It was this railroad that brought mail to the steamers that then continued on to Disston, Big Bayou, Manatee and Tampa, although, as we have seen, on a somewhat less than regular basis. During the Civil War years, all railroad building stopped, and the state fell far behind the rest of the country. When the United States was spanned in 1869—the east and west branches joining up in Utah—Florida could claim only about 450 miles of track, most all of it in the northern part of the state.

Changes in the direction of a local population or economy are brought about by some kind of impetus, whether from within or without. In the case of Point Pinellas, that stimulus was certainly the coming of the railroad, which would finish off forever the pioneer era and start certain towns, at

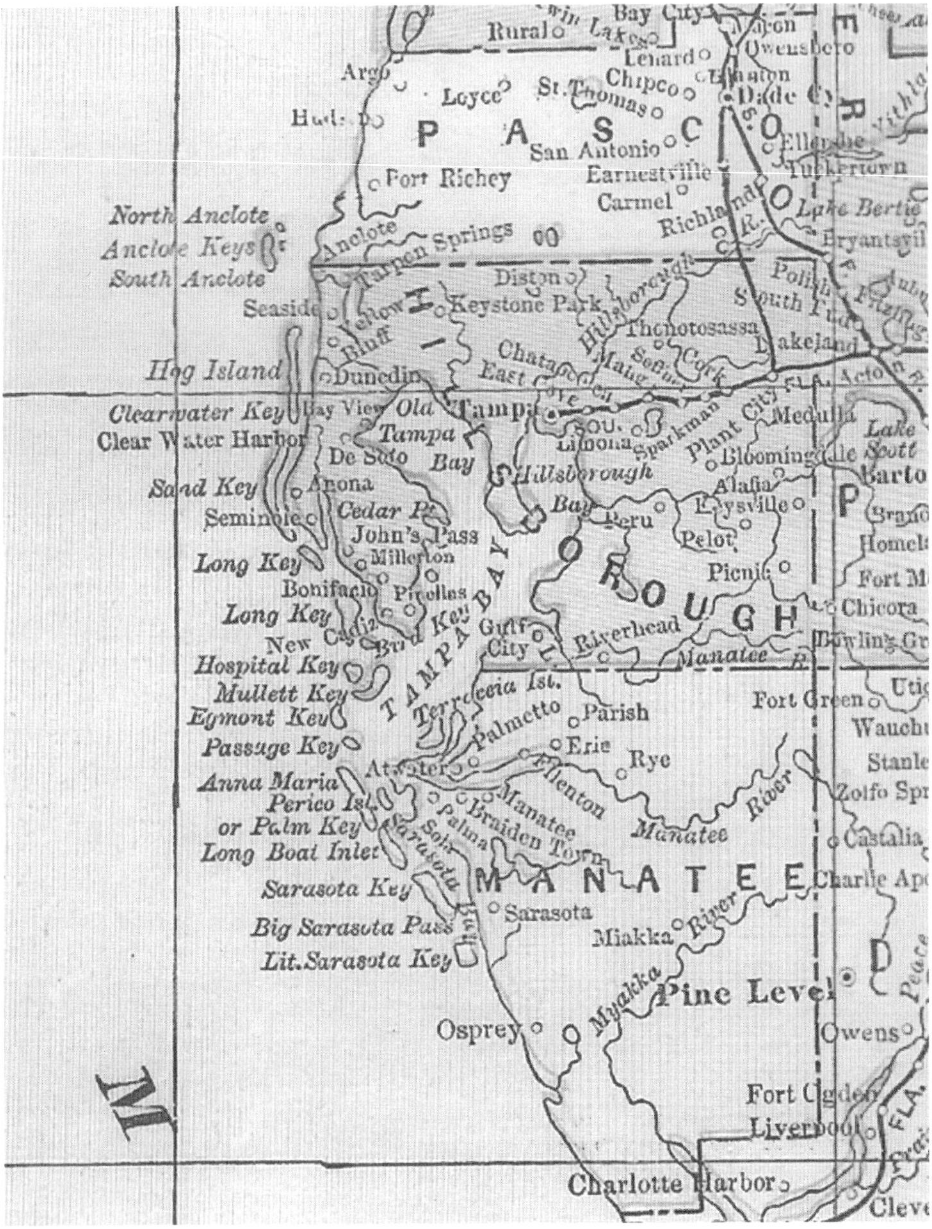

Map of Tampa Bay showing Bonifacio and the many keys along the coastline. *Courtesy Jan Dutton*

least, on the way to growth and accomplishment. It was the logical time for this next step, and men of vision realized it. Disston, H.B. Plant and Henry Flagler were three who were on the leading edge of the movement to bring the southern regions of Florida into the mainstream of commerce and communication. Flagler built his railroads down the east coast, and Plant brought his to Tampa. It apparently never occurred to Disston that a railroad to Point Pinellas would go anywhere but to Disston City.

What happened was this. A Russian immigrant, whose name is spelled in as many ways as transliteration from the Russian allows (Petrovitch Alexewitch Demenscheiff, Piotr Dementieff, Pyotr Dementyev, etc.) but known here as Peter A. Demens, had gotten somewhat inadvertently involved in the building of the Orange Belt Railroad from the St. Johns River to Lake Apopka in 1885. When the financiers behind this venture went broke, Demens took over the project and completed the thirty-four-mile link. This small success inspired him to think in bigger terms, to request a charter to continue the line for another 120 miles to the Pinellas Peninsula. In this, of course, Disston and his board, who were rightly concerned about the incursions Plant was making on what they considered their own territory, the west central coast, supported him.

Disston offered Demens some sixty thousand acres of land and his financial support, and the deal was done. His only caveat was that it should be done quickly. This backing gave Demens not only some credibility but also some delusions of grandeur, and he decided not to stop at Disston City, but to push the line on, with a series of expensive causeways and bridges, to Mullet Key (today's Fort DeSoto) and a deep-water terminal.

While all this was going on at the highest levels, the local folk knew only that something was in the wind, and the sooner it blew this way, the better. In the spring of 1886, Will McPherson described Disston City as one of the "prospective termini of the O.S.S. & G.R.R," and editorialized: "We are confident, from the reports received that we are just upon the dawn of a mighty boom, the result of which will be to bring such crowds of . . . health and pleasure seekers as was never seen before upon these beautiful bays. The O.S.S. & G.R.R. have given positive assurances that they intend to extend their road to the Point." At this juncture, of course, absolutely nothing was positive.

By June, John C. Williams, a large landowner in the area of Paul's Landing (which would become St. Petersburg), "has let a contract for the clearing of eighty acres of his land at that place, one half of which is said to be for the O.S.S. & G.R.R., donated by him to that company." The Disston City folk could not have known what bad news this would turn out to be. It seems that when Demens approached Disston about giving further acreage and money to make that extension to Mullet Key, the response had been an unequivocable denial. Disston hadn't really taken Demens' ultimatum seriously, still convinced that if the railroad was coming to the Point at all, it had to end at Disston City. Demens, wishing to increase the pressure, began looking for alternatives and found one in Williams, who readily gave him not eighty but two hundred fifty acres of waterfront land, so that the railroad would run right down through Paul's Landing and out onto a wharf extending far enough into the bay to reach a twelve-foot depth of water.

These three men were playing a game of double bluff that gained none of them much of anything in the end. Disston is often criticized for not taking more seriously Demens' ploy. There were probably two or three reasons why he didn't. First, of course, he thought it was obviously ridiculous to bring the railroad to such a nowhere place as Paul's Landing, a settlement without even the amenities of Big Bayou or his own Disston City. Second, he thought Demens would abandon the Williams deal and come back to him on his, Disston's, own terms. Third, Disston was at heart a boat man; he loved his steamboats and had no particular feeling for the railroad, no matter how much he realized its importance to the area's future.

Disston was by no means the most popular citizen in the area. During a long editorial discussion of the seemingly endless problem of a name for the town, Will wrote, "Who is this man, H. Disston, more than an ordinary land speculator? He bought up all the vacant lands for a song and is selling them out at stiff prices. What has he done or is now doing to build up this place? We wait for a reply."

It is not difficult to imagine the dichotomous emotions of Disston City folk at this juncture. They don't like Disston, they don't know Demens and they certainly have no control over the games the two are playing. A tone of desperation invades this early 1887 comment: "We learn that the committee to solicit subscriptions for the proposed railroad are doing but little. All right, gentlemen, if you do not want any railroads here you can keep them out, and you can keep out immigration also, and your poor sand ridges and flats will be a legacy you can hand down to future posterity at a value of fifty cents per acre."

There is no question that the Plant people were moving ahead. The Florida Southern line was averaging twenty-nine carloads of oranges per day for the Northern markets, and the prices for which the oranges were being sold were "very satisfactory." The Point was getting desperate to participate in this good fortune, and cared little who brought it to them. It was obviously a favorite topic of conversation: "If you want to start a lively discussion all that you have to do is to go into one of the stores and commence to talk about the railroad."

The Orange Belt had, by this time, been completed to Oakland, where it connected with the South Florida Railway at Longwood, "a station between Sanford and Orlando. Two trains are run daily each way." Despite every kind of disaster, Demens was pushing onward. The deadline Disston had insisted upon in his agreement with Demens was the end of the year 1887, and given the challenges the road builders faced, that was going to be extremely difficult to meet. The rain poured down in torrents, shipment of materials were constantly being delayed, the equipment that did turn up was defective, cost overruns were prohibitive, yellow fever outbreaks struck throughout the vicinity and above all, there was never enough money. In February of 1887, Demens found himself literally broke, and only with Disston's help was he able to borrow another $100,000 to forge ahead. Again and again Disston came to the rescue of the desperate company, with money, with extensions of deadlines, with every kind of assistance that would, he was sure, guarantee the eventual arrival of modern transportation to Disston City.

8. The O.B.R.R.

In actuality there was nothing much modern about the Orange Belt Railway system. Every bit of the equipment was substandard, bought at the most bargain prices Demens could negotiate. The rails themselves were at first no more than sixteen pounds per foot, incredibly flimsy compared not only to later weights, which approached and exceeded one hundred pounds, but even to the standards of the day, twenty-five to thirty pounds. The line was of narrow gauge construction, the width between rails about three and a half feet, rather than the standard four feet eight and a half inches. All the rolling stock was bought second hand from other lines that had converted from narrow gauge to standard dimensions. A passenger coach consisted in width of two seats, a tiny aisle and another seat, barely room to move about.

The wood burning locomotives could achieve some fifteen miles per hour, if the wood was sufficiently dry. If not, one could move along as fast by walking beside the train. It was not unheard of for passengers to get out and chop wood to keep it going. Axes were carried aboard for just that eventuality.

From the very beginning the Orange Belt was a technical failure, due not only to the almost obsolete narrow gauge configuration, but also, simply, to wretchedly poor building techniques. The gangs of construction workers were not markedly skilled. First came the choppers, who cut down any vegetation along the projected path, followed by the graders. Then a gang came along to lay cross ties, and finally another to spike and bolt down the rails. That was it. Those efforts completed, the train was moved along forward, without any serious attempt at leveling or firming the tracks, which of course resulted before very long in loose rails, wavy and uneven tracks, and frequent interruptions of service.

The operators were about as unskilled as the laborers. Frequent engine breakdowns were routine. All too often the woods caught on fire from the locomotive's output of soot and sparks. Cows were regularly run over, since the line had not invested in cattle guards, again bringing the journey to a stop. The O.B.R.R. was in fact known as the "cattle killer." Workers went out every morning to pick up cows killed the day before. Owners could claim the carcasses for nine dollars.

The O.B.R.R. was the largest narrow gauge railroad in the country, and the shabbiest. Still, Disston City longed for its arrival.

In early 1887, Governor Safford, who lived in Tarpon Springs, was here with a party of Orange Belt officials. "They spent two days with the people on the Point, inspiring considerable confidence that they mean business, and receiving some substantial guarantees in the way of help, in land donations. We are quite sure . . . that by a united effort on the part of the principal land owners here that we could soon have a road, but it will be in this instance as it always has been, many who are best able and should be most interested will do nothing. By our next issue we hope to be able to give more encouraging reports."

They kept their hopes up, and kept railing against the speculators. "We certainly have no desire to discourage immigration to this portion of Florida, but there is one class, who are apt to make themselves somewhat numerous, quite soon, that we don't particularly need—the land speculator—and it is our candid opinion that we have more to fear, and even now are suffering more depression, from our lands being bought up and held by this omnipresent class of individuals than from all other causes. They are the 500 per cent fellows. They buy the choice lands of the county at from $5.00 to $20.00 per acre and hold for $25.00 to $100.00. We do not need any more of such here. Let us keep our lands for those people who want to make their homes amongst us, and offer inducement to them to come, by selling, to actual settlers, at reasonable prices."

9. Not in Disston City

Demens continued to endure a series of crises. In August, the yellow fever epidemic was so rampant that workers deserted his gangs to escape the danger. And here is where Disston City itself may have helped to cause the railroad's eventual termination in St. Petersburg, due to its extremely strong stand against the yellow fever refugees.

In September Demens' creditors finally lost patience and chained locomotives to the rails, forcing him to come up with more cash. In October, his very life was threatened by hordes of unpaid workers. Still, amazingly, the work went on. The December 31, 1887, deadline had long been an idle joke, for by that date the line was still far north of the Point and far inland from the coast. But by the spring of 1888, the end was almost in sight; the Orange Belt reached Tarpon Springs. Demens pushed even harder, hiring crews of black laborers to speed the work onward. On April 30 they reached the edge of the Williams tract.

There was yet another halt while the two men hassled through further negotiations, but that was soon worked out, and the line completed the small remaining distance to its terminal at 9th Street and Central Avenue. The Stradas, with seventeen-year-old Sophie (who recalled the day her entire long life), came up several miles through the wilderness from their home on the Point to witness the arrival of the little wood-burning engine on June 8, 1888, in a part of town called Wardsville, because there was nothing there except E.R. Ward's store. But all that would soon change, and change so quickly the Disston City folks would be almost overnight left behind, contemplating their losses in a state of shock.

Many or most of them simply picked up and left. Baumeister went, and Norwood; George King moved his sawmill. The McPhersons would go, as would most of the English settlers. Paul's Landing, which was now in the process of becoming St. Petersburg (whether after Demens' first name or his home town is debatable), would experience an influx of homesteaders, tourists and merchants like Henry Hibbs, who brought his fish business over from Tampa and built an industry. The St. Petersburg population in 1888, at the time of the railroad's arrival, was something around thirty, certainly under fifty. Two years later, the 1890 census showed a head count of 273.

The tatty little railroad had two engines, so it ran the one hundred-mile trip between Pinellas and Sanford each way, each day, with stops at Longwood, Oakland, Tarpon Springs, Dunedin, Clear Water and Largo. The journey took twelve hours and was far from luxurious travel, but it served its purpose, and it changed not only the course of Disston City's history but the lives of all those who had chosen to settle on the Point. The mail came every day—every day! This alone obliterated one of the major social rituals of the community, gathering at the docks to meet the mail boats, which were often much delayed or never came at all. People hung around, waiting, visiting, an opportunity to catch up on the neighbors' activities and news. Now, trips to pick up the mail became daily errands, solitary trips to the terminal.

Arsenault calls the arrival of the railroad the end of the "face to face folk culture." Before this time, groups of people had settled, clan-style, where their livelihoods and kinfolk drew them. Fishermen and boatmen gravitated to the bayous; citrus and vegetable farmers set out their plantings along Lakeview Avenue; the cattlemen were inland and upland; and of course, the settlers drawn by Disston and his dream had gravitated to his City. Now the beginnings of homogeneity in society would set in at the site of the larger, growing towns, the places located along the railroad.

That was one effect, one that would take time to emerge, as would several others. The fishing and citrus industries, for example, would eventually benefit. At the moment, though, the Point was still a very long way from northern markets, and shipping rates were high. Neither was tourism much enhanced; there wasn't a lot, after all, to attract people to the area. Still, these things would soon happen, but not in "Distance" City.

The end to the story of the Orange Belt and the entrepreneurs, Demens, Disston and Williams, is about as disastrous as the curse of King Tut's tomb. The railroad itself expired in 1894, partly due to the great freeze that wiped out its commercial base of support, the citrus industry. Henry Plant took over the lease and operated it as the Sanford and St. Petersburg Railroad before buying it outright and making it part of the Atlantic Coast Railroad System.

John Bethell's memoir fills in some of the gaps regarding the end of the careers of Miranda and Torres.

Miranda was a man of great energy and was possessed of a lively imagination as all pushing men of affairs are wont to be. And if his schemes could have been materialized the lower end of this peninsula might have had a far different history as a result.

In his fertile brain the little village plat of Boca Ciega Bay soon became simply the nucleus of a Greater Disston... It was, maybe, a dream, but a dream that is likely to become under another name, a grand reality in the years that are before us.

Big lithographic maps of the greater city were issued, which, together with a variety of lesser literature, were scattered liberally abroad. An English settler was my authority for the statement that "next to New York and New Orleans, Disston City was the best known place in America as far as London was concerned."

A final chapter in the Miranda saga gives a hint of the prevailing public sentiment toward his ventures. An ad in the *St. Petersburg Times* placed by a political candidate in late 1903 states unequivocally that if elected, he "would never appoint William B. Miranda City Attorney." Bill Miranda died in February 1906, alone, in a hotel room on Central Avenue.

Bethell says that Torres removed to Seminole in 1888, and gives a sharp picture of the man's character: "In those young days of the town of Disston mass meetings of the populace were extremely prevalent, in which, whatever the matter in hand, Citizen Torres inevitably bobbed up with a lot of strongly worded 'resolutions.' And he carried off his part well. Railroads were planned—on paper. Water transportation lines were organized—without capital. Flying machines were not in the air at that time, but if they had been whole fleets of them—in imagination—would have swarmed around the young town. Unfortunately, everything else was mostly 'in the air,' and stayed there!"

What became of Torres after that? One report has him becoming a judge in Tampa in 1890, but we know that he ran for the city incorporation council in St. Petersburg in 1892. He probably did it all; Joseph Torres got around.

Demens himself had long ago left, deep in debt, for California, where he tried some new schemes involving newspapers and expatriate Russians. Williams, who had run unsuccessfully for mayor of St. Petersburg, died in 1892, somewhat bitter about the town he had helped to found. Disston, fully mortgaged and hit hard by the depression of the 1890s was more than bitter. He committed suicide in his bathtub in 1896.

Chapter III

The Fishing Village

IN A 1953 ARTICLE IN the *Gulfport Citizen*, Inez Jones Nuhn wrote that when the era known elsewhere as the Gay Nineties began, "along the waterfront of beautiful Boca Ciega Bay, a small fishing village sprawled—not the peace friendly type of village we know today, but a lusty settlement, where law and order didn't have too much of a chance and violence was the rule, not the exception, among the itinerant fishermen who laid claim to the fishing rights and privileges of the Bay."

This viewpoint, apparently rather widely held, found a contemptuous response from the descendants of some of those fishing families. Thirty or forty years later, Claudette Renney Dean wrote:

Anything that was built along the coast of Florida seems to be classified as a fishing village. The term is not offensive in its true meaning. However, today [it is] spoken with wrinkled nose as if speaking of a nasty on your shoe, and the people who inhabit these villages, no better. The reference to their homes as 'fishing shacks' reeks of stupidity. There were shanties built at points where the men camped out when they were fishing. These were known as fish camps. These were not their homes. You must realize fishing was only one part of their lives, a seasonal money crop but one which afforded pleasure and excitement. These men had many skills, they were independent, intelligent people and judged no man by what he had in the bank, but what was in his heart. First and foremost they were ship builders, a craft handed down from one generation to another. And their homes were built with the same care as the ships . . . The early homes were not built fancy, but serviceable. You must remember all, and I mean all, materials had to be brought in by ship. Even after they had their own saw mill it had to be sent away to be finished, so that nothing was wasted.

1. The Family

So who, exactly, were the people left in Disston City in the 1890s, after the railroad was lost and the grand town failed to materialize? Most of those who had come to take up the promise of the future capital of the Disston Empire had already left. The merchants, the newspapermen and the English folk were all gone. In essence, the town had moved back a decade and was once again inhabited by only its original settlers and their extended families.

James Barnett had finally succumbed to his War injuries in September 1886. Called "our old Neptune" by the *Sea Breeze*, he had continued his maritime ventures, buying and selling boats, right to the end of his life. Or renting them, as to a Mr. Dye of John's Pass, who "got one of Capt. Barnett's boats to go home in. When near Boca Ceiga Pass, he went forward to lower the sail, when a puff of wind struck the boat and upset it. The groceries were spilled out, and all lost, a sad experience for Mr. Dye, who is a poor man." Dye sat on the boat about two hours before it drifted into shallow water, where he righted it and eventually got back to town. "Not wishing to try his luck again on the water, he started for home by land, where he arrived Sunday morning."

James' obituary states that he left only three children, for Julia had died at seventeen in January 1885. Sadly, even Barnett descendants often seem to forget Julia's very existence, but perhaps there is more to the story. She had been married in August 1884 to a man named Tom Sawyer, then about twenty-five. Sawyer and his brother John were Key Westers with connections to the Roberts and Curry families, and antecedents in the Bahamas. John remained in Key West, where he became a prominent businessman and sat on the city commission, while Tom had been around the Point for some five or six years, though he returned often to visit his home and family. Julia is traditionally assumed to have died in childbirth, but a tale told by one of Henry Slaughter's daughters gives a different slant on her life. In this version, she disgraced her family by becoming pregnant, running off and having the baby, only to be brought back by her brother Henry, much to Rebecca's displeasure. Rebecca, it was said, never forgave Henry and never spoke to him again. Unfortunately, this is an unverifiable family legend.

In 1880 Henry had married into the vast Nash family, whose history paralleled that of his own. They, too, had trekked southward from Georgia immediately following the Civil War to homestead just north of the little fishing village and produce eleven children. Mary Nash Slaughter was the fifth of these, joined through brothers and sisters to the Arnolds, Leonardis, Lowes and to Joseph Torres. Henry and his wife Mary would have eight children themselves by the end of the decade: Minnie Clara, Margaret Aurelia, Grace Louise, Christine Rebecca, Inez Lucy, Florence, Robert Taylor and Henrietta.

Henry, who has been described by his descendants as a boat captain, had the usual variety of occupations common to Disston City residents of that period. He had, as noted, been the surveyor in the 1880s platting, and listed himself as a teamster in city directories, but early in this decade we find him "building a small lighter for Mr. Steinwinder to be used to float a sand pump for driving piles for dock and bridge work."

Joseph Steinwinder had come here in 1887 from Alabama, and found work on the crew building the Egmont Key yellow fever quarantine station. That job over, he began to operate a sawmill at Lealman, and would later move it to Gulfport. Steinwinder was of exactly the pioneer stock needed in the area. He ran his sawmill, fished, built his own house from trees he felled himself and lived into his robust nineties. Along the way he would marry Sophie Strada in 1892 and have four daughters and a son.

The other Slaughter children were all off living their own lives, most of them, however, close by. Martha Jane and Alex Leonardi had eight as well: Henry, Florence (a boy), Melissa, Viola, Nelly and Lorena, Harold and Vera. Alex's sister Mary Emma had married into the old Pinellas pioneer family of Neelds, who had bought the *Sea Breeze* from Will McPherson, but never continued its publication. The Neelds were fishermen, farmers and merchant sailors who carried mail and lumber to the Point, and occasionally indulged in "plume hunting," a devastating pursuit that wiped out many of Boca Ciega Bay's rookeries in response to the current fashion's demand for feathered hats and gowns.

Alex Leonardi had developed during this decade into one of the leading lights of the community, serving in several public and political capacities while employed in the construction of the "large hotel at Bellaire" (today the Belleview Biltmore).

Another Leonardi sister, Ellen, married George Meares, who was homesteading in the old area near Big Bayou, while Evelina, the youngest of Vincent's girls, married Joseph Strauss. Alex's brother Eugene married Vinnie Fripp, the daughter of an old Disston City family, just after she celebrated her seventeenth birthday with a dance at the Waldorf. The couple moved to "Sara Sota" and took along Vinnie's mother. The Leonardis often staged "musicales," charging a five-cent entrance fee; Vincent, a well-known fife player and probably master of other instruments as well, died in 1890 at the age of sixty-five.

Frank Futch and Sarah Melissa (Slaughter) and their family had by this time moved to Charlotte Harbor, near Punta Gorda. Their children—birth dates unknown, except that the youngest was born in 1911 when Melissa had reached the legendary age of fifty-two—were John, Albert, Oscar, Rufus, Leola, Charles, Robert, Rosa, Elonzo, Rayford, Daniel and Connie Futch.

A new family, the Nobles, arrived from Georgia in 1890, but were apparently not very popular. One of them "[moved] into the building given by Mr. Tomlinson to the people of Disston City for a place of worship and claims to have bought the property. The good folk of the town are wondering who had any right to sell the same." Minnie Clara Slaughter would marry a Noble son, James Thomas, when she was only fourteen and he twenty-one. The couple soon left for Lee County, where they raised a family of eleven children.

By 1900 James Barnett, Jr., though twenty-seven, was still living at home. Rebecca had applied for and been granted a widow's pension of $60 a year, based on James' service. Mary Elizabeth, on the other hand, had married her sister Julia's widower, Tom Sawyer, had two children (Chester and Gladys), divorced Tom, married Jackson Quinn, and had another son, Raymond. The last Barnett child, Laura, was newly married to John Campaign White, son of a very old Florida family.

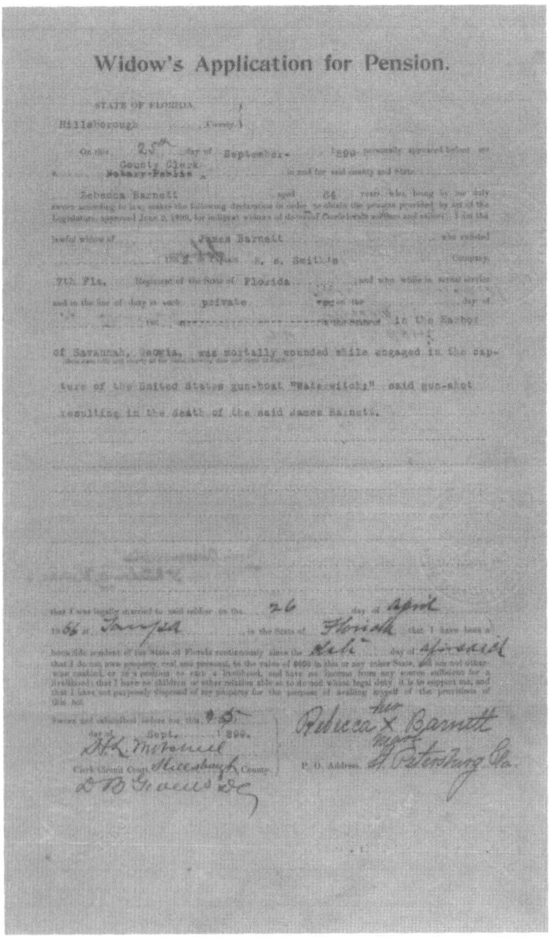

Widow's Application for Pension.

STATE OF FLORIDA
Hillsborough County

On this 25th day of September 1899 personally appeared before me a County Clerk in and for said county and State

Rebecca Barnett aged 64 years

lawful widow of James Barnett

7th Fla. Regiment of the State of Florida

private

in the Harbor of Savannah, Georgia, was mortally wounded while engaged in the capture of the United States gun-boat "Water-witch;" said gun-shot resulting in the death of the said James Barnett.

that I was legally married to said soldier on the 26 day of April 1866 at Tampa in the State of Florida

Sworn and subscribed before me this 25 day of Sept. 1899.

Clerk Circuit Court, Hillsborough County.

Rebecca her X mark Barnett

P. O. Address. St. Petersburg Fla.

Rebecca's Application for a military pension, 1899, signed with an "X".
Courtesy Sherrie Lynn Shamo

First of the Whites to have contact with Disston City was Joshua White, born at Fort Brooke in 1851 to a family long associated with a plantation around Curlew Creek. Joshua was a boat captain whose travels occasionally brought him this way. One trip is known for certain, and that is when he carried a cargo of two thousand coconuts to a proposed plantation on Long Key. Joshua had married a woman named Louisa Sontag, or, in the English translation, Sunday, some ten years his junior and widely accorded credit as being the only literate woman in the settlement. "Miss Lou," who would become the town midwife, claimed some relation to the German writer Goethe through her sister Frances' marriage to his grandson. The White children included John Campaign, Dolly, Ann (who apparently died young), Louise, Mabel, Barney and Herbert. In 1895, John married Laura Barnett and their first child, Rose, was born in 1898. The White home was located on the waterfront at the foot of 52nd Street, and we are left a wonderful drawing of it by a grandson, Richard Bozeman, Dolly's son.

Drawing by Richard Bozeman (1906?-1985) of his grandfather Joshua White's house on the bluff.

Bozeman's graphic illustration of Joshua White's home on the bluff gives us the finest sense of just how these fishing families lived. The two-story house set just back from the water's edge was a simple but efficient board-and-batten construction, built of pine heartwood with oak heartwood for decorative trim. This pine timber once grew in vast forests, which were entirely logged out by 1930. The Southern longleaf pine, called the finest timber tree of all, had heartwood exceptional for its honeyed patina and tight grain (today builders go to great lengths to raise the remaining sunken logs from the south's rivers to build expensive and elegant homes for their wealthiest clients). Such heart pine houses are notable for their durability and many still exist in modern Gulfport.

Elevated against flooding a century before laws had to be written to require such precautions, the White house stood tall and cool, porches back and front and a breezeway through the center providing constant ventilation. The lower floor had two rooms, a living and a dining room either side of the hall and a kitchen attached at the back, with a pantry still further beyond. The second floor consisted of one large and two small bedrooms with another hallway between, which served as a workroom for domestic projects, such as sewing.

The front porch was for sitting and the back porch for work, for there we find butchering hooks and racks for tools and materials. Outside the back door were both a pump and a cistern, though the wash pot and clotheslines were located at the front of the property, nearer to the edge of the bluff, possibly because of the fire danger. Along the shore there was a dock and room for the net spreads.

The entire back of the property was efficiently utilized. Running northward from the west side of the house, we find a grape arbor, fish smoke house, meat smoke house and lastly, privy. The Whites grew the same type of grapes, scuppernong, as had others such as the Puigs. These are a sweet species of muscadines, which can be eaten fresh off the vine or made into various condiments or wines. Across the northern border, which is now marked by 31st Avenue, there was a chicken hut and run. Other livestock pens and sheds were further to the east, past a small barn and kitchen gardens. Joshua also had a tiny grocery store at the northeast corner of his property, for by this time the earlier merchants had abandoned Disston City and there were no other shops left to provide the basic necessities.

White's home (demolished in the mid-1920s by Alvah C. Roebuck in order to provide a better view of the Bay for his residence at 5233 Dellett), probably slightly better than typical, was in the most heavily populated area of the late nineteenth-century settlement. The few remaining residents were clustered between 49th Street and 52nd Street, for five or six blocks north of the Bay.

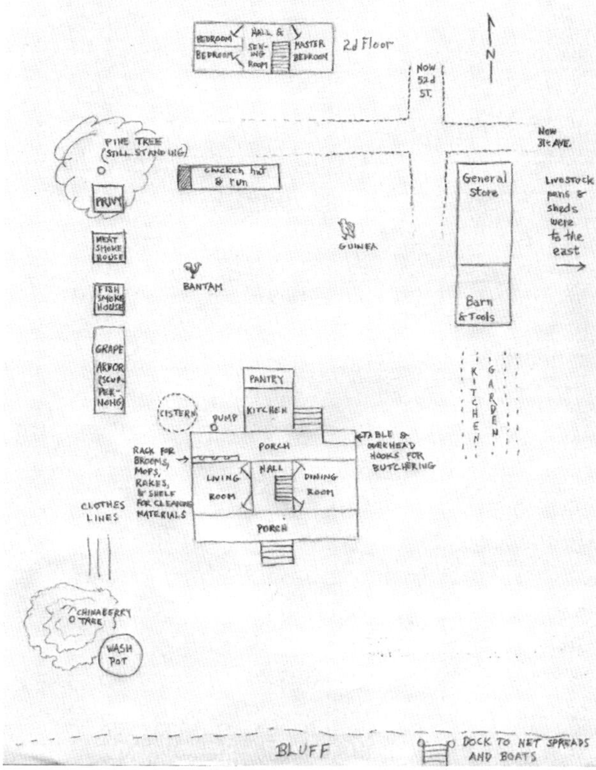

Bozeman drawing of the White property with outbuildings and their usages.

Only much later, after the arrival of the trolley, did the main part of town shift westward to its present location.

Other long-lasting arrivals were the Renneys. William was the first member of this family to come here. He had been born in 1855 in Key West, son of John and Lenore Lowe Renney, and orphaned at three. Raised by his maternal relatives, he returned to the Keys and became a diver and sponger. Soon he added boat captain to his careers and began sailing north to Ozona, where he met and married Elvira Dixon. Elvira, born in Quincy and descended from a family who had been in Hillsborough County at least since 1824, claimed the rights of a free dealer, a woman who could buy and sell property and conduct business independent of her husband's consent.

The exact date of the Renneys' arrival in Disston City is unclear, some recollections claiming it was a direct result of the Sponge Wars at Tarpon Springs, which did not really begin until the 1905 incursion of immigrant Greek divers. These so-called "wars" represent a series of events, not always considered important enough to mention in many histories, but which were in fact a complex and crucial factor in the founding of this and other localities. Once more the old Key West families play a part.

Some of the best sponge beds in the world are found along the west coast of Florida, where, for decades the Conchs had been sailing on their various missions. After the great hurricane of 1848 it is said they found many sponges thrown ashore, and, never lacking in enterprise, put together a small fleet of boats and men to do some harvesting by the simple hook and bucket method. Soon a small industry developed, with a marketing center in Key West, where the hauls were brought for sale.

One of the wealthy citizens attracted to Tarpon Springs by the Disston venture, John K. Cheyney, felt the industry had potential and would provide a good economic base on which to build. With Disston backing, he formed the Anclote and Rock Island Sponge Company, hired as his first employee none other than William Roberts and bought a boat from one of the Lowes. Not willing to stop there, Cheyney investigated all possibilities that could enhance his project, including a mechanical diving suit recently invented in Europe. The Key Westers and Bahamians who were used to hooking sponges in shallow water did not at all care for the idea of being submerged in heavy artificial diving apparatus. Consequently, the industry began importing divers from Greece, soon numbering in the hundreds, to work the sponge fields off Tarpon.

The Spanish-American War, which came altogether too close to Key West for it to remain a viable trading market, brought the fleet to Tarpon, where the Greeks continued to arrive and their ventures increased in size and profit. They thought the locals backward and lazy, long-bearded, gun-toting "layabouts" who worked only as much as they had to, and lived in a kind of ignorant drunken poverty. The "hookers" protested that the weighty-suited, bottom-walking divers would destroy the sponge beds, but the invasion of 500 or so young, strong, noisy and excitable Greek males was perhaps the real cause of their resentment.

Obviously a bad situation was brewing. After the war, most of the Key Westers left Tarpon Springs and returned to their home base, or perhaps elsewhere as in the case of the Renneys, some Robertses and Lowes. They did not, however, cease to hate the Greeks. Whenever possible they attacked Greek boats, "like a swarm of hornets" they captured crewmen and burned the boats. The battles were small but incessant, with harassment, beatings and destruction by both sides.

So the Renneys may well have begun to establish a home here some years before the worst of the Sponge Wars, perhaps while William continued to do business at Tarpon. Eventually William Renney's activities were entirely centered here, around a boating business conveying passengers and freight. The Renneys had a large young family, William Aaron "Ade", Samuel Perry, George, Lawrence D., Percy, Almiron, Fred and Martha, an outgoing sociable group who always had a place in their homes for one more.

Finally, the Robertses were still with us. William Roberts, nephew of both John Bethell and Abel Miranda, and Virginia (Young) had seven sons and a daughter: Christopher, Walter Minton, Frederick, William, Andrew, Carrie, Percy and Louis.

2. Cultivating the Crops

Many of the *Sea Breeze* news items were devoted to the current crops, a subject of paramount interest, after all, when it furnishes the citizens' very sustenance. But it also provides an interesting record of the farming ventures of the day.

Though commercial gardening was never very profitable here, tomatoes, cucumbers and eggplant were among the produce being shipped from little farms along Lakeview. "We saw one of our gardeners receive a big check from his commission merchant the other day." After buying a "small bill of groceries" and using the check to pay, "the merchant took it and handed back ten cents, with the remark, 'that makes it right.' Who would not be a vegetable grower?"

In the fall Will reported on the state of the MacPhersons' dwarf banana, pineapples and 'russet' oranges. The fine autumn rain was the cue to plant out strawberries, cabbage, collards and rutabagas. "Sow onion seeds," he advised, since the northern onion crop was said to be a failure, and Floridians could have a crop to sell "before their northern brethren can commence to plant. Force your plants and vegetables into market early."

And, "We are decidedly in favor of the no fence law as to hogs. We firmly believe that the annual expense of fencing against the few contemptible razor backs that run at large on the Point is more than the whole tribe are worth. We have lost sweet potatoes enough to pay for a half dozen or more. We believe that there is money in hogs (the trouble is to get it out of them) which increases the longer they run at large . . . We are willing to help raise a fund to buy up the whole lot, and have a grand shooting match, if some better way can not be thought of, to get rid of these worthless pests."

The rain came back in April: "Splendid showers . . . oranges are getting scarce . . . fine weather for vegetables . . . the farmers look happy now . . . sweet potatoes are abundant but too cheap for those who wish to sell." John Bethell's date palm was in bloom, and George Meares was shipping cucumbers from his holdings at Lakeview and 22nd Street. His neighbor, John Donaldson, "our colored friend" brought "some excellent new Florida syrup to town."

The acres of watermelons were "beginning to vine, and about the same amount in cucumbers which have commenced to bloom, and turnips—we are afraid to tell—well we will say that we measured one that was twenty-eight inches around and still growing. No telling how large they will be by next fall, but we understand that the fence is to be moved so as to give them room to grow in."

"All on the Point report good success with [grape] vines as far as we have heard. The mocking bird seems to be the greatest enemy to the fruit." Puig, for one said he would have had twice as many bunches on his two vines if it were not for the birds, who seem to think they have a perfect right to all they can eat.

Puig was still trying to make a go of New Cadiz, and we are left a remarkably picturesque record of life in the neighborhood by an early tourist whose letters to the Trenton, Missouri *Tribune* include the following tale:

A Mr. Thomas, of New Bedford, Mass.: "took a horseback ride across the peninsula to Disston City, and a mile to the east of Disston he made the acquaintance of an old citizen by the name of Puig, a Spaniard." Despite Puig's long residence, "he speaks English with evident difficulty. He has on his small farm, as I hastily viewed it, oranges, lemons, dates, palms, bananas, pecans, scuppernong grapes and a fair sized cabbage patch. But I am ahead of my story."

I learned from Mr. Thomas that transportation would be furnished to Mr. Puig's place, from St. Petersburg across the peninsula, and thence by sail across the bay to Long Key, beyond and to the west of which is the main gulf." So a group of gentlemen set out, "with baskets for shells, and well selected lunches," to await "the coming of our conveyance [which] came in due time [and] consisted of a rather heavy road wagon—not a spring wagon—with two spring seats, and drawn by one mule. The driver, a Mr. Kimball, a relative of Mr. Puig, called the mule Jim. With this outfit, four of us and the driver, started for Disston, some five or six miles across the peninsula. The mule, Jim, was of regulation color—a yellowish brindle, with a stripe along his back; but his gait was slow. Jim carried his head low, and his ears flopped forward like a mule already fatigued. When the driver would hit him on the right side, Jim would make a graceful curve to the left, and when hit on the left side the curve was reversed, but in neither event was the speed perceptibly accelerated.

The trip across the peninsula, some five or six miles, was very enjoyable. We got all the fun we could get out of Jim. The country is rolling pine land with the roll not very distinct. I observed two kinds of trees somewhat mixed with the pines; they are both called oaks. One has the genuine oak leaf, while the other has a leaf and bark much like the hackberry; but they call it oak, all the same. These oaks shed their leaves in the fall, and now the new leaves are nearly full size. I noticed a small shrub one or two feet high, beautifully covered with white bloom, which our driver said was a species of the pawpaw. I also noted a small scrubby brush which our driver called the willow oak. With the exceptions named, the woods we passed through was long-leafed pine and the ever present saw or scrub palmetto.

After an hour's pull Jim brought us to Mr. Puig's plantation, his residence being within a few hundred feet of the bay. This bay is not the Tampa; but has an unpronounceable name written Boca Ceiga or Four Mile Bayou. Long Key, of which I made mention in a former letter, lies between Boca Ceiga and Pas Agrille. When we had reached the plantation, and I had extracted a promise that Jim should be fed and watered, we entered a small sail boat with Mr. Kimball as sailor but there was no wind and it was about three miles across the bay to Long Key. Mr. Thomas is a sailor, but he proved to be a rower also, and he and Mr. Kimball who was our guide as well as sailor, rowed us across and down the Key until we struck a breeze from the gulf and our route was at once made easy.

"We sailed down through Pas de Agrille with the southern end of Long Key on our right and Pine Key on our left, and in full view of the light house on Egmont some eight miles to our southeast, we pulled for a sand reef some mile or two to the south of Long Key. Before I left our landing place I made a note of our surroundings and the shape of the low sand key, so I could return by the shortest route, and started up the Key in quest of shells. Within two hours I had my basket full of the pick of the gulf coast. At 3:10 we were on our return to the Puig plantation, which we reached in good shape at 4:15. Mr. Puig served us with lemonade, and gathered from the tree in our presence, a lemon for each, as he expressed it, nearly as large as pumpkins.

Jim was found to be all right, and after a fresh watering was hitched on to our heavy wagon and we were soon on our way to St. Petersburg which we reached by dark.

3. The Sea Folk

Boats were everybody's transportation, most people's means of livelihood, and many folks' recreation, so they got a major portion of the *Sea Breeze's* attention. Reports from the newssheet tell us that bigger boats continually dropped by, though on no set schedule. A steamer en route to Memphis might lie at anchor off Mullet Key, while a schooner loaded with lumber touched at the wharf, and another came in from Key Largo with a cargo of pineapple sprouts, cassava cuttings and banana roots. The sharpie *Mystery* of Cedar Keys brought some samples of millet, which was being promoted as a profitable forage crop, capable of growing "on high pine land, without any cultivation, and the cattle are very fond of it." The "sharpie" configuration was that of a sailboat fifty to sixty feet in length, with a topsail, main, gaff, and jib, and a flat bottom with a keel. Sloops were single-masted sailboats, while yawls, ketches and schooners had two masts. In yawls and ketches, the small mast is aft of the main, with the steering apparatus forward of this mast in a yawl and behind it in a ketch. If the forward mast is the smaller of the two, the boat is called a schooner, although schooners could have three, four or more masts.

Delia stopped on her way to New Orleans, and a brick mason came up from Key West on the *Ben S. Curry*, and left the same evening for Clearwater. He told the locals there was little work in his line there, for though "things are booming," most of the building was being done in wood. The boat then took a load of watermelons to Key West, and brought back some pineapples, bananas and mangoes.

T.A. Whitted, familiarly known as "Ott," came over from Palma Sola for the holidays, bringing a load of lumber. "Thinking he would have no use for shoes in this wilderness, he left his (a right new pair) lying on the bank when he started. He was compelled by the storm to land at Mullet Key, and had his boat swamped twice in the breakers, but the storm calming down he reached Disston about 7 o'clock that night without further accidents."

Whitted was at that time about twenty, and had come with his family from Iowa in 1878 to farm in Manatee. A job at George King's saw mill had brought him to Disston City in 1884, and when there wasn't a lot to do there, he "helped the mailman in bringing mail from Tampa to Big Bayou in a small sailboat." In 1887 he married Zephaniah Phillips' daughter Julia, and the next year they left Disston for St. Petersburg, following the railroad as so many did. Along with the fish merchant Hibbs and Joseph Torres, he ran on the "wet" ticket for the first city council in 1892, and lost to McPherson and his anti-saloon party. In later years, his son Albert would of course become St. Petersburg's hero pilot, after whom the local airport would be named.

We read in many historic sources that H.B. Plant, the man who brought the railroad to Tampa, effectively wished that Pinellas would never become much more, as Arsenault says, than "a refuge for weekend excursionists, mullet fishermen, and a few foolhardy citrus farmers." He was well on his way to realizing that goal in the 1890s, for fishing, in Pinellas and certainly in Disston City, was truly the only remaining vocation available to residents. The expertise of the locals as fishing and hunting guides was well known and promoted, even by Plant himself, at his elegant Tampa hotel. But scratching a living from the Gulf and the Bay was not, and never had been, an easy or profitable life. Foremost of the difficulties was the process of getting a catch to market. Now, however, two new factors had improved the fisherman's options: the railroad, of course, and the arrival of Henry W. Hibbs's fish company in St. Petersburg.

Hibbs, born in 1862, was a North Carolinian, although like so many others, he had ties to Key West. When he brought his fish business to St. Petersburg from Tampa in 1889 and opened a fish house on the Orange Belt Railroad pier, he offered locals an outlet for the sale of their catches. No longer did they have to contend with shipping by boat or rail to Tampa or even more distant markets. They responded enthusiastically, with about a thousand pounds a day brought in for processing, which by the end of the century had become ten thousand pounds or more. Interestingly enough, the entire estimated poundage processed in the year 1900 was about three million, while at the beginning of the Second World War, Clam Bayou alone was shipping out some five million pounds annually.

The locals trusted Henry Hibbs, for they knew him and he knew them all. He gave them credit when they needed it and paid them fairly and promptly. He also tried to keep up with every possible modern improvement, as in the matter of providing ice for shipments. At first he had relied on ice brought in by the railroad, never a particularly dependable method, but soon he built his own ice plant near the foot of the half-mile long St. Petersburg pier. He overcame the problem of transporting the ice to the end of the pier by the simple expedient of constructing what amounted to a wheeled platform rigged with sails, which was used successfully for many years and only abandoned after it ran down and killed a tourist in 1913.

Men of the Hibbs Fish Company bringing in a catch on the Gulfport pier.

Hibbs operated on a larger scale than most of the other middlemen who had jumped in to take advantage of the growing industry. He himself owned some of the offshore vessels that went out beyond the Bay into the Gulf after grouper, red snapper and mackerel. In 1892, when St. Petersburg incorporated itself and held elections for the first town officers, Hibbs made the mistake of embracing the party which was not sounding the rallying cry against demon run. George King, Arthur Norwood and Will McPherson became city leaders; for the moment, Henry W. Hibbs did not, though later, in 1894-95, he would serve a term as mayor of that city.

Sometimes enterprising locals made a little more by selling directly to Point residents through the simple method of catching ten or a dozen, spiking them onto a palmetto frond, and going house to house offering them for five cents apiece, a considerable advance over Hibbs' price, but obviously not practical for dealing in quantity.

When there was some slack time, most fishermen turned to building their boats, particularly the little skiffs used in mullet fishing. Of course, some became extremely proficient at the trade and ended up as actual professional boat builders, as did the Sawyers, for example. But the homemade skiffs were the backbone of the local industry. These were small flat-bottomed boats designed for use with oars in shallow water. They were usually about sixteen feet long, with a bow cap on them and a net table in the rear, for loading the several hundred yards of net carried on each. The oars, too, were fashioned by the men who used them, into fourteen- to eighteen-foot sections of two-by-four or two-by-six whittled down to a four-foot blade on one end and a handle the rest of the way up. With no other form of propulsion, the skiff was poled along through shallow water, and paddled through the deeper parts of the Bay, which was heavy hard work indeed.

The grassy flats to the west of the settlement, which early on acquired the nickname "Fiddlers' Flats," were a good source of shellfish. Clams, stone crabs, oysters, coquinas (found in the Gulf, not the Bay), scallops and so forth were neither plentiful nor meaty enough to provide a diet staple, but they added a different taste now and then, as did the meat of the turtle. Now illegal, "turtling" excursions had been a feature of this coast for decades if not centuries. Moonlight nights on Blind Pass provided occasions for party-like trips after the big ones, the 600- to 700-pounders.

The killing method was cruel by today's standards. Turtles were turned over on their backs in the sun, and kept that way until they were very hot, then a bucket of water was thrown onto them, forcing them to blow. They were immediately decapitated by waiting axes. The killing of a turtle was a community event; everyone brought pans to collect pieces of meat, which were then chopped fine and fried in flour and seasonings, a welcome delicacy.

The eggs of these turtles were as big as ping pong balls, another treat the fishermen enjoyed through the simple expedient of puncturing them with an ice pick, shaking in some salt and pepper, and tossing them down raw.

Not everyone, of course, could quite (literally) swallow this.

So fishing was often the only way to avoid starvation, even to make a few dollars. Almost every man and boy in Disston City, and well into early Gulfport, was at least a part time fisherman—when the mullet were running. Each month of the year brought a different kind of catch. Amberjack and sheepshead ran in January and February; grouper and trout from November through March; bass, mackerel and kingfish spring and fall. Flounder, jewfish, redfish, shark and snook put in occasional appearances, and the king of game fish, the tarpon, was in season from May through the summer. And then there were the mullet, which were taken all year, except between November 15 and January 1, the spawning season.

Much of the netting was done right along the beaches. Joshua White's great grandson Nathan described some of the process: "The seining of mullet was done up and down the beaches, but they didn't go offshore for that—you'd take the mullet and if you'd have a good northwester in November or December, it would drive these spawned fish out into the gulf and as you know the mullet, both male and female have roe in them, the male had the white and female the yellow, and it takes the mixture of the two discharged into the water and this makes them hatch out, that's as far as I know about it."

Joe Roberts, grandson of William Roberts and Carrie Bethell, was one for whom catching mullet was a livelihood and he knew them well. "The mullet is a migrating fish, and if he takes a notion to go to Sarasota, it don't take him very long to get there. Mullet roe," he added, "is as good as caviar. Is, in fact, caviar."

Nathan White said, "The fishermen would then haul and seine them on the beach. They would put one end on the beach and make a big half moon circle out to the gulf and come back, and wrap the net around the post and pull the net in going up the beach. It was unbelievable the amount of fish they pulled up onto the beach." That, of course, was during the days when it was said there were so many mullet in the Bay that they made a roaring noise when a whole school of them crossed a sandbar. It has long since been against the law to put one end of a net on land.

They also did some netting away from the beach, making a cradle with the net and roping the fish within. In some ways, the very abundance of the Bay worked against those who depended on it for livelihood. The huge catches, particularly as the season wore on, drove the prices down to almost nothing, perhaps a penny or two a pound. Walter Roberts recalled, "I once saw my father catch 500 mullet with a cast net in little more than an hour. The fish

Netting from land, as once practiced.

averaged two pounds each, and one cast of the net would bring in 15 or 20 mullet."

Richard Bozeman wrote this dramatic recounting of the mullet-mens' lives:

> *When the sun refuses to shine and clothes haven't dried in weeks, when the icy rain of a November squall hits the face like buckshot and even the blacksnake won't stick his forked tongue out of his pit, the time is right for mullet to search out the still water protected by flying mangrove roots, for that is where mullet spawn. All nature now conspires to protect these stars of the sea by sending the worst weather of the year to pound the bays with lashing rain and churn the air with buffeting winds. This is the time when only the hardiest of men stand tall in their oiled-silk slickers and pole their skiffs into the tempest to frustrate nature's plan for the mullet.*
>
> *Two men, in separate skiffs, each with a lantern, a poling oar, and four hundred yards of net, glide out on a moonless night in search of flashes of phosphorus. When the glowing water is found, the two skiffs start from a common point and quietly move in opposite directions, paying out net as they encircle a shoal of mullet. When the circle is complete, the two skiffs move to the center of the enclosure creating a great commotion with oar against gunwale and knife against kettle to frighten the fish into wildly ignoring those faint blue-gray lines that let their heads through but stop them at the pectorals. In this position the strings of the net enter the gills, preventing them from closing, so*

that the fish is unable to separate the atoms of oxygen from the atoms of hydrogen and consequently drowns.

Once the strike is made, the circle is opened by the two skiffs moving in a reverse direction taking in the nets as rapidly as may be before the sharks with their triple-rows of razor-pointed teeth rip out square yards of net and gulp down scores of fish. As each net is taken in over the stern, horny hands extract the fish from the meshes, the nets being dropped in the stern, the fish being thrown to the center of the skiff, but eyes ever alert for an electric eel, a man-of-war, or other paralyzing creature of the sea. The horn on the hands, which results from years of pulling on wet hemp and being stuck by fins and cut by gills, offers no protection against the shock of eels or the poison of sea nettles.

When the haul is completed the skiffs are poled to the fish house, the place where ice has been stored; there the fish are packed in crushed ice to await transportation to market, and the men pole out to the bay again in the hope of making another haul before the season is over. So pass the nights and many winter days of mullet fishermen.

The mullet man's wife walks down to the net-spread with her husband and joshes with the other wives while their men pole from the cove to the bay. With forced laughter over un-funny jokes, the wives return through deep sand and sandspurs to their homes. There is a reluctance to enter the now empty house which her husband and his brothers built of heartwood; its destruction by termites or post beetles is one problem she does not have to worry about. Fire is another matter.

As the evening shadows lengthen she knows yesterday's wash-pot water is now cool enough to turn out under the clothesline to form a hard crust over the sand. The hog her man slaughtered before setting off for mullet has to be butchered, the hams and bacon sides salted for him to hang in the smoke house, the loins prepared for the oven, the guts emptied, scraped, washed, and boiled for sausage casings, and the offal spread round the rose and jasmine bushes. The kerosene lamps must be lighted now so the children can learn some grammar, memorize the spelling of words, and do their sums, while she coaches them without missing a stroke of the flat iron on yesterday's washing. On Saturday nights there is dough to knead and set for Sunday's light bread—in case the preacher comes. (On other days there are clabber biscuits, hot from the oven three times a day.)

There are always necessary chores to be done, necessary in more ways than one: she must not let her mind dwell on the hazards of her man's occupation -- the chances of his being stung by a ray, bitten by a barracuda, even drowned . . . These dangers she will not consciously admit to herself, but she cannot put them completely out of her mind as long as her man is on the water. Must get him to burn out the privy when the mullet are gone. Tragedy strikes the mullet men too often. There was that sad funeral for the jolly young prankster who bought wood alcohol from a passing bootlegger who said it was corn liquor. How many beds and bosks are going to miss him? He was good looking. Strong, too. No more of that. Her man wouldn't drink wood alcohol, would he? Nor would he stop at New Cadiz to call on that woman they say moved in after she got too diseased to continue plying her profession in Ybor City. Kill her, if he does!

Thankful for one job that won't have to be done tonight: bathing the children. Too cold. A lick and a promise will have to do this time. Cold is not all bad: there'll be no more houseflies, sandflies, mosquitos, and gnats until spring. Soon he'll be gathering oysters and cutting cabbage palms for us. If only she could take him some hot coffee brewed from freshly ground beans. Maybe bake a pie of dried apples and raisins this cold night; maybe he'll return tomorrow with a good haul; maybe enough for us to afford screens like they have in the windows of that dude fish camp. Couple of 5000-pound hauls ought to do it . . . Too hot most of the year to bake pies and cakes in a wood-burning oven. Must get him to lay in more stove wood and kindling before long. Anyway the best desserts hang on the trees and vines in the yard: oranges, loquats, bananas, peaches, guavas, mangoes, cherries, grapes, melons. In the morning before the sun is up, the day's supply of vegetables will have to be brought in from the kitchen garden, washed and prepared for cooking: squash and carrots, okra and tomatoes, egg-plant and potatoes, corn and beans, spinach and beets, cabbage and onions. Wonder if he could be persuaded to plant some sugar cane this spring. There will be fish to dress and fry, a chicken to catch and make into purleu (must save the down for pillows), and four vegetable dishes to fix. The children must be properly fed, though their father might not be home for a week. There's breakfast to make and lunch boxes to fill with sandwiches and—fruit for the school children. If this cold weather holds, it will be a good time to make soup. Eggs must be gathered from the chicken hut evening and morning, washed and candled. There is milk to be churned into butter. Then there is that bolt of percale from which sheets must be cut and hemmed, pillow cases run up, and maybe some nightgowns made. And she will embroider monograms on table linens in her spare time.

The "chicken purleu" was known in the settlement as a social occasion. The men would build fires and put on huge pots of rice while the women cleaned and boiled the chickens with rich seasonings. As the meal was put together, the men would fish or hunt and the women take the opportunity to visit.

4. End of the Nineteenth Century

Inez Nuhn called Disston City a lusty, violent place. There certainly was no formal government or law enforcement of any kind and would not be for years to come.

When disputes occurred, they must have been settled by the immediate participants. There doesn't seem to have been any real serious crime, although at this time it is difficult to make definitive statements. Two factors, however, mitigate against the probability of much of anything beyond the spontaneous drunken brawl. One is the interrelation of the entire population and two is the longevity of rumor and innuendo in this very tightly bred society. In short, if there were murders in Disston City in the 1890s, we would know about them today. On the other hand, we can be almost assured that domestic violence was so completely common that it was not remarked on at the time and has remained only a matter for speculation, a speculation that derives in part from the unusually high number of spousal exchanges.

There was the alcohol factor. *The Sea Breeze* never missed the opportunity to inveigh against "Demon Rum." From the earliest issues, when it was stated, "We have no saloons on the Point and do not need any . . . Devil's den in which to retail liquid poison to our people who may be weak and unwary enough to patronize them. How many women and children on this Point think that their condition would be benefitted by a rum shop being started at their door? How many households would be made happier? We are quite sure that the people here do not want anything of the kind, and we trust that all will refrain from giving the move any encouragement."

This sentiment would remain in place for many decades. One of the first acts of the newly established town government in 1910 was to formalize the "dry" status. This is a somewhat two-faced position, however, as the locals never, throughout history, lacked for something to drink.

More often, though, the families took care of each other. Everybody had a cow and a garden and nobody went hungry or thirsty for lack of sharing. A Slaughter remembered that: "You could always get a mess of fish to eat and vegetables out of some one else's garden if you didn't have any of your own. No matter how bad times were, we had it better than a lot of people in other areas." The very fact that the community survived those decades, without law, without government, without a police force or jail, is an indication in itself that some means of societal pressure must have existed, for we do know quite without doubt that many if not most social occasions ended in drunken fights, which apparently went just that far and no further. There is no residual feeling of animosity between descendants of the various clans, just a kind of half-humorous acceptance that some were a little less respectable than others.

Certainly there were guns in every household. The men carried them, as has been seen, when they hired out on the periodic cattle drives still held by companies such as Lykes, who maintained a great portion of Pinellas as open range well into the twentieth century. Snakes had not disappeared, still invaded people's lives with terrifying regularity, and were as often as possible shot on sight.

Florence Slaughter, one of Henry's daughters, remembered a snake encounter during 1897, her first year in school. Her teacher, Mrs. Weihman, had given the younger children a recess so she could hear the lessons of the older ones. "While playing we heard something rattling, and I made all the other children stand back while I went to look for the thing that was rattling. I soon saw one of the largest rattlesnakes I have ever seen. It was coiled and ready to strike. I will never know why he did not strike me as I was in striking distance. I was only five years of age and knew nothing about snakes. But I thought I had to protect the other children."

Records of Pinellas natural history agree with little Florence that the vicinity was home to a particularly large and deadly variety of rattlesnake—the diamondback—which could reach a length of eight feet. There were also, unfortunately, water moccasins and cobra-like coral snakes. And alligators, naturally.

So even the children coped with a life that could be harsh and dangerous, but they had fun, too. They played the games that children have played throughout most of the years of human history, games which require little or no equipment: tag, hide and seek, guessing games and hopscotch, London Bridge and drop the handkerchief. What toys they had were homemade too, such as dolls, seesaws and jump ropes. They played on the beach, swam in the shallow clear waters of the Bay and fished off the old wooden pier where the steamboats and sharpies and schooners tied up. Even herding the cows down around toward the Bayou must have provided a little excitement. Or this, also from the Slaughters: "There were plenty of orange trees and orange groves in Gulfport at that time and us kids used to go and get a bunch of oranges and stuff them in our bosom, in our shirts and our pockets and then we'd go and sit in the shade or if it was night, sometimes we'd build a little camp fire and talk and eat oranges, then we'd all get up and go toward home."

Women and children shared many of the household chores, as the men were so often away at sea for long hours or days on end. It fell to the women to do most of the gardening, the plowing and planting and weeding and harvesting, and naturally the preparation of the food thus provided. Care of the animals, if any, was their job. Chickens and cows were part of nearly every homestead, producing eggs to be gathered and milk to be churned into butter. Children could help bring water from the early wells with their basic windlass mechanics, and later with hand pumps. They also, like Henry Slaughter, were responsible for making salt, and keeping the wood box filled. Everyone in the family worked to cultivate and harvest the citrus. Providing some comforts to the inside of the home was entirely the province of the women, and sewing clothes and linens foremost among these duties.

The adults combined pleasure with work whenever possible. Most of the younger men, Florence Slaughter Jarrett recalls of her Nash uncles, had ox carts, not only for their chores but also for excursions and amusements, such as races. Among the other social occasions that attempted to turn work into play were quilting bees, hog-killings and cane grinding sessions. There were, of course, the events that mark the milestones of a community's life, the christenings, weddings, funerals and holiday picnics. There were barbecues and fish fries when the catch was good or the hogs were killed and hay rides in the fall. There were races with sailboats and horses and the faithful oxen. There were parties and dances, too, the square dances gradually being replaced by the newly introduced and somewhat scandalous round dancing favored by the English colonists.

Bertha Strauss Wells, a granddaughter of Vincent Leonardy, recalled the festivities during cane grinding time, when "we had lots of company, all coming to drink juice, chew cane and listen to my Uncle Ed tell ghost stories. At other times we and some of the neighbors would take dinner and have picnics, fish fries and oyster roasts on the bay."

The Fourth of July, for instance, was celebrated in grand style—orations, racing, sports and games like baseball, followed by a dance at night. One year, described by Will McPherson, the event was held near Big Bayou in a belt of timber selected as the most convenient place because of its "dense shade, afforded by the large oak trees." A committee cleared the underbrush to make way for tables, awaiting "the lavish spread of good things which our lady folk had prepared." William Neeld made the introductory remarks and read the Declaration of Independence "in a high tone of voice and in a very enthusiastic manner," and the crowd sat down to a dinner of chicken, iced cakes, "and, oh, those melting delicious pies!"

"After dinner the crowd went to the water's edge, where the tub race took place. Mr. Bethel rode the barrel, and Walter Roberts was the only one to paddle off in a tub. The Bayou was full of white winged sailboats loaded to the waters [sic] edge with joyous living freight. Next came the shooting match, which was very interesting to 'the boys.'" And finally, "the crowning event was the dance at night . . . For pretty and witty girls, fine and handsome young men, and genial old fellows, I'll stake my money on the Point."

As much fun as it was, "We have heard several of the young men around here say they were glad the Fourth would not come again for a whole year. They walked to the Bayou, ran around all day, attended the dance at night and then home. The next day they were so stiff they could scarcely move."

Christmas time was the occasion for more happy celebrations. "We understand that more amateur theatricals are in preparation. A little higher flight is to be attempted; 'Hamlet,' with the part of the Prince of Denmark left out. The performance will be held about Christmas week. We hope that the brilliant success which attended the last performance will not be lacking in this."

Appropriate ceremonies were held at the schoolhouse, worked up by the Disston Sunday school. After an opening of "declarations," one written by Arthur Norwood and another by Edward McPherson, and a song by Miss Jessie Anderson, Santa Claus appeared, a curtain was removed to reveal the tree, the "showiest ever seen on the Point," and the distribution of presents began.

"The tree was set afire once by one of the candles, but was extinguished without any damage being done," after it was "stripped of its precious load," and folks soon "departed for their homes declaring themselves well satisfied with the way things turned out."

Citrus cultivation suffered during the decade from 1890 to 1900, which saw perhaps the coldest weather ever recorded in Florida. Year after year the freezes grew stronger, and in 1894 and again in 1895, truly devastating frosts enveloped the entire state, laying down an unheard-of blanket of actual snow. Bertha Wells wrote, "When the 1895 freeze came the snow sifted through the old shingles of the house and some drifted in the corner of the open porch. Mother asked how come all that corn meal got out there; she had never seen snow before."

Folks in Disston City may have lost some fruit, even some trees, to the great freezes but citrus was never a real economic factor here. Cold or not, the fish would provide.

Chapter IV
The New Century

LIFE HAD BEGUN SPEEDING UP even before the corner was turned into the twentieth century. New inventions and discoveries—electricity, the telephone and the automobile, to mention a few—were transforming the very nature of life. Never before had anyone been able to speak to others at a distance, to ride in a car, to fill their homes with light whenever they wished. These were not improvements on existing technologies but entirely new ideas, simple at first, of course, but still representing an amazing step into the future, the beginning of a period of unprecedented development that would link individuals as well as communities. Never before or again would such a brief period see quite as many advances. After that, as has been said, everything else was simply engineering.

Not all of these modern conveniences had come to Disston City. Not any of them, in fact. It would be another decade before anyone owned a phone, an automobile or had household electricity here. Elsewhere, as in St. Petersburg for example, little settlements were becoming semi-modern towns, but Disston City did not see the old rural village patterns much disturbed at first.

A charming story from the diary of George Lizotte telling of a 1902 Christmas party illustrates that simplicity. Mr. Lizotte, one of the earliest settlers of what would become St. Petersburg Beach, recalled the joys of his childhood Christmases in France and wanted to bring some of that happy spirit to this pioneer outpost. "I have a scheme," he told one of the many Robertses, who was visiting him on a fishing trip, "Why not have a celebration here? I can round up a bevy of children with their parents at Disston City, who have not the faintest idea what it means to celebrate."

A Roberts brother found a suitable tree, while Lizotte and his friend sailed to Tampa, where they bought colored glass balls, candles, tinsel and toys "from wax dolls to mechanical monkeys." On the day of Christmas Eve, they went to Disston City and "rounded up the few famlies then living there, but most of them had large families and the prospects were good for a large crowd." They had worked all day to decorate the tree and set out the toys and candy.

"At dusk the children and their parents, mostly fishermen, began to come in and I can still hear their joyous acclamations as they sighted the tree all lighted up with innumerable candles and covered with toys and stockings of candy." George Roberts then made an entrance dressed as Santa Claus, and, "I shall never forget the happiness expressed by those children when one after another received appropriate gifts. Cigars and cigarettes were on hand for the men, boxes of candies for the ladies. Dozens of small hands soon emptied the pail of candy." One of the Roberts men made a punch, which Lizotte suspected was "not all orange juice," and the men, animated by this concoction, "sang familiar songs and smoked cigars," until midnight, when they left, carrying the children, now asleep but still "holding their toys to their breast."

Such simple pleasures would have been the memories of a lifetime for the Disston City fishing families and their children.

1. Frank A. Davis

Life was moving at a quicker pace in St. Petersburg, where the advancements were coming fast and furiously. Much of this was due to the entrepreneurial adventures of another newcomer, Frank Allston Davis. Davis was born in Vermont in 1850 and started his career as a teacher. In his late twenties he moved to Philadelphia and began an association with a firm that published medical textbooks. This led to the founding of his own company in 1879.

After the death of his first wife in the 1880s, Davis married a woman younger than his son, and adapted her family, consisting of three even younger sisters, to his household. A decade later his health had become a concern and he was advised to relocate in Florida. This he did. His first stop was Tarpon Springs, where his undertakings were marked by both successes and failures. His rheumatism did get better, but his attempts to bring the town into the modern world were not met with total enthusiasm. Davis apparently had a real desire to publicize what he, following the eminent Dr. Van Bibber (whose famous article the Davis Company had published), considered the ultimate health resort location in the entire country. In Tarpon he met Jacob Disston, brother and financier to Hamilton, and together they worked to promote the Pinellas area, printing books, magazines and brochures of essays, poems and photographs, mostly at Davis' own expense. He firmly believed that the little town of Tarpon Springs needed a few modern conveniences, and so he built an electric plant there. The natives were not impressed, and "remained loyal to their kerosene lamps," as his biographer wrote.

Unwanted there, Davis moved his household and his attentions to St. Petersburg. In 1897 he was granted a municipal franchise to build a power plant on what would become known as the "electric pier." Great excitement reigned in the city, for by the end of the year, St. Petersburg would have thirty-two streetlights in the area around Williams Park. A contemporary account raved, "By this enterprise every part of the town is brilliantly illuminated . . . a success in every particular. No pains had been spared by the company to provide the latest scientific devices." One of Davis' own officers was more realistic, and described it as "the most primitive and out-of-date aggregation of machinery that had ever been collected . . . but . . . the light it gave was certainly wonderful to behold."

Throughout all this, Davis managed to keep his book publishing business going, though it was tricky at times, like in 1900 when he was forced to declare bankruptcy. Even his descendants suggest that not all was exactly above board in Davis' business dealings. However, regulations were slightly less strict in those days, and barely a year went by before the F.A. Davis Company was re-incorporated.

Frank Davis would, of course, be the man who eventually in a sense made Gulfport, for it was he who would bring the streetcar here, when he decided to extend his business into transportation. B.F. Measey, secretary and treasurer of Davis' company, wrote about those days in a long recollection published in the *Times* DeSoto edition in 1914. "Feeling secure in the electric light and power project, Mr. Davis naturally looked around for other 'worlds to conquer,' so applied to the city council for a franchise to operate a trolley system, which no one but Mr. Davis seemed to think was a necessity in any way, for at that time, while the walking was not as good as it is at present, still the people were used to it and could not see where revenue was to come from to operate such an expensive luxury as a trolley line."

Called by one who knew him well, "the finest salesman I've ever met," Frank Davis must have put all of that charm and those skills to work when he hit the borders of Disston City sometime around the beginning of 1905. Measey goes on to explain why this location was chosen: "After a careful study of the geography of the Pinellas peninsula, Mr. Davis concluded that at least some time it would be profitable to have a trolley line from St. Petersburg to a point on Boca Ceiga Bay, where boat service could be installed, making Pass-a-Grille the point where in the future, whether near or far . . . there was sure to be a flourishing seaside resort, and with the glorious climate with which providence had blessed the Pinellas peninsula, St. Petersburg must grow, people must flock there by the thousands and tens of thousands and ultimately both the electric light and power company and the trolley line would be moneymakers of the highest order."

But Disston City was a different world, far apart now from St. Petersburg with its electric lights and telephones, the latter, incidentally, introduced by none other than Arthur Norwood, who had rigged up a phone line between his two stores on Central Avenue. (Seeing that, naturally everyone wanted a telephone, and by 1899 there were eighteen subscribers to the infant service.) All these wonderful new facilities, combined with the easing of the late nineteenth century economic woes, and the influx of soldiers and their accompanying hordes of reporters, hangers-on, and families during the Spanish American War, had contributed to an astonishing rate of growth for St. Petersburg. Disston City, way out there in the woods and denuded of its once-glorious visions, was left further and further behind.

2. John F. Chase

Before the town would shake off its lethargy and truly enter a new era, a time in which it finally ceased to be the ill-fated Disston City and took on, for a while at least, the equally ill-fated name of Veteran City, another player had to enter the game. This was Captain John F. Chase (1843-1914).

Chase was born in Maine, and was still in his teens when he joined the Fifth Maine Light Artillery as a cannoneer. During one of the worst of the Civil War battles, at Chancellorsville, he suffered incredible shrapnel wounds, which partially blinded and crippled him for life. With an arm and an eye completely destroyed as well as almost fifty other injuries, Chase was pronounced the most severely wounded survivor of the entire Civil War. His bravery throughout this attack resulted in his being awarded the Congressional Medal of Honor for meritorious conduct in 1888.

After the war's end, he returned to Maine, where he set to inventing a great variety of things, some of which were conveniences for people with disabilities. He achieved dozens of patents, the best known of which was for a kind of collapsible hoopskirt/bustle combination.

In 1895 he came to St. Petersburg with his family, having earlier investigated the area. His business ventures included peddling foodstuffs from a horse-drawn wagon, and, eventually, a partnership with sawmill master George King in the steamboat business, which involved ownership of the *Anthea*, a seventy-foot steamer later bought by Davis for use on the Veteran City/Pass-A-Grille run. He continued to follow a rather military lifestyle from his home at 6th Street and 1st Avenue North, taking it upon himself to help guard nearby Mirror Lake (then Reservoir Lake) against sabotage or contamination during the Spanish-American War.

In 1896 Chase applied to the St. Petersburg Council for franchises to proceed with an electric power station and a streetcar. He was turned down. Obviously his and Davis' interests were coinciding, and indeed they were soon involved together in Davis' Florida West Coast Company, which, in 1901, did succeed in opening a horsecar line along the pier to facilitate movement of passengers and freight from ships to shore. But the big adventure from Davis and Chase would be the Veteran City promotion. This was Chase's idea and Davis' money, or at least money he had raised from other people, though Chase used his many connections to veterans' organizations to promote the sale of land. His first, rather tentative, ads requesting "property of all kinds" were placed in the *Times* in early 1904: "I think I can find you a customer among the many Grand Army men who are coming here to settle."

With this new goal in mind, Davis became extremely interested in the idea of a transit system, and once again a streetcar line was proposed. This time, he succeeded, and with the backing of his financier friends (including Jacob Disston and George S. Gandy, who had some years earlier designed the Philadelphia transit system) formed the St. Petersburg and Gulf Electric Railway Company in December 1901.

3. The Streetcar Line

Now they had to decide where to go with it, for a trolley system had to connect to a water service in order to provide some reason for its existence. Pass-A-Grille with its many assets, white sand beaches, fishing, swimming and shelling, not to mention a decent hotel for meals and accommodations, was a logical destination. B.F. Measey recalled his first trip to Pass-a-Grille, "made in a little motor boat, with a lame engine, loaded down to the water's edge, taking hours to make the journey from St. Petersburg . . . I remember my first dinner, served by Mr. Lizotte, which was certainly unique in every way, both as to the service and menu . . . a good shore dinner garnished with stone crabs, for which his hotel is now so famous."

The departure point was the critical choice, and to make it Davis undertook to survey the coastline all the way around Pinellas Point. By a great stroke of serendipity, the young boatman he hired to take him on this mission was a some-time employee of Joshua White, a fellow named Walter Williams, whose life and family would become indelibly linked to the history of Gulfport in years to come. With Walt Williams' guidance, Davis and his Philadelphia backers found that the most suitable location was a site just west of the present small settlement of Disston City. A pier 700 feet out into the bay would provide enough depth for the boats he envisioned to serve the tourist trade. The land at that point was not terribly attractive, for there was a long stretch of low-lying mud flat extending from the water's edge northward for some distance. A serious landfill job would be required to make much of anything of the site, but for the moment it would do for a destination, and the streetcar line could be begun.

Measey wrote, "I was driven along the proposed line of the trolley from St. Petersburg to Gulfport, very few houses or inhabitants to be seen along the route as then proposed, almost impassible thickets through which we had to force our way . . . through the flat woods, with water up to the horses' knees. All this Mr. Davis pointed out as the site of a future great city, but I failed to see anything that impressed me with the fact that Mr. Davis would ever see any of his prophecies fulfilled."

Construction began late in 1902, and went along rather nicely, until it hit Booker Creek at about 9th Street and 6th Avenue South, where it bogged down, quite literally, for awhile. This first section was finally opened toward the end of 1904 and soon enough it got on down to Tangerine Avenue, where the straight shot westward was begun. A brochure of the period called this segment "the fruit belt, and a beautiful residence section of St. Petersburg." It was a good distance, all the way through woods and groves, sand and streamlets, but the company persevered and soon enough the cars began to run, although perhaps the scenery didn't quite live up to its promise. The land along the trolley route in the Tangerine area was so low and so wet that some people, including Henry Slaughter, grew rice there. One early rider, who apparently wasn't aware of the beautiful residences, etc., described the terrain as "uninhabited junglelike countryside, exotic and steamy."

When the route reached a point directly north of the proposed boat pier, it made a sharp ninety-degree turn southward, down into the empty forests of western Disston City. This location was sometimes called "rattlesnake curve," one of the highlights of the devious route, another of which was "jackass curve," after a stubborn mule who often slept alongside or on the tracks. There was a ditch at the bend where a "considerable population" of alligators lived, and their habit of sunning themselves would in the future amuse the tourists but make the conductors rather nervous.

Davis' and Chase's advance work was well done, for they had brought their proposals to those residents who were currently of importance, and had received from two of them the gift of ten acres apiece for the right-of-way. The rest of the subject land was now the property of the St. Petersburg and Gulf Railway, through Captain Chase, who had purchased some 200 acres for his own personal dream, a retirement community for soldiers of the Civil War. The Union side.

The trolley track down through Gulfport toward the Bay.

4. The Town

Chase's plan to create a haven for retired Union Army veterans in the midst of this sparsely inhabited and completely southern community has today an air of total unreality, though apparently then it seemed like a completely logical and potentially successful venture. His 200 acres were cut out of the middle of the Disston City territory, essentially the area today bounded east and west by 52nd and 58th Streets and running several blocks northward from the shore. They were to be sold as home building lots, a minimum of sixty by one hundred feet, at a price of "$100 and up," and small farms for fruits and vegetables at sizes between two and a half and five acres. All were to be platted and laid out by the railway company, which promised to give 10 percent of the proceeds from the sales to the town itself for improvements to streets and parks.

The idea of establishing a new community just for veterans was not unique at that time. With several hundred thousand survivors still living, and many actively involved in organizations such as the Grand Army of the Republic (G.A.R.), a sort of forerunner of today's veterans' lobbying bodies, there was considerable potential for ventures of this kind. Two or three existed

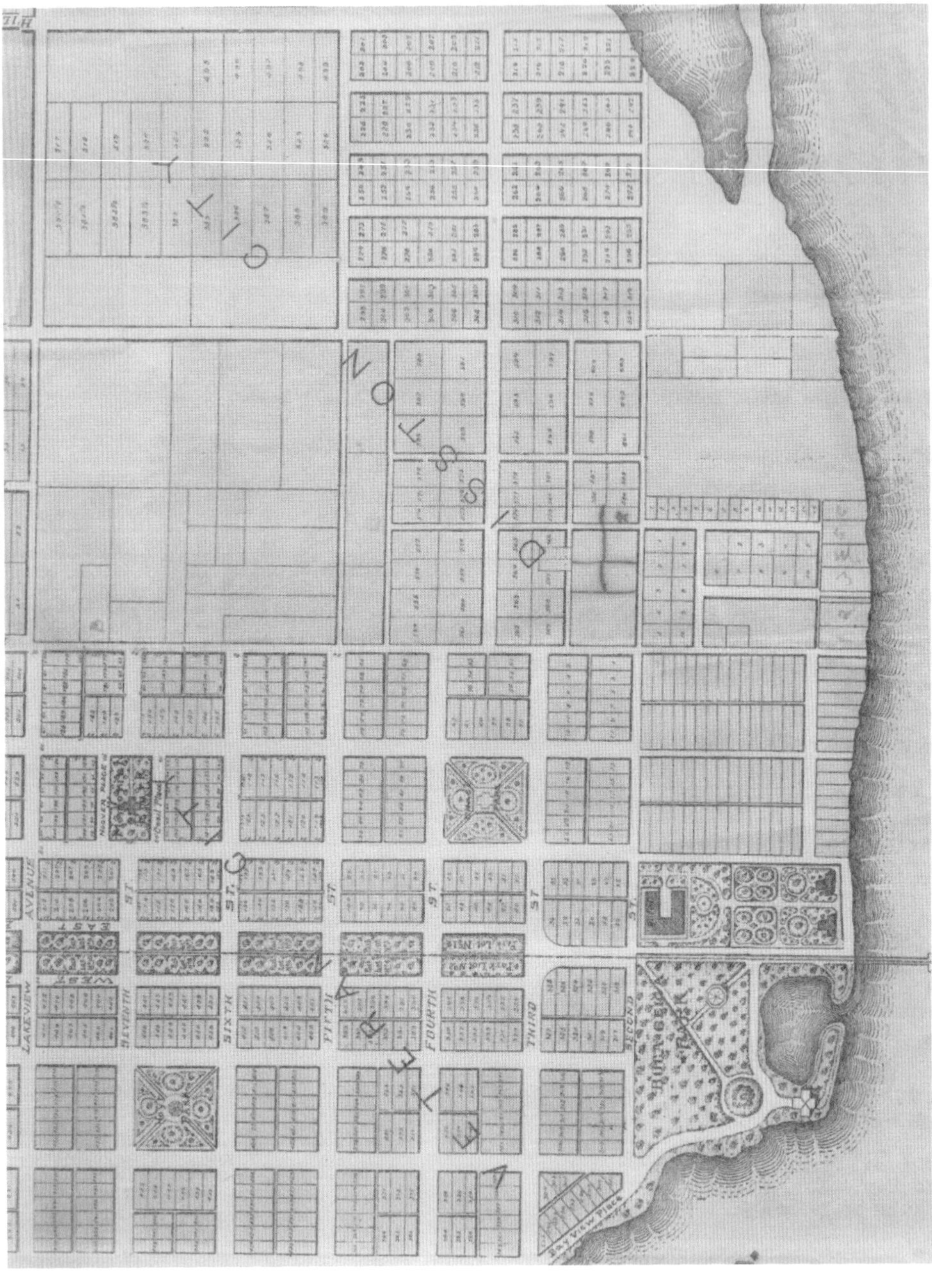

A 1905 promotional map for Veteran City and the St. Petersburg and Gulf Railway.

elsewhere in the South when Chase introduced his promotion in September 1904. He did make some effort to include Confederate veterans, perhaps after realizing they would be a potentially more accessible market. His announcement, reported in a March 1905, issue of the *St. Petersburg Times*, also alludes, without further elaboration, to a "special location for our colored population."

"Veteran City is the healthiest, most genial spot in the world, will be a haven of peace, rest, and comfort that will add another span, and one filled with happiness and content, to the lives of the old veterans who will gather there," said the *Times* of the proposed development. The editorial writers also went on to support Chase against the local critics who felt that any development out there in the country was to the detriment of their interests in St. Petersburg.

In the promotional plat map of 1905, everything below what would be about 29th Avenue today was set aside for public green space. A further seven of the twenty-four blocks in the subdivision were also reserved for this purpose. There was a large "Boca Ceiga Park" to the west of the trolley line and another landscaped promenade to the east. Both sides of the tracks were handsomely planted, creating park-like islands ninety feet in width in the middle of what was then called variously Boca Ceiga or Davis Boulevard, now Beach Boulevard (Today's maps show these dimensions still pertain; the park width totals 190 feet). Beyond this promenade there was to be a fifteen-foot easement and the future residences would be set back yet another fifteen feet from the proposed sidewalk line.

There was a block-sized park where Chase Park stands today, yet another at the location of Hoyt Field, and a smaller landscaped area in the position of the current City Hall complex. Many modern aspects of the city, then, owe their origins to this preliminary (and never realized) plan. When baseball began to be played regularly in the town, in 1908, the games were held perhaps on one or the other of these parks, which were still in rather primitive shape. The first game, in fact, was lost to the Lealman team by a score of twenty-five to twenty-one, due, the players claimed, to the fact that the grounds were "no good" and they had to spend most of their time hunting the ball in thick palmetto and scrub.

These early promotional maps and brochures promise that the waterfront was being "extensively developed" with sea walls, public parks, drives and avenues, and "setting out tropical and ornamental trees and shrubbery." What actually existed there in fact was still nothing much but tidal mud flat. The old Disston/Miranda wharf had just about rotted away by 1901, the same year whatever remnants of the Waldorf Hotel that remained were carted away for use in building fishermen's homes. Cattle were still free range in the area until well into the 1910s, when the town insisted the Lykes Company haul them away over to Maximo.

Some 212 building lots were located in the platted area, and a few "streets" in the Veteran City development were cleared, somewhat, to provide access to the potential viewers of the available lots. These were effectively no more than breaks in the palmetto scrub, paths of sand dug out of the undergrowth. As such they would remain, until the town incorporated itself and began a program of improving first the sidewalks and then the roads within its jurisdiction.

Parts of the settlement were completely untouched by Chase's grand plan. The later homestead area of the Slaughter/Barnett family was located well away from the swampy site of the streetcar's prospective terminus. This land, between 49th and 52nd Streets, from Lakeview south to 25th Avenue, abutted the Veteran City boundaries and was of course still part of Disston City territory, which ran eastward as far as 45th Street. Northeast of Veteran City was "West Oakland," most of which today is part of St. Petersburg, and due north was "Gulf View," now within the boundaries of Gulfport. Westward, where far into the future, modern South Pasadena would arise, was then pretty much *terra incognita*.

The entire town had been focused between 52nd Street and Disston Avenue from the water northward. It was here that all the late nineteenth-century activity had taken place—Will McPherson's paper, Torres' store, Baumeister's, Locke's, White's and the homes of the English colonists. Now that would change, for the center of town would shift westward, and homes and businesses would spring up along the streetcar line, particularly on Boca Ceiga/Davis/Beach Boulevard.

The two civic-minded citizens who donated the twenty acres of land for the trolley right-of-way were Mr. Woodworth the early postmaster, and a rather shadowy but ultimately extremely important personage, Alonzo Augustus Hoyt.

A new social class had emerged, slowly, in the late Disston City era, its leading lights Hoyt and Woodworth. A.A. Hoyt remains a mysterious figure barely discernable from the mists of the early twentieth century. Born in Vermont of German ancestry, he served in the Civil War and later under Custer. In many sources he is called Reverend, but no record of any actual ministerial connection can be found. Possibly he has been confused with the Reverend J.P. Hoyt, a prominent St. Petersburg clergyman of the period.

Arriving here about 1896, Hoyt immediately began to take on the role of elder statesman. Apparently a widower, he had a grown son, Charles, who remained in Vermont. In 1901 he married a woman named Elizabeth, sixty years old to his sixty-three. In July 1906, when the town officially became

Veteran City, it was he who succeeded Woodworth as postmaster, a position he held for a couple of years, until it was taken over by Malcolm McRoberts for the last thirty months or so until the final establishment of incorporated Gulfport. The recollections of Mary McRoberts Roberts, who was often referred to as the postmistress by virtue of her standing as the postmaster's daughter, include the "Reverend" Hoyt, whom she says "never received as much as a free ride" in compensation for his gift of land. The residents did appreciate the gift, though, and perhaps that led to the naming of the future ball field for him (not, as some have said, for Waite Hoyt, a left-handed Yankees pitcher of the 1920s).

Much more will be heard of Mr. Woodworth, now fifty-one, during his off and on career as a foremost citizen, *Times* correspondent and perpetual political figure. Hoyt and Woodworth were joined by a couple named Wetherell, who for awhile seemed to be part of everything that was happening, as were the C.W. Thomses, "Judge" Leon B. Cooper, Mr. and Mrs. Brightman and whoever happened to be the current school teacher, a position held first by Miss Leila Curtis, and after her departure for St. Petersburg, Miss Linnie Sessions.

The F. M. Wetherells had arrived here from Michigan, and the Brightmans from Rhode Island. The Wetherells bought a house formerly belonging to a family named Cook in the vicinity of 51st and 29th, but didn't stay too long, removing themselves to Nassau in the middle of 1902. Mrs. Wetherell, however, came back during 1903, saying "Disston City was good enough for her," and immediately resumed her place at the head of local society, such as it was. Mr. Wetherell had some kind of position with the "government gardens" in Barbados, and was away most of the time.

The Brightmans bought the "south half of the Henderson forty," where they set out an orange and peach orchard (Robert and Henrietta Henderson were sixty-ish Massachusetts people who came here to grow fruit. Their land was in the area north of 28th Avenue and west of the Boulevard). Interestingly enough, this project was superintended by Hoyt himself, since he owned the north twenty acres and had just built a new house upon it, a place described as having a pleasant outlook on the Bay, hence, no doubt, its name, "Bayhead." In the course of this construction, Hoyt was severely cut by a falling plank, and, there being no one else around to help, closed the four-inch gash in his leg by stoically taking "several stitches" in himself.

The Thomeses would become one of the few families to remain in the area over an extended period of time. Charles W. Thomes, in his early sixties, was probably the gentleman described in the earlier adventurous visit to the Kimball/Puig plantation with Jim the mule, as well, of course, as the eventual salvager of the Waldorf Hotel remains. Born in 1848 in New England,

Thomes served in the Civil War as a fourteen-year-old drummer boy, then in the White House itself. He was one of the group of men who trailed Lincoln's assassin John Wilkes Booth, and was in on the capture. From 1865 until his removal to Florida in 1898, he sailed on whaling ships out of New Bedford, Massachusetts. His wife, Elizabeth Madeira Daniels, was the daughter of a Maine clipper ship captain, her middle name perhaps reflecting his travels. She had a brother, John, who also lived in the area and was, in fact, famed for building an extremely strange structure known as the Daniels castle on Disston Avenue. John was a self-proclaimed soldier of fortune and writer, having served in some seven wars, so he said, primarily in the Caribbean. He had designed his odd home to recall a place in which he had been imprisoned, Moro Castle in Havana. The so-called Castle Chalon survived until the mid-1920s, then went into the memories of several local people and town mythology. A Thomes grandson described it as "a rambling thing that looked like a 12-year-old boy built it out of boxes and boards."

The Thomeses had seven children, one of whom, Delia, recalled the trip south as having been made by boat from Boston to Savannah, and then on by train to St. Petersburg, arriving "black as stoves." Another daughter, Abbie Mitchell, was part of a family that would become of great importance to Gulfport, the Webbs. Abbie married Samuel James Webb in Massachusetts, where he had worked as a machinist, sometime around the turn of the century. Their first three children, Grace Muriel, Lillian Ethel and Samuel Wesley, were born there in 1901, 1903 and 1904, long after the elder Thomeses had moved to Disston City and just before the Webbs themselves arrived to take up residence here.

The Woodworths had a son with the unusual name of Ariel, who died, tragically, of typhoid fever at the age of nineteen in 1902. From the tenor of the Disston City Items column in the *Times* during the 1900s, it can be assumed almost certainly that Mr. Woodworth himself was the correspondent. His news, mostly concerning his various shell-selling and chicken-raising businesses, centered around this small group who were also members of a "literary club" that met in his home, and their doings; Mrs. Wetherell's various boarders, Judge Cooper's paralytic stroke, assorted Thomes illnesses, Mrs. Hoyt's travels and Ariel's death, of course.

The 1903 Thanksgiving dinner, for example, was held at Mrs. Wetherell's and her guests were: "the Reverend" Hoyt; all the Woodworths, including brother George, sister Mrs. Pearson and her daughter Bertha visiting from Boston; Tim Kimball and his sister Mrs. Puig; the teacher Linnie Sessions; and Professor Arthur G. Reynolds. This latter gentleman was an English bachelor, "biological collector and naturalist," who would live in the town simply forever in "peaceful reticence," all the while keeping the lowest of public profiles.

Perhaps Jim the mule had met his end, because Tim Kimball now had a horse and wagon. The horse was young, nervous and widely considered to be mildly demented. It fully met expectations one day when Tim drove into St. Petersburg and encountered a bicyclist. Startled, the horse bolted through the window of Singlehurst's store, and the wagon came apart as it hit the curb, leaving Tim with only the shafts and a couple of wheels. Nobody was badly hurt, but there was little or nothing left of the bicycle.

Most of the same people gathered at "Oakwood," the Woodworth home, for Christmas, but the next year, 1904, Mrs. Wetherell and the Woodworth women removed themselves to St. Petersburg for the winter, leaving almost no one in Disston City but William and his chickens.

5. The Big Day

At any rate, the super salesman Davis sold Hoyt and Woodworth on the benefits of an electric streetcar, which were no doubt obvious. The benefits of the Veteran City development were probably somewhat less apparent, and, reading between the lines of history, never appealed quite as much to the residents. The two projects opened together, on April 5, 1905, with a daylong celebration. Sophie Steinwinder spent the morning slicing bread, a chore she said was made easier by the fact that Frank Davis was working right alongside her, slicing ham, for the great party. Newspaper reports contradict her memory, placing Davis in Philadelphia that day, so perhaps it was Captain Chase, or more likely, another member of the Railway company. The ham, though, was probably correct, since the weather had been so stormy the fishermen couldn't get out and there were no fish available for the proposed fish fry.

The heavy rain and dark skies cleared, leaving a pleasant, breezy spring day, and the ceremonies began at 11 a.m. Cars had been running from St. Petersburg since 8:30 that morning, bringing people to the clearing by the shore where the picnic and speeches would be held.

First, a dedicatory prayer was given by Reverend J.P. Hoyt of the St. Petersburg Congregational Church. Next a flag was raised to the top of a sixty-eight-foot flagstaff, that duty shared by Daniel Hoover, a captain of the G.A.R. (Company B, 9th Pennsylvania.Cavalry.) and a Confederate opposite number. Mr. Hoover, a sixty-two-year-old widower from Washington State, was the first veteran who actually bought into the proposed development, having arrived here in March, a month before the official opening. There was as yet no streetcar service, so Mr. Hoover camped out in a tent awaiting the coming of the trolley that would bring the building materials for his house. Not many other old gentlemen would be as game or as determined.

A little side note to Mr. Hoover's life while in his temporary shelter near the beach involves an adventure he had with five ladies from Tampa, who were returning from an excursion to Pass-a-Grille one day and found themselves with some time before the next car was due to arrive to return them to town. They met Mr. Hoover and he offered to show them some of the interesting sights in the immediate vicinity, one of which was a large colorful grasshopper. The ladies were suitably impressed and frightened by the strange creature. Bending too near, one of them had the terrible experience of feeling the grasshopper jump down the front of her low-cut dress. She shrieked for help from her friends, but none of them wanted to touch the nasty thing, so, after some moments of screaming chaos, Mr. Hoover himself undertook to reach in and remove the grasshopper from the lady's bosom.

Fortunately he was elderly enough to get away with it. Back to the celebration. After the flag raising, Alonzo Hoyt, described as "a noble old veteran himself" (Co. C., First Vermont Cavalry) made an "eloquent address of welcome" and the guests finally got to eat the lunch provided by the railway company. Then came the serious speech-making, with the "famous orator" the Honorable E.R. Gunby of Tampa, a future Bull Moose party candidate for Congress, pontificating for quite some time, followed by Chase himself, and closing with a valedictory prayer.

In Mr. Gunby's keynote speech, he had said, "It is the purpose to make this a city where [veterans] may temporarily abide and build their cottages or palaces—where they may remain in a climate the best on earth—where many a veteran now traveling in the sunset path to the gates of the golden west may find a home until he is prepared to enter another mansion already prepared and to find a welcome from those who are gone before." Hearing this, it is perhaps no wonder that few chose to settle in the town, given that its express purpose seemed to be to provide a place in which to die.

Though planned with good intentions, Veteran City was a bust from the beginning. Civil War survivors were now well into their sixties, and though a few came and looked, far fewer bought into the scheme. Most of those who finally made it this far south found more attractive locales, such as Tampa, which was becoming quite a city, and particularly one with a reputation as a good place for military retirees. By June of 1905, five lots had been sold, though none of the buyers stayed around to play any kind of a role in the life of the community. Even as the venture approached its first anniversary, perhaps only a couple of dozen lots had been purchased.

This entire period at the midpoint of the decade was one of general growth and prosperity, especially in real estate ventures. Veteran City stood alone as a failure for several reasons. Chase had incurred the wrath of local real estate agents for working at their profession without a proper license. Davis' finances were suffering. They upped the promotional ante by offering one year's free passage on the St. Petersburg & Gulf line for every thousand dollars spent in making improvements on Veteran City homesites. They increased their advertising, buying half-page spreads in the *Times* featuring huge typefaces and almost frantic offers to sell the lots at rates now billed as $20 down and $10 a month. They reorganized the Florida West Coast Company, bringing in a new board of directors with Georgia-born contractor Walter Fuller as Vice President.

Not only did the lots not sell, but there was competition from the current owners. For example, in 1906 Daniel Hoover sold two of his lots on the east side of the track at 4th Street (27th Avenue) to an even older gentleman than himself. Albert Balch, then seventy-nine, who came from Wisconsin with his wife Madeline, paid Hoover $250 and set about building an imposing two-story structure there.

The Balch house, now 2632 Beach Boulevard.

Over the next few years more and more desperate devices were employed to attract buyers. In 1907 a gala day was held, and a thousand people came out to Veteran City to be entertained with music and fed sandwiches and cakes, tea and ice water, cigars and oranges, while being encouraged to bid at a land auction. About thirty lots were sold that day, the prices ranging from $90 to $225 ("half their actual value"). A couple of years later, when another such auction was held, the price had bottomed out at $49. The attraction this time was a drawing for a free lot, which was won by a lady who may or may not ever have claimed her prize.

Chase kept trying, but perhaps without his initial vigor. Always the inventor, he had a new project to consume his time and effort, a fifty-foot long, ten horsepower "flying machine." He spent much of 1909 trying to market his design for this plane all over the country. It was a far cry from those early inventions of collapsible hoop skirt/bustles, and a far cry from Veteran City.

Nothing was going to save Veteran City.

6. The Casino

When one stepped off the streetcar at the Veteran City station—the station being a little building located on the east side of Davis Boulevard between today's 27th and 28th Avenues—there was nothing much in sight beyond the simple boarding platform, where wooden pallets laid either side of the track. Even the promotional maps of 1905 could not pretend that any great metropolis lay at the end of the ride. Potential passengers had to slog down through mud flats to the shoreline and wait to be lightered out to the launches in small vessels to board the excursion boats. Sometimes, when the tide was particularly low, people had to wade out to the lighters.

Measey writes: "As the trolley neared its terminus at what is now known as Gulfport, another problem of serious importance presented itself, which was the building of the dock and pavilion to accommodate the tourists and others who might patronize the line. This meant more money and entailed upon those who were doing their best to construct and build, with the little amounts that were being slowly paid into the treasury, a burden that was hard to bear, but by hammering, contriving and economizing, the wharf was built with the pavilion thereon, presenting at that time quite a handsome appearance, and the builders felt repaid for the effort that they had put forth."

Even before such amenities, they had come, the tourists and visitors and excursionists, for the trip to Pass-A-Grille, a couple hours by trolley and boat. Paul Boardman, quoted in Hurley's *Surf, Sand, & Post Card Sunsets*, called the trip

The Veteran City Station, original terminus of the streetcar line.

"over the crystal clear waters . . . a dreamlike experience in itself." But as soon as possible the tracks were extended down to the shore and beyond. By August the wharf was finished and lighted, a new "electric dock," and we see in old pictures how it reaches far out into the water from the landside wilderness.

At first the ferryboat service did well and employed many of the town's men. It was run by the trolley company, using Davis' seventy-five-passenger *Anthea*. As the venture prospered, the launch *Jennie* was soon added with a regular schedule of four departures a day from Veteran City (9 and 11 a.m., 3 and 5 p.m.) and four returns, leaving Pass-a-Grille an hour later. By the beginning of 1906, the twin-deck *Uncle Sam* also joined the route, leaving Veteran City at 7:30 and 9:30 a.m., 2:30 and 4:30 p.m., and arriving back at 9 and 11 a.m., 4 and 6 p.m.

In the meantime plans were announced for the building of a "two-story pavilion" and the pier was extended from its original 668 to 800 feet, to a point where the water's depth would support the landing of the freight and excursion boats. By February 1906 fast-working crews had got as far as the top floor "resting place" of the pavilion. An artesian well was successfully brought in, after some effort to strike a flow, sufficient though limited, at 129 feet. In a month, the new facility was ready for business.

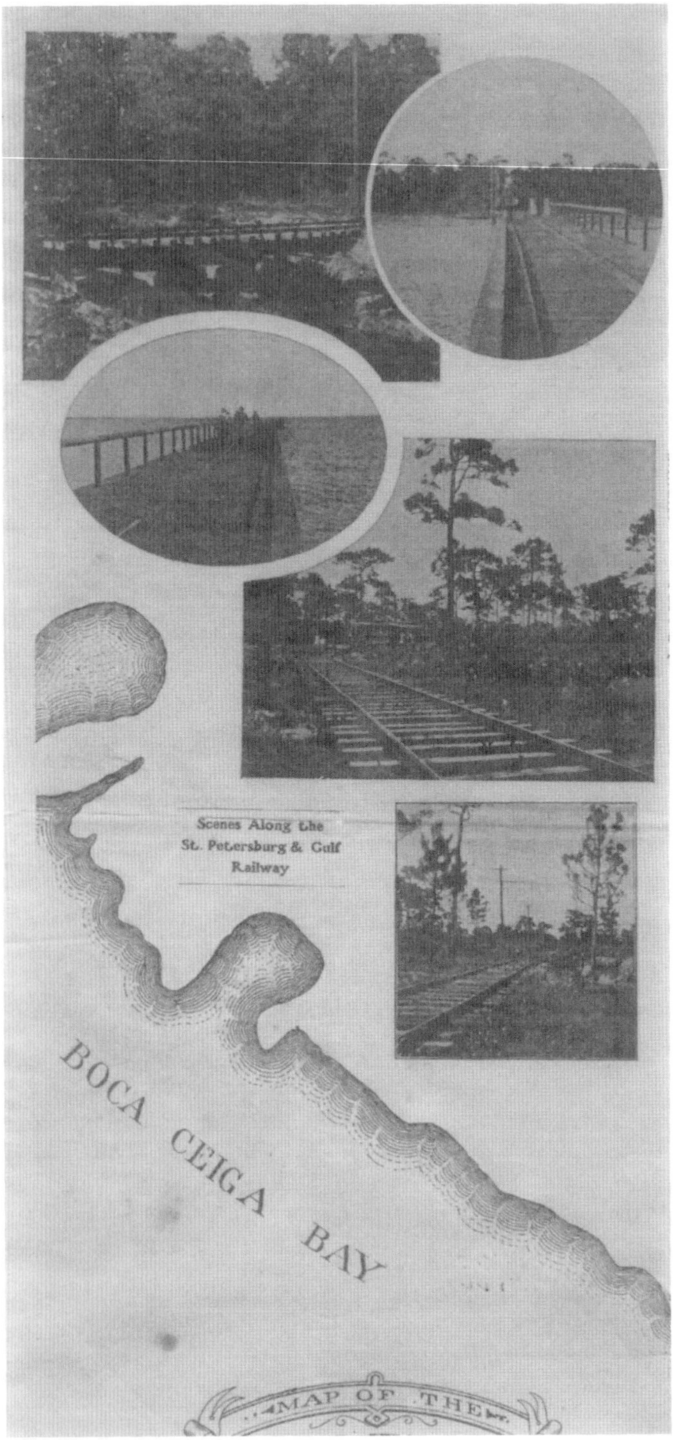

Scenes from the 1905 promotional map showing the end of the trolley tracks before construction of the Casino.

Opened "informally" with a dance on April 9, 1906, it would come to be called the Casino, after the Italian designation for a community gathering place. Not then, certainly, and not ever did it have any function as a place to gamble, as the name today implies.

It was unique. Unfortunately no records remain of its designer, for in those days construction was truly "vernacular;" that is, it was more or less put together by men who were skilled carpenters but not trained architects. Planning was informal, to say the least. The physical design of the building featured roof trusses of four- by twelve-inch pine, bolted together in such a complex pattern that blacksmiths were required to be on the building site to fashion the bolts as needed in as many as thirty different sizes and lengths.

The Casino, newly built in 1906.

The structure measured 102 feet long by 67 feet wide, and the lower floor featured on the landward or north side a large area for performances, dances and community functions, with a 23 by 12 foot stage and seating for 500 people. The interior had a rough-hewn appearance, the wooden walls and open beams of the peaked roof left in their natural state. Southward, or seaward, a "soda fountain" sold a wonderful variety of souvenirs, shells and trinkets, as well as candy, drinks and tobacco. In addition to the refreshments, there were billiard and triviola tables and slot machines, which apparently involved primitive motion picture viewing rather than games of chance. A ticket window and post office boxes formed the business part of the operation, which was originally leased to B.C. Steele of Philadelphia. On the second floor, the open-air pavilion, 32 by 67 feet, gave a breezy southern view of the bay, and shortly the billiard tables and slots would be moved up there to make room for the "Palace Ice Cream Parlor" on the first floor. No wonder people began to come to the Casino as a destination in itself as well as merely passing en route.

The Casino viewed from the south, or waterside.

Beyond the main building the passenger platform continued more than 100 feet to some small further buildings, waiting rooms and service sheds for the boat line. Alongside the tracks to the east was a walkway for pedestrians, while the trolley ran out to and beyond the Casino to the west, so passengers could step directly from the pier to the waiting boats.

The pier, the Casino and all the accouterments, now called the "Electric Dock and Spa" stood on pilings of sturdy pine, well built and stable. It immediately became so popular that original plans to shutter it during the summer were shelved to accommodate all those folks who flocked to the dances, parties, minstrel shows and meetings in the pretty pavilion, at an admission charge generally between twenty-five and forty cents.

But by late 1906 Davis' interest in the project had waned concomitant with the public's lack of interest in the Veteran City development. He had turned his attention to improving his St. Petersburg facilities by building an impressive new electric pier there. After these ten or more years of frantic activity and expansion of his streetcar line, Davis withdrew almost completely from further ventures when the sudden economic downturn of 1907 cost him nearly everything. By the end of the decade, all his holdings had been placed in receivership, and their management turned over to Walter Fuller, who would become the next important player in the game.

When the company's boats to Pass-a-Grille ceased to run, the Casino's function as a way station on the popular excursion route was voided entirely. Steele sold his operating interests in October, and the business changed hands again four or five times in the next few months. Soon, even the advertising rights to almost everything the Florida West Coast Company owned had been sold to a man named Frank H. Emerson. Beneath *Times* photos of the wharf and the stage curtain lined with advertising posters, he boasted, "I control the space in the trolley cars, too." The Casino was reduced to primarily local events, like church services and meetings.

As usual, it soon rose again and throughout 1907 and 1908 a great variety of entertainments took place including a gala ball with a Japanese theme, a demonstration of sleight-of-hand and slack wire walking, a play presented by the Chicago Theatrical Company, magic shows and a dance held by the fraternal order of Woodsmen featuring perhaps the strangest of amusements, contests for the "tallest, shortest and heaviest ladies." In the spring of 1909 it was for several months transformed into a roller skating rink. While this ended the parties and dances, forcing them to relocate to St. Petersburg or Pass-a-Grille hotels, it was a popular event, with as many as 200 people enjoying the free skating some evenings.

Perhaps by no coincidence, just a couple of months later the pier was strengthened by the addition of 180 new pilings.

The Wintersgill brothers, Elmer, forty-five, and Lester, thirty-five, arrived in town in the spring of 1907 and formed the Mary Boat Company to restart the excursion service. They bought the *Uncle Sam*, had it refitted to carry 200 passengers, and gave it a familiar captain, none other than Will McPherson, twenty years after his *Sea Breeze* adventures. In 1908 better uses were found for this large boat with a cargo capacity that could go as high as twelve thousand feet of lumber. It was put out to charter and the Wintersgills set about building a new ferry, smaller but with more amenities, such as an icebox under the forward deck. This would become the long-running and popular *New York*, which would ply the route for years. It was joined in 1909 by the gasoline-powered 180-passenger *Gypsy*.

The *Gypsy* coming in to dock.

The Veteran City/Pass-a-Grille boats carried freight as well as passengers, and sometimes cows. They did make money, even at the reasonable rate of thirty cents round trip. So with Fuller now owning the streetcar line plus the Boca Ceiga Boat Company, which he had created to serve it, there was inevitable conflict brewing between the official service and the locals who offered their craft as a means of transportation to waiting tourists. A sorry bone of contention escalated into serious hard feelings and eventually lawsuits between the Wintersgills and Fuller.

Claudette Renney Dean wrote the following some seventy-five years after the events, indicating just how much the promoters rankled her ancestors. "He [Chase] was nothin' but a carpetbagger. He run his streetcar and goin' to get rich on Disston City and then got mad 'cause nobody bought his lots, and run the streetcar down. Then he got mad because the Gulfport people that had the ships here all the time tried to steal his trade takin' people over to the beaches and back. Yes, we got Chase Park from him but that's because his daughters didn't want to associate with people in Gulfport so they moved to St. Pete." The Chase daughters mentioned were Lena and Beulah, thirty-seven and thirty-three respectively in 1905, and both unmarried.

Beulah Chase actually did live in town for awhile, at about 56th Street and 26th Avenue, where she kept chickens. One morning she was awakened early by a great deal of squawking, and, going out to investigate, found a skunk tail hanging out of the coop. This she grabbed, pulling out the animal, which she then battered against the side of the building and finished off with a hatchet. The skunk measured almost three feet long, a record size. Beulah "had to use soap and water and meal vigorously for several hours, but before too long she was again able to go out."

7. How the Town Changed

Since the trolley was Veteran City's main connection with the outside world, the motorman was something of a town crier, bringing news and messages to those wanted in St. Petersburg for whatever reason. If you were late getting ready for "the big trip," you could send someone ahead to warn the motorman and he would wait, just as long as was needed. Many people recall sitting aboard while someone finished dressing or doing some other last-minute chore. No one seemed to mind much. It certainly beat the alternative. Mary McRoberts wrote: "When on occasions storms and high waters washed out the tracks . . . we were forced to venture to St. Petersburg on our own. I remember one time when my parents had urgent business in town and walked all the way. They stayed in St. Pete until the service was resumed."

The ride from St. Petersburg took between half an hour and an hour, depending on whose version one believes, though the variance may be accounted for by better and worse runs—cattle on the tracks, disconnections from the electric service or just plain failure of that service. It supposedly ran half-hourly in each direction, but that is very unlikely to have happened in actuality.

For the fare, it was a really good deal. Though the exact price varied some over the years, it began at fifteen cents out from St. Petersburg and ten cents return, and only three months later was lowered to ten cents each way. In the evening, after 6:00 p.m. it was only ten cents round trip. It left St. Petersburg about eleven and ran as far as there were passengers and then turn around and go back. Children paid a dollar a month for their transportation to school.

A very early trolley.

One of the Robertses, an early motorman, recalled that it wasn't an easy job: "Streetcars used here years ago were all second-hand and far from being in good condition. Brakes were hand operated and many times once they were set it was difficult to release them. The motorman ground on the brake handle and often had difficulty stopping a car. Seats ran crossways, with no aisle, so the conductor had to walk on the running board to get to the passengers to collect fares." The cars were very small and open, carrying only about twenty people, but even so were never crowded, averaging perhaps two hundred passengers a day. While there was usually plenty of business on weekends and holidays, sometimes as many as one thousand riders on a good day, otherwise the cars frequently ran empty from one end of the line to the other. So, despite the occasional memorable weekend, as in December 1909 when a record three thousand people made the trip, the streetcar line never made money and continued to be subsidized by those checks from Philadelphia.

Tourists traveling out to the Casino for a day's excursion at the beaches often remarked that it seemed much cooler once the car crossed Disston Avenue, which amused the locals, who realized that was because the pavement stopped there, and beyond that point the tracks ran over grass and through the woods all the way to the water.

Tourists gathering rice shells on an excursion to Gulfport. *Courtesy Ernie Riske*

There was a pavilion along the way, a simple open-sided structure with a floor and a roof, built as the tracks were laid to provide a place for a picnic in the woods or an evening dance. Later residents referred to it as "the colored people's dance pavilion," but there is no indication that it had any formal designation as to the race of its users. Its life was short, for in November 1909, it burned to the ground and was never replaced. The damage loss was estimated at $200. (One later report suggested that the establishment of "a Negro casino on the waterfront" had actually been the driving force behind the movement for indignant citizens to incorporate. Perhaps the reference is to this building as no other possibility has come to light.)

The Pavilion and a switching spread somewhere near the Gulfport border. *Courtesy Webb family*

Since there was only one track, a switching spread was constructed somewhere along the way. Unfortunately it didn't often happen that two cars encountered each other exactly at this point, for the schedules were not always rigidly in effect. When such a confrontation occurred, it fell to one of the cars to back up, which entailed un-hooking and re-hooking the electric connection and a considerable loss of time. Probably it annoyed some people, but for the most part, the riders regarded it as an unavoidable happenstance and sat it out with a good-natured shrug. Life was a little more relaxed then.

The first improvements were made as early as the spring of 1906, when the track was leveled along some of the "rough places," and telephone connections were installed along the line, so that there was some means of communication if help was needed. Later, two switching locations were added within Gulfport's limits, one in what is now Clymer Park, just south of Gulfport Boulevard, and one at the Tangerine entry point.

Although the rickety condition of the tracks and second-hand cars left some passengers in doubt of their safety, there were fortunately very few serious accidents. One recorded collision happened in July of 1908 when two cars met unexpectedly near the sawmill. The conductor's leg was broken and one car was so badly damaged that it had to be taken out of service. A few months later, while pushing a flat car loaded with wood, the trolley hit a horse that had panicked and run onto the track. The horse was killed and again the car irreparably damaged. There were other incidents, derailments, wrecked cars, injuries, even one fatal one in 1906, but not within the Gulfport boundaries.

What did happen, with some regularity, was that a pole would get knocked or blown down, the wire would sag and hit the car, dragging the pole along with it, till someone (quite often a passenger) would get out and hold it up until the car passed. And when automobile traffic came along, there was the occasional incident of damage to the rails. Anchored only lightly in the sand, they would spread easily when run over by an auto.

The streetcar began a regular mail service, daily and Sunday, in August 1907, delivered directly to the Veteran City stop, which also served as the post office, at least until the Florida West Coast Company reorganized itself enough to begin some serious clearing work in the vicinity and needed the space for offices to oversee the thirty or so men involved in the project. From there the first sidewalk in town, built in 1909 of shell at the expense of the adjacent property owners, was laid some seventy-five feet northward toward the Balch house, which stood—and still does—on the corner of 27th Avenue.

Another of the most important new benefits to the town as a result of the streetcar line was the sawmill, built about 1907 within the big curve where the trolley struck south from Tangerine. F.R. Singlehurst bought it out in 1908 and began the final clear-cutting of the remaining lumber in the district. There was a little narrow gauge side rail off at an angle from the sawmill, running in the direction of today's 58th Street and 15th Avenue, which was used to help haul in the logs from the nearby sites, though mules were still employed for the rougher terrain. In later years, it was often assumed that this track had some relation to the trolley, but it did not, except that Singlehurst had had the engine towed out to his location by the combined power of three streetcars.

A most important function of the trolley was to haul freight, especially building materials, from one point to another, by means of small flat cars it pushed or pulled. Between 26th and 28th Avenues a side track was built to allow for parking of these cars. This was a great advance on the tedious method of trekking into town with a horse and wagon or oxcart. Some materials, as usual, did continue to arrive by boat in the time-honored method, but the new access to ready-milled lumber caused a real upsurge in home building in the immediate area of the freight car siding, which is why so many homes along that part of Beach Boulevard date from the period 1905-1910.

There seems to have been no formal delivery of the building materials in this era of personal integrity and trust. You ordered something and probably paid for it, it came and you went and took what you needed when you needed it. Sometimes three or four freight cars were parked there waiting for purchasers to come along with their teams. When a flat car was once again empty, the trolley hooked it onto the rear and brought it back to town for another load.

Just the thought of being able to get from one place to another without fighting the torturous paths of sand and mud that passed for roads was enough to make the streetcar system a very welcome addition. The state of the roads in West Hillsborough was as abysmal as it had been in the days of Will McPherson's editorializing, and the politicians in the eastern or Tampa part of the county had no particular interest in seeing them improved. No money was wasted on a region with so few voters and so little political influence. But it was exactly that question which would eventually cause the residents on this side of the Bay to band together and secede from Hillsborough County a few years into the future. In order to prove the difficulty of reaching the county seat by land, a group of motorists, including Frank Davis' son Alonzo, set out in 1907 to drive there from St. Petersburg. It took more than three days of coping all the way with one problem or another, be it streams to ford, wildfires or no available gasoline (Albert Whitted, showing his daredevil nature early, once made the trip on his motorcycle in a matter of hours, but that was mostly due to a spell of dry weather when the sand roads were packed down rather than swimming in the usual mud). The trip from Veteran City to St. Pete was not quite as onerous, but still not one lightly undertaken. The tracks may have crossed the several little streamlets along the way, and walkers could use the footbridges, but horses and wagons or oxcarts still had to wade.

Without any contest, the prime advantage of the new transportation system affected many livelihoods—especially those of the fishermen. Now, at last, a catch could be shipped directly, in a matter of minutes, to the markets of St. Petersburg or the boat connections for Tampa and beyond. This was more of a boost for the town than all the potential developments in anyone's dream. The tourists, too, availed themselves of the fishing pole racks mounted on the sides of the cars. One story from 1909 illustrates how the sport fishing tourists used the car line. Apparently a lady landed a seventy-one-pound, five-and-a-half foot long tarpon on an excursion and insisted on bringing it back to town with her. Some gentlemen obliged her by lugging it aboard and arranging it in a seat. Before the trip was over, several reports came in to the St. Petersburg police regarding a "shot up body" on the streetcar.

8. The Residents of Veteran City

On June 21, 1907, Rebecca Arnold Slaughter Barnett died after a fall in her home. She was laid to rest in Glen Oak cemetery, and with her passing, the pioneer era was truly gone, though many of her forty-plus grandchildren remained in the area to assume positions of importance in the ensuing years.

One of these, Viola Leonardy, had in 1902 married Elisha Henry Weathers, one of the more interesting new arrivals to the area. Born in Augusta, Georgia, in 1873, he ran away to join the circus at the age of twelve. Till the late 1890s he pursued this life, learning all the skills that it required, becoming accomplished at such arts as magic and walking the high wire. But with the onset of the Spanish-American War, he decided to have a try at soldiering, and after some unfortunate adventures, including an injury from a horse's kick, ended up in Tampa in 1900. It is unknown how or why, but he made his way to Disston City, arriving there in 1901.

Claudette Dean wrote of him, "He loved to entertain and was always putting on shows for the residents. It was during one such event while he was sitting in a chair perched on a high wire, that he invited all the people to his wedding, then proposed to his intended. Guess he figured she wouldn't turn him down after [that]." After his marriage to Viola, "she put an end to the high-wire act and he became a millright [sic] and carpenter and went into the building business, building many of the first homes on Pass-A-Grille. His skill on the high-wire was not wasted. He was called on to do any work on towers, water tanks, places where men of less skill would have been put in great danger."

Viola's younger sister Lorena had married Henry Slaughter's brother-in-law Angus Lawrence Nash at the age of fourteen, and after ten years had several children, with more to come. Angus was the youngest son of the widowed Christian Nash, who still lived on Tangerine Avenue, and it is there the couple settled. Nelly Leonardy had just wed Frederick Roberts; thus both Lorena and Nelly had strengthened the interwoven ties between the Slaughters and the other local clans.

Henry Slaughter's daughter Maggie was married to Frederick Roberts' brother Walter. Another daughter, Grace, married John Guy Morrison just a few days before her grandmother's death, the ceremony held in Walter and Maggie's home. She wore "blue china silk trimmed in white Valenciennes lace" and her bridesmaids were her sisters Florence and Inez, in white muslin and pink silk with white lace, respectively. Guy Morrison had arrived here from Pennsylvania as a young boy and lived as a boarder, supporting himself, from the age of thirteen. It was noted that the couple received "handsome presents, some of them expensive."

Though Christine Slaughter was only nineteen, she had been married for three years to Lawrence D. Renney (L.D.), a motorman on the trolley line. Lawrence received great praise and commendation from Chase himself for saving Mrs. Chase's life during a frightening incident aboard one of the company boats in 1906. Mrs. Chase and a small boy had been pushed into the Bay by the large crowds and were being carried away by a strong tide when L.D. jumped overboard to rescue them. Later, Lawrence and Christine found work managing the Wintersgills' Boca Ciega Yacht Club. Both the Morrisons and the Renneys lived on Disston Avenue.

Lawrence Renney's brother Sam would also achieve a kind of fame when in 1909 he tangled with an old alligator named Queen, who seems to have lived for awhile in back of a St. Petersburg store. Sam was attempting to rope the eleven-foot long gator to ready it for transportation on the "12 o'clock freight car" out to the ostrich farm, a popular attraction located along the trolley line around 40th Street (admission: adults fifteen cents, children ten cents). Said to be as much as seventy-five years old, Queen's life in captivity apparently hadn't lessened her ferocity, for she clamped onto Sam's arm and whirled him around mercilessly while bystanders tried everything to make her let go. Prying at her jaws with a crowbar failed, but a good whack on the nose with an iron rod finally worked, and Sam was freed, his hand "chewed to a pulp" and never of much use again, though his alligator adventures were far from over.

Walter P. Fuller was invited along on one such adventure and described it in a 1971 letter to Sam's son Bill.

An alligator farm had recently opened on South Fourth Street, and there was a cash market. The owner wanted two or three big ones to draw crowds and a lot of little ones to sell to tourists. We first went to Maximo Point to Tzar Bennett's place. The old man had a large tract of land on the waterfront, heavily fenced, and mostly kept in its native state, which was a heavily wooded 'jungley' area. The old man's wife was blind and on her account, he was desperately afraid of fires. Incidentally, about once every two weeks, the old man trundled a wheel-barrow to the Gulfport car line at Tangerine, rode the streetcar line to St. Petersburg, did his shopping and reversed his route. Sam picked his 'shopping day;' however, something alerted the old man and he didn't go.

Sam and I crawled through the fence at a point near a little pond, which had a big alligator hole on it. His equipment was a horse and wagon, a long pole with an iron hook on the end, a crowbar, and some good stout rope. He probed around until he hit the alligator, stuck the hook through the reptile's lower jaw and we were hauling his majesty out of the hole when Mr. Bennett burst through the Palmettos in a hysterical rage and brandishing a double-barrel shotgun. He pointed the gun at Sam and screamed 'Get off my land.' Sam calmly looked down the muzzle of the gun, slowly walked up to Mr. Bennett, ducked and grabbed the gun and took it away from the owner. He then soundly slapped Bennett's face and calmly said, 'Old man, don't you ever point that gun at me again.' He then unloaded it, gathered up his gear, we crawled through the fence and Sam gently tossed the gun at the old man's feet.

We then drove out to Joe's Creek, which reached Boca Ciega Bay by a route that ran slightly south of the Light House Restaurant and Bar at the corner of Park Street and Tyrone Boulevard. There was a huge alligator nest at this point, and the eggs were just hatching. We got busy catching the baby 'gators' and putting them in two sacks. At this point, an enraged mama alligator, about ten feet long, came out of the creek with a rush and grabbed Sam's right arm between the wrist and elbow, in its powerful jaws, and clamped down, and started to roll. When a gator catches a live animal, it holds it in its mouth and turns over sideways very rapidly until it breaks important bones and renders his victim powerless. But Sam wrapped his arms and legs around the gator and rolled with her. A pine tree and palmetto clump stopped this rolling and Sam very calmly told me to put the forelegs of the gator over her back and tie them. The gator is then helpless, so he coolly told me to get the crowbar, put it between the jaws and pry her mouth open. He pulled his arm out and he tied the gator's jaws shut and we trussed her up and heaved her in the wagon and tied her down. Only after we had gotten all of this done did Sam tear up a shirt and bind his wounds. The scuffle had torn almost all of the skin off of his arm, and he was bleeding profusely. We drove to town and only then did Sam go see a doctor.

Some man! The most courageous one I ever saw!

Inez Lucy Slaughter was seventeen and would soon marry Tom Sawyer's nephew Courtney, who was described by a descendant as "a little short stubby man, not a good-looking man," but a fine builder of fishing boats. The Henry Slaughters had their final child, Willis Irving, and moved into the Disston Avenue house built by Dr. Jason Taylor (after whom their first son was named), a well-known citizen of the period, who had spent some years in town before his death in 1908.

Rebecca's three Barnett children were still in town as well. Mary Elizabeth's two children by Tom Sawyer had been raised by Rebecca and were now grown. Chester worked with his father Tom in their fish camp located in town, and occasionally traveled with him on visits to his family in Key West, before marrying Ruth Roberts, cousin to Walter and Fred. Gladys would marry Roland Girard in June of 1909, her "pretty pink and white wedding" held at the Disston City school, which was decorated with smilax, pine and white oleander for the occasion. Crowds overflowed the interior and followed the couple to the Casino for a reception. Elmer Rousseau, son of Mabel White, was best man, Mattie Renney maid of honor, Vera Leonardy a bridesmaid and little Lilly Quinn flower girl.

The Girards were not new to Pinellas, having been here about as long as anybody, some say since the great storm of 1848, when, one story has it that the patriarch of the clan, John Francis Girard, fresh from Paris, lived with the almost legendary early settlers of John's Pass. The first of his children, John

Francis, Jr., was born in Tampa in 1859, and two more boys soon followed. Conscripted to carry supplies to Cuba, John and his schooner *Estrellita* disappeared, leaving his wife in desperate straits. She began a frantic search for him, during which her two younger sons died of yellow fever at Key West. John, the eldest, survived and went along with his mother into a second marriage to a man named Carter. In 1883 he married Mary Williams of Key West, who, descendants claimed, had some connection to Rebecca Arnold. They had twelve children, one of whom died in infancy. The surviving six boys were James Roland, William Otis, John, Jr., Stephen, Theodore and Jerome, the youngest boy and eleventh child, born in 1906. The girls were Mary Birdina, Leila, Pearl, Grace and Emily.

James Barnett, Jr., was thirty-four, still at home in his mother's house and even after her death showing no inclination to marry.

Laura Barnett and John Campaign White were building a new house next to his father Joshua's place down on the bluff, but in the storm of March, 1909, it was lifted off its foundation and carried several feet, suffering considerable damage and a broken chimney. As the house was "not quite paid for," he suffered a serious new "financial burden." It could have been worse; Joshua's house was "a complete wreck," as was the old Baumeister house and several others in the area.

These members of the immediate family were joined by several newcomers who found their way to Veteran City in the period 1905-1910, though none of them seem to have come because of the planned development. Still here were a few of fthe original settlers, like the Woodworths, Thomeses and Steinwinders. (It was in the Steinwinder home on 51st Street in 1909 that the first indoor Catholic mass was said within the town, by the circuit-riding priest who served the area). William P. Woodworth had remained one of the very few residents in Veteran City during its early years, but he, too, gave up for awhile in 1907, briefly relocating in Tarpon Springs before he came back in better form than ever. Now he titled himself "Judge" and claimed the presidency of the Florida State Poultry Association. He also seemed to resume his correspondence with the *Times*, writing again about the Wetherells, who also came and went, and Daniel Hoover. Old Mr. Hoover's cottage was described as about the prettiest place around, a neat little home set in ten acres of gardens, orange trees, and attractive landscaping, while "Uncle Dan" himself achieved some local fame for his agricultural skills, producing one year no less than eight superb varieties of peaches.

Woodworth, like the Whites and the Leonardys, suffered from the 1909 gale. His "large house" was lifted from its foundation and carried several feet to the northeast, breaking up the floors and tearing to shreds all his careful landscaping. Mrs. Woodworth received a serious back injury in the incident, and while Mr. Woodworth was "thrown across the floor," he was not "especially hurt."

One important new family, in terms of the effect they would have on the future town of Gulfport, were the Webbs, who were connected to the Thomes/Daniels family. Originally from the town of Luton in Bedfordshire, England, several children of Henry Joseph Webb immigrated to America in the early 1900s. These were Willis, born 1867; Henry, born in 1873; Samuel James, born 1875; and a sister Elizabeth, called "Tizzie." Another brother, John, perhaps older, stayed in England. They came first to Canada and then New England, where Tizzie remained, while the three brothers eventually wended their way south to Florida. Henry, who was married to the former Lucy Young (1874-1912) had two children born in England, May (1900) and Lillian Grace (1902) and three born in Canada, Sidney Willis (1904), Florence Lucille (1907) and Evelyn Elizabeth (1909).

Henry Webb (1873-1930?)

Sam and Abbie (Thomes) Webb arrived here in 1907, followed by Henry and Lucy. The Henry Webbs lived on Disston Avenue and the Samuel Webbs on Davis Boulevard. Much more will be heard from them all. Willis and his wife Amy also continued to live in Gulfport for decades to come, though following a rather more retiring lifestyle than that of his younger brothers.

Samuel Webb (1875-1931) and his wife Abbie (Thomes) Webb (1883-1939). *Courtesy Webb family*

But of all the newcomers of this time, few would compare to the Wintersgills. Brothers Elmer and Lester, sons of a German immigrant, were men of many skills and vocations who had probably begun their careers in Pittsburgh shipyards, where their father Ralph had certainly worked. When they moved south, it was first to manage a hotel in Jacksonville, then on to Veteran City in 1907. Ralph came along with them to live with Elmer, who had recently married a widow named Mary White. In late 1907, Lester helped Elmer build an eight-room home, which still stands on the southeast corner of Beach Boulevard and 25th Avenue, and was recognized as a "substantial addition" to the Veteran City development. Lester's own home was a block or so further south, also still in existence.

The Wintersgill family at 2620 Beach Boulevard: Ralph at right, probably Elizabeth Wintersgill McRoberts standing in the light dress, her daughter Mary and Lester's daughter Elsie seated on the steps. The other women may be Elmer's and Lester's wives Mary and Louellen. Malcolm McRoberts may be one of the two gentlemen standing at the left.

In 1910 Lester Wintersgill was thirty-eight, had a wife named Lou Emma, a school-age son Washington and a daughter Elsie, then about fifteen, who would one day marry Louis Roberts, brother of Maggie Slaughter's husband Walter and Nelly Leonardy's husband Fred. Elmer and Lester's older sister Elizabeth and her husband Malcolm McRoberts also arrived to take up residence across Davis (Beach) Boulevard, not far from the original trolley terminal. They were in their fifties and had a household consisting of a son Harold and daughter-in-law Clara, with their three little children, Malcolm, Ralph and Elizabeth, and an unmarried daughter, Mary. Malcolm Senior had succeeded Alonzo Hoyt as postmaster in March 1908.

The Wintersgills put up a boat works just east of the Electric Dock, which would evolve into the first Boca Ceiga Yacht Club. This structure, built on pilings, was at the end of a private wooden pier at the foot of 54th Street, and consisted of several slips covered with a corrugated metal roof. It lasted till the late teens, but has been the site of one or another municipal piers almost ever since. Lester was the more active member in this endeavour, captaining the *Florida* and a variety of other boats on their fishing and ferry service runs.

The *Florida* captained by Lester Wintersgill.

On one such trip, we are left a hilarious account of a rather rough passage to the grouper banks some fifteen miles west of Pass-a-Grille by a man who said that one "sick friend was offering $50 for the sight of a pine tree, and Alonzo Hoyt was praying that the government would erect a boardwalk to the grouper banks." In the end, Lester brought the boat safely through the weather with no damage beyond that to his passengers' good humor and digestions. On another occasion, just as he was docking at Pass-a-Grille, Wintersgill's quick thinking saved the life of little Della Crawley, who had fallen into the water, and possibly those of his entire passenger complement. As dozens of horrified onlookers rushed to one side to see if the girl surfaced, the boat tilted dangerously and threatened to tip over completely. Captain Lester shouted for them to move away from the rail, the boat righted itself, and Della swam competently back to the pier.

While not always as colorful as Lester, it is Elmer who was something of an entrepreneur. He had become in 1908 the first person in town to have a kind of electric service, when he hooked up a one-half horsepower motor to the streetcar wires and had himself an automatically functioning pump. And he was quick to take advantage of a spring 1909 transportation strike in Pittsburgh when, surprisingly, he was able to acquire a line of three, twenty-two-seat "autos" and put them into service there, no doubt a fairly profitable venture.

The Wintersgills brought with them from Jacksonville a Swedish man named Robert Sjustrom, who became the manager of the Mary Boat Company. Sjustrom bought Veteran City lots at 52nd Street and 26th Avenue and went to work at once to build a residence for his motherless children. Almost immediately they became involved in an adventure, when his thirteen-year-old daughter Clara eloped with a man ten years her senior. The lovers had set sail for Tampa on the *Manatee* and Robert Sjustrom, after alerting the sheriff, was right behind them on the next boat. The man went to jail and Clara was ignominiously brought home.

Sadly, Robert died the summer after their arrival, leaving his brood of children complete orphans. In addition to Clara, now fifteen, there were John, nineteen; Olga, seventeen; Oscar, thirteen; Emma, twelve; and Alice, nine. Lester Wintersgill stepped forward to act as their guardian until each of them reached the age of twenty-four. John found work as a carpenter and Olga became in essence the head of the family.

In 1909 she participated in an almost incomprehensible contest held by the *St. Petersburg Independent* to determine the most needy people in the town and surrounding areas. Olga won in the county category, receiving $50, which she said would enable her two youngest sisters to continue to attend school (Clara was apparently a lost cause). She also said she had hesitated to enter because she felt an even more worthy contestant was "little Henrietta Slaughter, who needs the money badly." Henrietta did enter the next contest and lost badly, finishing last.

Other families who added to the mix of the late Veteran City population were the Schludeckers, the Ermatingers, the Cussons and the Millers. The Schludeckers were German immigrants who had arrived in this country about 1888 and in the immediate area about 1906. Albert and his wife Emma, who were in their mid to late forties at the time of incorporation, had seven children, six of whom came with them from Pennsylvania; the youngest, Charles, was born here. The oldest girl, Rosa, had been sent out to work when she reached sixteen, and was employed as a servant in St. Petersburg; while Otto, just twelve in 1910, would eventually become the second husband of one of Joseph and Sophie Steinwinder's daughters, Helen.

Albert (1866-1945) and Emma (1863-1940) Schludecker. *Courtesy Alfred Hammond*

The Schludeckers lived in a big old unpainted house near Disston Avenue north of Lakeview in an area that came to be known as the "German settlement." There they farmed and in later years operated a small dairy serving the immediate neighbors, for, without transportation during certain times, Albert had to walk his milk route. He left a diary covering some of this period, which demonstrates exactly how grueling the routine was of the small farmer.

In it he recorded the early morning, midday and evening temperatures and weather every single day, followed by a listing of his chores. It is an indelible record of unrelenting hard work; sowing and reaping, harrowing and hauling, clearing new land for himself and his employers, the local homesteaders who used him to do their heaviest work. Day in and day out Albert dealt with the difficulties of cultivation in this climate, over and above which were the occasional setbacks of fires, rampaging hogs, dying livestock and rattlesnakes.

On Sundays he paused just a little, for after chores usually involving the chicken yards (which he wrote as "shiskenyards" in one of the few remnants of his German education), he would go into town to collect the mail, then take the time to "read and write." Holidays were for others, not him. On Thanksgiving, his sons had a "holiday afternoon," so they all set to work grubbing out palmettos. A few days before Christmas, he bought a rifle for the boys, which may have served as a present. There is no mention of any gifts for Emma or the girls, or, in fact, any celebration of the day itself, beyond a walk through the woods.

He hired himself out to the Whites and their in-laws the Bozemans, the Browns and the Ritcheys, among others. At one point he mentions charging Mr. Brown only $12.25 for three months work, "and then he kicked." If something needed to be transported—luggage, crops, people, a bedstead, anything—it was Albert Schludecker who was called upon to do the hauling.

At one point in 1909, Albert must have become completely fed up with this hard life, because he wrote a long letter to the *Rural New Yorker* complaining that the promoters' promises of easy farming here were totally false. You will need, he said, ten times as much money as you might think, five times as much fertilizer and still you will have only one chance in a dozen to get a profitable crop. And don't believe it when they say there is never a killing frost, because there is. Of course, word of this heresy got back, and for a while Albert was not the most popular man in town.

The Ermatingers, a large and somewhat wild family of Swiss descent, came to Veteran City when they bought ten acres on Disston Avenue, with a grove and some chickens. Though a hatter by trade and a city person by birth, Mr. Ermatinger and his boys attempted to make some money with the chickens. Son Elmer, in *Pass-a-Grille: A Patchwork of Memories*, said the following: "Once I had to deliver 25 chickens . . . It was a very hot day and when I got there, the chickens were all dead! I'll never forget that. Also after school I would deliver the hats that had been sold and my father would give me ten cents for each one. Many a time I walked ten blocks to save the nickel carfare."

The Cussons were: Alexis, forty-eight in 1910, his wife Josefa, and their children Raymond, twenty-two; Antonia Marie, popularly called Nita, twenty; and Leon, eleven. Mr. Cusson, said to be associated with the American Cigar Company, was a native of Canada and his wife Josefa was from New York. Mrs. Cusson, who was of Spanish ancestry, would become known for her entertaining, inviting once in 1909 "all Catholics" to her "lovely country home" for an afternoon party of cards and refreshments. Before long the youngsters were a mainstay of the social columns, Miss Nita dancing in "blue crepe de chine and white lace" and Raymond entertaining parties of friends at local restaurants.

A gathering held at the Cussons' "Bay View," in December 1909 celebrated Nita's engagement to a St. Petersburg man, Harry Scott. This magnificent event was described at length in the *Independent*. The house was "aglow with light and color," a frieze of bamboo vine covering the walls of the reception room and twining up the stairway, while festoons of red hearts decorated doorways and pictures, and were draped from chandeliers. Cupids, dolls and other trinkets were "nestled in the foliage." The menu included creamed oysters, sandwiches, relishes, coffee and cake, and the guest list was not drawn from Veteran City neighbors, but consisted entirely of downtown society and members of St. Petersburg's fledgling yacht club.

The Millers had been around for some time. This recollection of Albertus Miller, ten years old in 1902, and possibly a relation of the Everett Miller who had moved his family into the old Baumeister house about that time, sums up life here in the last days before the "settlement" disappeared forever into the officially incorporated town of Gulfport. Even at that young age, Albertus was a main provider of the family's food supply.

My mother would say, 'Son, can you get us a couple of rabbits?' And right outside from us a little ways there's all kinds of rabbits. They were just everywhere. I could go out with a twenty-two rifle and, say thirty minutes I'd be back with a couple and I'd skin them out and take them to her. She might say, 'Son, the tide is about right for, can you get us a couple of quarts of scallops?" I could trot on over to Boca Ciega Bay and, at that time, that was before any of the dredging or anything, and scallops were very very plentiful all over the flats. I could wade out a foot deep of water on those flats and that little short grass and the scallops would be everywhere. I'd take a croaker bag with me and put all in it. I could drag and then go to shore and open them. I got to be very good at opening them. It wouldn't take me long then to get a couple of quarts of the muscles out of the scallops. That is all you eat of that clam fish. Then at the northeast corner of Boca Ciega Bay, there was a fresh water creek ran into it [Clam Bayou] and every high tide would push that water back and then the tide would go down and the fresh water would run out again. Right in that area there were several beds of oysters. So we had all the oysters we wanted during the oyster season. And my mother would tell me that she'd like some oysters to fry. Why, it didn't take me long to run down there and get them. And then out in that grass, on those flats, occasionally there would be an area, oh ten feet or maybe 50 feet across where there'd be no grass, be just pure white sand. And wading out to them you'd disturb the sting rays and the flounders. And usually they'd made it to one of those bare spots where the sand was and they'd flop the sand around with their fins and throw it up over their back in attempt to hide. And we'd have a little spear in our hands, I used a one-pronged spear when I could see them. And you just shove it on down through them and then get him and take him off that barb and put him on a string so you drag it behind you. And it didn't take long to go out and get a half a dozen flounders and during that length of time you'd kill at least that many sting rays.

Well before 1910 just about everyone had given up on the Veteran City concept. *The St. Petersburg Times* had written, "Veteran City has, since its founding, been a pretty place to see on a map and is situated in a beautiful location overlooking the waters of Boca Ceiga Bay, but work on clearing and developing has gone very slow since." All the efforts to promote the area had failed and the big investors had left the little settlement to fend for itself. The town returned to its old ways. The fishermen went off for days at a time, the ladies got together and had porch parties, the children went to school, holidays were celebrated. There was now something like one hundred inhabitants. It was time to make the move. It was time to form a real government.

Great good fortune allows us a look at a happy event just at the end of this period. The Woodworth home was the scene of a party to celebrate the coming of the new year, 1910, and the new decade. Bertha Pearson was the young hostess, presiding over a gathering of the town's youth, all locals, unlike Nita Cussons' St. Petersburg society parties. The older Steinwinder girls were there; and Olga Sjustrom; as well as Carrie Roberts, at eighteen the youngest child of William and Virginia's large family; and Elsie Wintersgill, who was fourteen or fifteen. Among the boys were Almeron Renney, Andrew Roberts and John Sjustrom. Carrie's future husband Clarence Stefanski was there, and sixteen-year-old Edward Brantley, who would soon become the extremely youthful captain of the *Gypsy* (and, much later, mayor of St. Petersburg).

It's a pretty picture that comes to mind, these youngsters, singing and dancing, and dining on hot chocolate and cake. At midnight they ran out to the beach to welcome the future, which would be in their hands, and that future would be Gulfport, for not many months later, on August 30, 1910, the call would go out to organize a municipal government.

Chapter V
Incorporation

1. The Call Goes Out

Alonzo Hoyt was the main organizer of the incorporation effort, and it was he who would call the October 12, 1910, meeting of registered voters and be elected its chair. It was also he who designed the rather strange town seal, showing as it does a row of mythical skyscrapers that would never, thankfully, materialize. He, however, did not succeed in a bid to become Gulfport's first mayor and never again served the town in any political position.

It all began in August of that year, Wednesday evening the twenty-forth, when Hoyt brought together as many of the locals as he could round up to broach the subject. He and Woodworth were there, of course, and Elmer Wintersgill. Henry Slaughter and Jim Barnett attended, with Alex Leonardy and his daughter Lorena's husband "Laus" Nash, Henry Weathers, Joshua and John White, Walter Roberts, Jack Quinn, Guy Morrison, Sam Webb, Roland Girard, William Blackshear (who would marry one of the Steinwinder girls), John Daniels and the Stefanskis, Alec and his grandson Clarence. Alexis Cusson came, farmer Charles Perrington, Lee Allen, Elmer Rousseau and a "Mr. Estes," probably a dry goods merchant from Georgia named Emory Easters (also spelled Esthers). Estes or Easters and his wife Martha were in their forties, and had three teenage children, Katherine, Eric and Hortense, at seventeen the current town schoolteacher.

Hoyt gave an impassioned speech in favor of incorporation and then called for a vote. Some obviously abstained because only twenty-one votes were cast, the result being a positive verdict, sixteen for and five against. They then went on to consider a name and "after some discussion" chose Gulf Port.

Not everybody was enthralled with this decision. The *Times* editor Straub, for instance, wrote a couple of weeks later, "Inasmuch as no benefits of incorporation can possibly ever reach these districts named, my good friends Wintersgill et al, will not deny that it looks very much like a thrifty plan to

The seal of Gulfport, designed by Alonzo Hoyt.

make several miles of surrounding country pay most of the taxes necessary to do whatever it is they want done at Veteran—excuse me—Gulfport." Straub was particularly annoyed because the new incorporation included some land he owned and "expected to build a town on someday." This property would now not be available for his own development plans; it had been, as he said, "en-Gulfed."

The vitriol against this "absurd territory grabbing" continued for some little while. Complaining that Gulfport proposed to take in so much land that it would overshadow St. Petersburg, making the latter a suburb of the former, Straub suggested instead the incorporation of Pass-a-Grille, which was already world famous. Let that absorb Gulfport! He, of course, also owned considerable property in Pass-a-Grille and would have proceeded with incorporation there if only there had been the requisite twenty-five qualified electors in residence to put forward the proposal.

Hoyt, Woodworth and the Wintersgills were not put off. They went to the *Times* competitor, the *Independent,* to publish the required notice in the issues of September tenth, seventeenth, twenty-forth and October first. Publisher Lew B. Brown at once editorialized in his paper in support of the endeavor, though adding, "The limits of the new city are large, taking in quite a bit of choice farm lands, and there has been some little opposition to assuming city taxes by a very few of the property holders." He approved of the new name, calling it "very pretty and appropriate," and credited its choice to "Captain Wintersgill, the knight errant of Veteran City, always awake and scrapping for every possible benefit and point."

And so the meeting day came, and thirty of the thirty-eight registered voters gathered at the Casino. Hoyt was elected chairman and Woodworth secretary.

"A vote was taken by written ballot which resulted in a decision to incorporate, twenty-three votes being cast in favor of incorporation and seven votes against incorporation."

"William P. Woodworth, Elmer E. Wintersgill and Alonzo A. Hoyt were nominated as candidates for Mayor. Mr. Woodworth refused to be a candidate for any office whatever, and Mr. Elmer E. Wintersgill was elected by a vote of twenty-one, against seven, for Mr. Hoyt. On motion of Mr. Hoyt, duly seconded, the election was made unanimous."

"Mr. A.L. Stefanski, Mr. Lester E. Wintersgill, Mr. Joshua White, Mr. Henry Slauter and Mr. Henry Weathers were nominated for the office of aldermen and, there being no other candidates, they were declared duly elected." Sam Webb was nominated for Clerk and John White was nominated for marshal, also without opposition.

The incorporation document was duly filed with the office of H. Clark Crawford, Secretary of State. The new mayor Wintersgill went over to St. Petersburg the morning of the thirteenth and was sworn in, so that he could administer the oaths to the other officers that evening at a meeting held at his Boca Ceiga Yacht Club. Gulfport had become a town, officially, and now had a government of its own and a territory some eight miles square. Exactly as Straub suspected, the founders had included as much land as possible, three or four times today's area, to take in enough settlers to provide some kind of workable tax base.

The *St. Petersburg Times* continued to rail against this usurpation, stating: "Gulfport is perhaps the largest town in Florida, territorially speaking, and for population per square mile it is undoubtedly the largest on earth, and for good hard American cheek it will perhaps compare with any in the county, the taking in of large areas of valuable lands that can never receive any benefits of the corporation whatsoever and are taken only to be taxed, and being nothing more or less than a hold-up. But hold-ups are seldom satisfactory to anyone in the long run and the thing will right itself in time." Hoyt was called the "head booster" of the "immense territory" of thirty-eight citizens, which was a misstatement as, counting women and children, there were a great number more citizens than voters. However, perhaps women and children did not count, and there may well have been just about 38 adult white men in the territory.

The *St. Petersburg Independent* was a little kinder, pointing out what a suitable name Gulfport was, since the location was the best of points on the west side of the peninsula for embarkation to destinations in the Gulf of Mexico. "Veteran City is No More," said the headline of October 13, followed with a story about "the little Boca Ceiga town" now "organized as Gulfport."

Note that at this point the spelling of Henry's name as "Slauter" is first seen. His son, Willis Irving, who also used that form, once explained the change as a mistake on his own birth certificate. Since Irving was born in 1901, and this document written in 1910, it seems unlikely that his father had adopted the mistaken spelling. Other suggestions do come to mind, including the possibility that Henry may not have been completely literate. A petition signed by him in 1917 shows a careful, belabored and almost childish handwriting, spelling out "H.L. Slauter." Whatever the case, from then on, various members of the family chose to be known by that designation.

Of the forty-three men who either signed or attended, at least twenty-six were related to Henry and to each other, or would be in the near future. Some other relationships were not close, but in that era and that society would have been considered no less than kin. Apparently unrelated were the following: R. Lee Allen, Daniel Hoover (that first brave purchaser of a Veteran City lot); F. G. Gleaton, younger brother to Thomas Churchill "Church" Gleaton (born in 1872 in Alabama, he had boarded with the Renneys on his arrival here in 1902 and often fished with the Nobles); W. Bruce Livingstone (forty-six, who with his wife Minnie and daughter Sheila, had earlier that year taken over management of the Casino); H.E. Mitchell; Charles E. Perrington, a forty-eight-year-old widowed farmer from Maine who lived along Disston Boulevard just north of Tangerine; B.F. White (no doubt another of that clan, possibly a brother of Joshua); Charles E. Willetts (sixty-nine, never married, a former Union Army Major originally from New York who came to Gulfport in 1897); William P. Woodworth; Alexis Cusson and Alonzo A. Hoyt. Thomas Ausson remains a mystery.

Schludecker's diary continued to give a priceless picture of life here at the time of incorporation, an event in which he took no part. That very day, in fact, he was struggling to plow with a recalcitrant horse, who "would not go any more," even after "a licking." He wrote, reverting to German for the lower case I's, "i wish i never come to Florida to do such plowing with such a horse." Albert ignored family matters, such as the marriage of his oldest daughter Rosa, but he was careful to note the harvest of a fifty-two-pound watermelon and a sweet potato that grew to six pounds two ounces. This happy achievement is followed only a couple of weeks later by another disaster: "the wind blowed the barn down."

2. The First Councils

The five men elected to become the first town council took the designation "aldermen," and would receive a salary of twenty-five cents for each meeting attended and a fine of fifty cents if they were absent. (This system remained the same for many years, although the amounts were raised slightly.) It is not clear just what terms they agreed to serve, as the minutes of those first three or four years have been lost over time, and resignations and reappointments occurred regularly. It seems likely that there were staggered terms, with perhaps three of them having been selected to serve one year and two of them two years. In the election of 1911 three seats were open, Slauter and Stefanski being the two who were not required to stand for re-election.

At any rate, the structure of this government was such that the mayor was not a member of the council, and did not chair or even attend their meetings. He also served as municipal judge, and in this capacity he could require the attendance of witnesses, administer oaths, "inquire into the truth or falsity" of allegations and determine from the evidence the guilt or innocence of the accused, as well as decide the penalty. This was obviously a position of considerable power.

A president of the council was elected by its members to conduct the meetings; sometimes this office was held over a period of time and sometimes a chair was elected at the beginning of each session. Alec Stefanski was the first man named to this position. Of all the citizens' choices for council, one of the most surprising is that of this sixty-four-year-old immigrant of Polish descent who was said to have served with Troop A, 3rd New Jersey Cavalry, in the Civil War. Stefanski, a relative outsider, must have had some remarkable characteristics to be so honored. Spelling was apparently not one of those characteristics. In a letter to the West Coast Telephone company dated December 8, 1910, and prepared by Sam Webb for Council signatures, his reads "A.L. SETFAMKI."

He and his wife Jennie, fifty-five, and two grandsons had arrived here from Ohio to build in Oak Park (the Childs Park area) in 1908. The wedding of his grandson Clarence to Carrie Roberts was held at the Roberts homestead, then at Maximo, earlier in 1910. Woodworth's niece Bertha Pearson was maid of honor "in white swiss over pink with pink ribbons," and Carrie's brother Andrew, the one to whom she was closest in age, was best man. The young couple went to live with the elder Stefanskis.

It was Stefanski and Elmer Wintersgill, who, as the town's two highest officials, went to the American State Bank on the morning after incorporation and borrowed $100 under their own names to provide Gulfport's initial funding.

One of the council's first jobs was to send the town's name change to the long-suffering postal service. First there was some concern that the new designation was too much like another town, Gulfpoint (shades of Disston City), and the name would be disallowed. But this time the authorities did relent, and as of December 22, 1910, mail could be officially and correctly addressed to Gulfport. The post office was established in the Casino, where the council met as well. Records show that the first postmistress was "Clara B. Giger," who served from the date of incorporation until October 1913. This must refer to John Bethell's daughter Carrie Alma, twenty-nine in 1910 and married to Arthur Geiger. No doubt the federal government was impressed with the increase in revenue from 1909 when a total of eight dollars in stamps was sold, to the 1910 proceeds of $25.

Morality was extremely strict in Gulfport, on the public surface at least. The very first week of its existence, a temperance meeting was scheduled, to "rally and strengthen" the anti-alcohol sentiment. Another early act of the council was the prohibition of the sale of any merchandise on Sundays. The *St. Petersburg Independent* responded by stating: "This will be a severe blow to people who are compelled to purchase their meals on Sunday, as they will have to eat enough Saturday night to last until Monday morning."

At one early meeting, council voted to order seven police badges, and almost simultaneously, to ban hunting. More sarcastic remarks from the *Times* editorialists were occasioned. "It will take not seven but seventy-seven to see that the ordinance against shooting in the woods which comprise about 99% of the territory of Gulfport is not violated." Even if the town marshal could possibly patrol the "vast areas" of the town, even if he could actually catch an offender, what would become of the miscreants in a community without a jail?

The whole business of shooting in town was a complicated issue. Game was still prevalent enough that hunting was a common occupation, so some allowance had to be made for such a popular pursuit. Yet, the waiver of restrictions was abused, and there were "a number of houses in which shot is lodged," so the prohibition was again issued in the late fall. The badges, handcuffs and other police paraphernalia arrived early in 1911, and the law enforcement branch of the town government was now fully equipped, although still manned by only one person.

In February the council drafted plans for a city hall and "lockup," and two months later voted $1,200 to purchase twelve lots for town purposes. Bonds totaling $4,000 would be issued as follows: $1,500 for the town hall and jail; $500 for building and repairing bridges; $500 for making or improving streets; $500 for sidewalks; and $1,000 for general expenses. Lester Wintersgill and Henry Weathers headed up a finance committee, while Mayor Elmer and Alec Stefanski became the "sanitation committee."

The *Times* never failed to ridicule these attempts at forming a functioning government. A news item snickered that the "Sanitary Committee" would "have a busy week" since it was they themselves who would "do the hauling away of the rubbish." And later the paper commented on the proposed jail as "alarming to the many sportsmen who have been in the habit of hunting quail in what is now Gulfport, but it has been suggested that the 28 citizens of that hustling metropolis be made special officers with headquarters at the jail to capture those lawbreakers."

Even the simplest improvements were the butt of newspaper jokes: "They have not started work on the sea wall yet, but it is rumored that six bags of cement were received this week by the Waterfront Committee." The "extensive municipality" was derided for wanting a road to link up with St. Petersburg's improved Lakeview. If they hadn't set their boundaries so far outside the center of their "burg" their road building wouldn't have had to be so extensive, the writer pointed out.

As one would hope, the *Times* was taken to task for its running series of snide comments on the embryonic community's efforts, but any criticism was treated lightly. "Certain citizens of Gulfport have objected to the vein of levity our editorial staff sometimes allows to creep into mentions of that city's affairs." He goes on to ask how could they be taken seriously when the paper receives letters such as one from a "lady taxpayer," who says "Gulfport council have had another spasm. Getting worse. We are now promised mounted police and as there is no money for horse, mule, donkey or goat, in my mind's eye I see them mounted on brooms, and pigs and chickens hiding." So the reports persisted in the same vein, poking fun at a council meeting held at the Casino ("a large audience chamber packed with 28 citizens of Gulfport and a stranger") to check the assessment rolls, "It was thought that now the place was a real city with a mayor and councilmen that values should be raised."

Straub's excuse was that he was "unable to secure a correspondent" there, so knew "almost nothing" about the place, except the "ridiculously all-pig foolishness of those Gulfport people who incorporated lands several miles from their burg simply to hold the owners up for town taxes." Eventually he became so involved in the fight for separation from Hillsborough County that his disdain of Gulfport was limited to the occasional derogatory comment. It was during the tenure of that first council that the long struggle for independence came to a head. After countless attempts to sever West Hillsborough from its overshadowing neighbor, voters approved the move on November 14, 1911, and by the first of the next year Pinellas County came into being. At that point Pinellas had a population of about thirteen thousand, which, while being only some 17 percent of the total population of the original Hillsborough County, paid more than 23 percent of the taxes. It was ready to stand on its own as Florida's forty-eighth county.

One of the council's most pressing concerns was the need for a local school. The Florida West Coast Company was persuaded to donate two lots toward this end. The school committee, chaired unsurprisingly by Superintendent Hoyt, met in the old schoolhouse, wherever and whatever that was, and declared themselves out of debt and up to date in repairs. They formed another committee to petition the county for the establishment of a separate school district, or sub-district. Lester M. Wintersgill (L.M.), Henry Weathers and Sam Webb took on this project.

L.M., called by the *Times* "one of Gulfport's hustling councilmen," got to work having the actual plans drawn up for a new building. The final proposal came to council in May and the building was to be forty by sixty-two feet, one story, constructed of concrete block, and to consist of four rooms each capable of holding thirty-two students. When Hoyt moved to St. Petersburg to run a rooming house on 5th Avenue North, Sam Webb took over as superintendent, and, in a special election held in December, Alex Leonardy replaced Sam as school trustee.

Halley's comet had been a national sensation when it passed in May, and thanks to Albert Schludecker's diary, we know that the local "peoples are scared the world will tumple." The next day he noted that it hadn't "tumpled," or he wouldn't have been writing.

Sometime during that summer Henry Weathers left the council, due to his "removal from the village," and an interim election was held to fill the vacancy. Hoyt organized this, as usual, with Mr. Thomes, Walter M. Roberts and young John Sjustrom acting as the official inspectors. The seat was won by a man named Henry H. Kolb, sixty-four, who served until the regular fall election and was never heard from again, politically, though he and his wife Elizabeth remained Gulfport residents for many years to come.

In September, the citizens met at the Casino to nominate officers for the coming year. For mayor, Elmer Wintersgill and Alonzo Hoyt were proposed; for council, Joshua White, William A. Renney, Henry Weathers (he must have returned), Alex Leonardy, Charles Thomes, Joe Steinwinder and a motorman on the streetcar line, A.W. McGee. Sam Webb was the only nominee for clerk, while the marshal's position had two contenders: Fred Roberts and Aaron "Ade" Renney.

The election was held on October 3, 1911, an event the *Times* described as follows: "The municipal band played in the square before city hall all morning, but as all votes had been cast by noon, they went fishing after dinner." Since at this time there was no city hall, or, for that matter, no square or municipal band either, the entire report is probably sheer hyperbole. The results were stated without further derogatory comment. Elmer Wintersgill defeated Hoyt (possibly contributing to Alonzo's imminent move to St. Petersburg) by nineteen to ten votes. Alex Leonardy received twenty-two, Charles Thomes fourteen, William Renney seventeen, and the conductor, whose name was now given as W.B. McGhee, also twenty-two.

Going by the council roster of early 1912, the new aldermen were Leonardy, Thomes and McGee, elected to the three open seats vacated by Lester Wintersgill, Joshua White and Weathers/Kolb, though why Thomes' lesser vote superceded Renney's is unclear, unless the figure was a misprint, or Renney resigned for some other position. Sam Webb was re-elected "clerk, treasurer and collector of internal revenue." And Ade Renney defeated Fred Roberts for "tax collector and city marshall" by the narrow margin of fifteen to fourteen.

Albert Schludecker was one of those who voted. He has left us in his diary his schedule for that day, as well as a complete weather report (2:00 a.m., seventy-eight degrees; noon, ninety-four; 7:00 p.m., eighty-rour; fair and hot). His first chore was to mow, then he harrowed what he had plowed the day before. After that he sorted potatoes, then raked his earlier mowing. Probably it was by now early afternoon and with the full heat of the day beating down, he went to town to cast his vote. On his return, he put in some time hoeing potatoes, and finished the day by hauling hay.

The year 1912 opened with a financial muddle. Some of the money raised by local trustees for the construction of a school, and supposedly placed in the hands of the school board, had somehow been used to pay for other things. With the contractor demanding his due, an accounting discovered that about $300 had been spent for "elections, interest, salaries, etc." Given the fact that the town had run for all these months on the $100 Wintersgill/Stefanski bank loan, it is not surprising council had resorted to this creative financing.

But the school trustees needed to come up with additional funds to meet their obligation, so Lester Wintersgill was dispatched to Tampa to work out a solution with Hillsborough County. With Elmer suffering from an unexplained but apparently not terribly serious illness, Lester had taken over as acting mayor.

Two rooms of the small red-brick school had been finished the previous October, though obviously with no amenities, for parents met there to work out a way to build a sidewalk so the children didn't have to "wade through water" to reach the doorway. Early in 1912 the rest of the building was completed, and now all four rooms were put into use. Mr. F.G. Tranberger was named the first principal, and a committee of parents got a seventy-five-foot flagpole erected on the grounds. By the end of 1912, sidewalks around the school were finished and new desks purchased for the students. Final cost of the project had totaled $3,500, though many niceties were still lacking. The Cussons held a box social to benefit the school library and raised $22.

Elementary school age children from Gulfport were allowed to attend St. Petersburg schools if they so chose. Town officials didn't like this much, announcing that some seventeen potential students had selected this option, costing the school a third teacher. The trustees petitioned St. Petersburg to disallow this latitude, without much of any effect on the situation, which would continue far into the future.

With the council minutes lost to posterity, the only municipal records from the early period come from the police logs and court dockets, scanty as they are, since the marshal's position changed hands about as often as did the council seats. Ade Renney could not have continued in it very long, as police records show that before the November election, it was held by one of the Robertses, probably Fred, who had lost the office to Aaron the previous fall. Most everyone in town had a turn during the early years, before the Renneys and the Nashes pretty much claimed it as a permanent job. The mayor's court convened just twice in 1912, once in June and again in November. Both cases involved shooting offenses committed by outsiders, who were fined and assessed court costs. In one of these, Marshal Renney received some satirical publicity. A Methodist minister and "leading and prominent citizen" of St. Petersburg was fined five dollars for shooting within Gulfport's limits. The enthusiastic hunter, hot on the trail of quail, didn't know he had strayed across the border, while the marshal, "sat on his porch" and watched, never saying a word in warning, until the illegal shot was fired. To add insult to injury, the pastor missed the bird as well.

Council also met infrequently at the beginning of 1912, due to Elmer Wintersgill's absence, no great loss, as there was reportedly "no pressing business," anyway. Soon, though, the aldermen abandoned their earlier bond issue and voted another, this time in the amount of $10,000, for further improvements: now $1,500 would still go to the building of the town hall and jail; $4,000 for road improvements; $1,500 for ditching and culverts; $500 for bridges; $500 for sidewalks and $500 for street crossings; the remainder for general expenses. They had discovered just how many services there were to provide and what a small tax base there was to do it with, though total valuation of the town's properties in 1912 was $100,760, a considerable increase from the $6,000 of the preceding year.

A June election regarding "good roads bonds" failed in Pinellas County by a vote of 505 to 489, despite Gulfport's posting "a splendid clean record of 14-0" in its favor. "The fine result is largely due to the active efforts of Mayor Wintersgill, who is always a booster," said the *Independent*. St. Petersburg had supported the road bonds too, but the north county held out and defeated the issue.

Having survived a year or two as a real town, the community turned its attention to whether the type of government they had chosen was the most appropriate. Changing from mayor/council to the commission configuration began to be a subject for discussion during the summer, and Lester Wintersgill was appointed to look into it, as variations in these systems were "not well understood." He was joined by Sam Webb and Alec Stefanski to form a committee to investigate the possibilities. What happened, perhaps as a direct result of this debate, was that friction developed between two factions, one of which wanted the eastern part of the town to secede and return to County control. Leader of the "divisionists" was Stefanski, who lived in the area in question. He said the territory was too large for the number of people, who were too scattered to share mutual interests, and he managed to convince eighteen of the twenty property owners there to sign a petition placing the issue on for referendum. He and his committee set to work to determine precise boundaries, and requested that council table the bond issue until this territorial dispute was decided.

By late August the secessionists had chosen a line one-quarter mile east of Disston Avenue as the town's proposed new boundary. This would return a section one mile by one and one-quarter miles to Pinellas County. When the usual meeting was held to nominate candidates for the fall election, the "prime factor in the movement," Stefanski, was put forth for mayor. This is a bit confusing, considering that Stefanski did not wish to be part of the town he was running to govern; however, possibly he thought that by being mayor he could more easily control the secessionist process, and then resign. The *Independent* reported the "lively fight" between "the divisionists and the anti-divisionists" or, in essence, between Elmer Wintersgill and Alec Stefanski, as causing "much excitement."

W.B. McGee (or McGhee or Magee) had resigned at some point during the first part of the year and his unexpired term would be filled at the election.

William Lovelace, a contractor; J.L. Nash; and a Stefanski supporter, D.A. Lawson, were named as candidates for that seat. Three councilmen would also be elected to serve regular two-year terms from a field of seven nominations: Henry Slauter, Lester Wintersgill, James Ritchey, Albert Schludecker, A.J. Singer (another Stefanski man), F.E. Haynes and A.T. Cornelius. Sam Webb had no competition in the race for clerk/tax assessor/treasurer. The marshal's position would be contested by Lawrence Renney, John C. White and brothers Fred and Andrew Roberts.

On the fifth of November, the hotly contested town election was held. The voting population had increased by 50 percent with the addition of thirteen new registered voters, and at least thirty-one of them turned out to vote, because Elmer Wintersgill defeated the divisionist Stefanski by twenty-four to seven. Lovelace took the interim seat by sixteen votes to Nash's eleven and Lawson's five. The top three of the seven contenders for the regular two-year terms were Lester Wintersgill with twenty-seven votes; Haynes, twenty-five; and Albert Schludecker, nineteen. Ritchey had come close with fourteen, but Henry Slauter garnered a mere nine votes, and Cornelius only four. Singer received not a single one.

Lester was chosen president of council. The town clerk's office was, at the moment, located at 110 5th Street, an address remarkably close to the Wintersgill residence on Davis (Beach) Boulevard at 5th Street (26th Avenue).

John Campaign White nosed out Fred Roberts nine votes to eight to return as marshal. Brother Andrew got five votes. Lawrence Renney did not have a listed result, so perhaps withdrew in favor of being appointed tax collector, which he was, as soon as the new aldermen took office. An interesting final note on the election was that all candidates with the exception of Mr. Haynes were socialists.

3. Building a Town

The Casino, under the management of the Livingstone family, had added a bakery to its facilities and continued to function much as before, though with a considerable increase in competition from the spate of new hotels being built in downtown St. Petersburg. The "Silver Kings" orchestra provided music for the dances, this group led by Lewis King, thirty, son of the old sawmill master, George King.

The trolley chugged along with the usual complement of misadventures. King and his orchestra boarded one evening, along with a group called the Jolly Fellows, for whom the band was going to play at a Casino dance.

The electricity failed, restarted, then failed again, this time seemingly for good. After sitting for a rather long while, all the passengers decided to walk the rest of the way, a couple of miles, for the final stoppage had occurred somewhere before the sawmill curve. They set off in the dark, and how dark it must have been, the band members in their white pants and shoes, stumbling along the rough track. Occasionally someone would wander away and be called back before becoming completely lost, and eventually, just after 11 o'clock, they all arrived, somewhat the worse for wear, and still determined to have their dance. Having seen them safely to their destination, the motorman returned to the car, got it started somehow, and brought it down to the Casino. It was now extremely late, and he insisted they stop the party they had waited so long to enjoy and get on or he would leave without them. Some contemplated finding a place to stay the night, but that was not an extremely likely possibility, so return they did, getting back to St. Petersburg sometime before morning.

Trolley #104, one of the first to be used on the streetcar line.

On another evening when many people were returning from beach excursions, two inbound trolleys got stranded on their way to the city, blocking all further traffic. By 10 o'clock some of the passengers gave up and walked the remaining distance. But the Mary Boat Company was still bringing folks back to Gulfport, and "scores" of people piled up on the pier, waiting for transportation that never came. Captain Wintersgill offered to take them around by water and some went with him, while others "watched the fish and wondered about sleeping accommodations." Finally, well after midnight, a trolley arrived and the exhausted beachgoers all got back to town.

The *Times* found the streetcar line another excuse for making fun of Gulfport. Reporting on a council meeting, an article said that the town clerk was "instructed to look up the charter of the Trolley Co. and see what rights it had. It seems that the noise of the cars annoy the city and they are thinking of getting the company to run its cars to the city limits only and have them stop there. The citizens can then walk the remaining 8 or 9 miles home." And at the next meeting, council supposedly passed an ordinance "requiring the trolley to stop at all streets where passengers desire to get on and off, which will be confusing until the chairman of the Street Committee gets signs up showing where the streets are."

Straub's continual derogation of Gulfport and promotion of Pass-a-Grille contributed to a new plan he published, suggesting that the trolley tracks be continued across the bay, building on the many sandbars and mangrove stands then in existence. However, failures such as the ones mentioned above were perhaps too frequent to take this suggestion seriously, if it was, in fact, meant seriously.

Although two additional cars, second-hand "double truckers" from East St. Louis, had been added, the trolley line had by this time fallen into some disrepair. The cars, never new to begin with, were in dire need of painting, and presented "a very poor appearance." Still they ran, mostly well patronized, back and forth to the Casino for excursions and to special events, like the Labor Day picnic at Oak Park. Some of the activities of this latter occasion present a startling picture of the contemporary idea of amusements: a fat men's race, a talking match for women and prizes for the oldest attendees.

There were now, or were soon to be, ten streetcar stops within Gulfport's borders. First was at Tangerine and 49th Street, called the Disston stop. Second was at 50th Street and Tangerine, a platform only, called the Ritchey stop, no doubt for the family of chicken farmer and alderman James Ritchey. Third was at Pinellas Avenue (now 52nd Street) and Tangerine, called the School stop. Fourth was at the turning point, Tangerine and Davis (Beach) Boulevard. This was called the Sawmill stop, though the sawmill had been dismantled, loaded onto a streetcar, and removed in 1911, when this location was logged out.

Fifth was at Davis and Lakeview (Gulfport Boulevard) called, after the road's original name, the Lakeview stop. Sixth was the Wintersgill stop at 25th Avenue and Beach Boulevard. Seventh was the old Veteran City station, at about Beach and 27th Avenue. Eighth was the original terminus at 3rd Street (28th Avenue) and Beach. Ninth was the Cusson store stop at 30th Avenue and Beach, where Alexis Cusson in 1912 opened a grocery store in a two-story building. The trolley's tenth and final stop was, of course, the Casino.

The Cusson store on Beach Boulevard, built 1912.

As the tourist business and excursion traffic increased, the schedule became more frequent, with arrivals and departures every half hour. Then something unheard of for that perpetually second-hand system occurred when a brand new streetcar was added to the ten ancient ones. It was so quiet, they said, that the drivers had to be instructed to give some warning when they were passing, as pedestrians and bystanders used to the rackety old cars would not be aware of the danger of being run down.

In the first month of 1912 alone, a woman tourist and a two-year-old calf had been hit by trolley cars. The calf was killed, but the woman was not badly injured and took the blame for walking in front of the car without paying attention to where she was going (and this was before the addition of the noiseless one). An even stranger accident occurred in February when a loaded gun fell from the pocket of a motorman while he was helping passengers board from the Casino dock. The gun landed on its hammer and discharged, firing a thirty-two-calibre bullet that hit the young conductor, who was rushed back to the city where he underwent surgery and made a full recovery.

Then, just before Christmas, the canine population got a present of sorts when new regulations allowed dogs to ride on the trolley, provided of course that they paid the fare. This was perhaps more of a move to keep them off than on, some folks having been in the habit of jumping aboard with dog in tow and no thought that the animal, too, might have to buy a ticket.

The *Gypsy* was now making the run from St. Petersburg to Pass-a-Grille (twenty-five cents round trip) on a regular basis, to meet increased demand. It had been brought here from Saugatuck, Michigan, a month-long voyage through Lake Michigan, down the Mississippi and across to Egmont Key from New Orleans, the latter part involving twenty-one hours of heavy seas. It carried a load of 160 passengers on Thursday, January 25, 1912, the largest number to that date ever to make a single trip. Young Ed Brantley was the captain during this period, while his father Clarence and uncle Dillon were homesteading on Coon Key.

The Wintersgills' Boca Ceiga Yacht Club was "a splendid new boat livery," with every slip filled, tanks on the high bluff to supply fresh water, and a ways for repairs. They had bought the *Maine* to add to the *New York*, which was running a regular schedule of six departures and returns daily, and Captain Lester's *Florida*, with its new twenty horsepower Fairbanks and Morse gasoline engine. This latter marvel of efficiency could make the passage between Gulfport and the beach in a mere twenty-five minutes. The inventive Elmer was busy as usual, now devising a storm warning station. He would receive communications over a "private wire" and then display the proper flags on a tall pole he had erected.

With all this activity, the *Independent* recognized Gulfport as a "hustling little city" and a "progressive little place." Actually there was so much construction going on that potential builders had great difficulty in finding workmen to carry out their projects. And it got busier when an "architect and land promoter" named Herman E. Wendell arrived from Ocean City, New Jersey, with his wife and children. Previously in Los Angeles he had designed and built homes in the bungalow style so popular at that time. Wendell began to acquire some large land holdings in Gulfport, and by summer he was embarked upon building a "cottage" for his own family and had joined with Lester ("father of Gulfport's development") Wintersgill to open a lumberyard, with stock brought from Tarpon Springs by lighter.

It was Wendell who finally put together a real plan for the sea wall project, a $60,000 undertaking that would add a projected fifty-five acres to the

The Wintersgills' Boca Ceiga Yacht Club.

downtown waterfront, and fill in a "small lake inshore from the Bay" near the track. B.F. Measey was involved as well, indicating some connection with the old Davis/Fuller interests, now fully engaged in the formation of a new town at the western end of Central Avenue, along the latest trolley line. There had been a contest to come up with an appropriate name for this development, and the winner, announced late in 1912, was *Davista*. The Gulfport branch of the company was called Pinellas Estates, and it was, much as before, formed by some "Pennsylvania capitalists," with Measey as president. Fuller said they would clear the land along the trolley tracks from 4th to 6th Streets (27th to 25th Avenues) and lay sidewalks, but the Gulfport council would spend the next several years pressing for fulfillment of such promises, fruitlessly, for the most part.

The sea wall was proposed to be three thousand feet long, with a boulevard and parkway to be constructed behind it. Pinellas Estates owned forty-one lots and sold thirty-three of them almost immediately, in a huge real estate promotion designed to fill the vacant tracts of prime Gulfport land. It worked; people bought them in bunches of fives and tens, showing that the town had finally become the investment opportunity so long sought in vain. The *Independent* stated that Pinellas Estates had "changed the physical aspect of Gulfport as well as the size and character of its population."

The Davis holdings still included some 10 acres east of the dock, with about 400 feet of water frontage. The old Boca Ceiga Park lands were now controlled by a group composed of Lester Wintersgill, Herman Wendell and St. Petersburg's "Mitchell the Sand Man." Late in the year Lester would partner with Sam Webb to build and open a real estate office on the Boulevard, but at the moment Wintersgill was running the business alone. He must have been one of the first persons in town to have a telephone, which was listed in April 1912, as number 400 ("three long and one short rings"). He even hired some help, luring Rusha Mae Steinwinder away from her job with Clara Geiger in the Casino post office.

Elmer Wintersgill and his McRoberts relatives had formed yet another new entity, the Bay View Park Development, proposing construction of a hotel in the spring of 1912. The project never came to fruition, at least in that form, for the eventual Bay View Hotel was still some two years in the future.

Strangely, and in contrast to all this activity, the Casino was in one of its periodic downturns, and faded somewhat from the limelight, hosting mostly private dances with sometimes as few as twelve couples, outings of state tourist societies, plus the occasional basketball game and Camp Fire Girls meeting. This girls' club was particularly active about now, at one point staging a mock trial there echoing some current judicial *cause celebre.* Sam Webb took the part of prosecutor and Lester Wintersgill prepared the defense. No record is left of who won the argument.

There was a chapel at Glen Oak Cemetery now, though it was still surrounded by woods and the site, unfortunately, of much random shooting and hunting. Because it was used by a variety of worshippers, a schedule was arranged to provide services for four denominations. Methodists met the first Sunday of the month, Baptists the second, Congregationalists the third and Presbyterians the fourth. Most of the locals had by this time transferred their religious affiliation to groups nearer home, so few of them may have traveled those three or four miles to attend services, but most of the old settler families did continue to use the burying ground for years to come.

A Methodist congregation had come together in Gulfport, meeting first in the infamous "prop college" and then in the Casino, but services were intermittent, depending upon when a visiting preacher was in town. The Gulfport congregation was part of the Seminole Circuit, served by ministers who covered a large territory. One of them usually appeared a couple times a month to hold services at the Casino, despite frequent "embarrassing interruptions" from the pleasure-seekers on their way to or from an outing.

Then a young theology student named J.H. Daniel agreed to preach on the first and third Sundays, and starting in the summer of 1912, townsfolk came in considerable numbers to worship at the Casino and listen to Mary McRoberts and Florence Slaughter sing "beautiful solos." When nearly ninety people showed interest in establishing a church in Gulfport, a building fund was begun. As in everything else in town in those days, Mayor Wintersgill was truly the force behind the church's development. This was particularly interesting in that Elmer had never joined the church or even claimed allegiance to any religious denomination.

Equally important was the contribution of the youthful pastor, still a student at Sutherland Methodist College, an educational institution located in Palm Harbor, which had itself been founded as "Sutherland" in the 1880s. A fire in 1921 forced the school to move to Lakeland, where it is known today as Florida Southern College. Young Reverend Daniel (presumably no relation to the castle-building soldier of fortune) organized a boys' basketball team that played in the Casino on a floor "made for dancing not basketball," where he at one point ran into the stage and "skinned up his brow so that he had to wear a bandage over his left eye" for some time afterward. The room was "too small for long throws," and it was generally agreed that an outdoor court was sorely needed, not to mention an actual church.

Some 150 people attended an ice cream social that summer, which raised $13.40 toward the estimated $1,200-1,500 the building would cost. With a $500 loan from the Home Mission Board of the Methodist Church now in hand, all were enthusiastic about the prospects of success and trustees met to draw plans and make a first payment on two lots. By the end of the year bids for construction were being taken by a building committee (Wintersgill, McRoberts, Roberts, Clarence Brantley and a Mr. Harris).

Luke Nash, then about fifty-five, and the second oldest of the huge Nash family, wrote a surprisingly literate and interesting letter to the *Times* in the fall of 1910, apparently in response to a political debate in which someone had bemoaned the loss of the "old rights." Luke, certainly with credentials of the earliest of settlers ("45 years experience" as he put it), talked about some of those old rights, such as the right to eat the fruit that was grown, since there was no way to sell it and nobody to sell it to. Then there was the right to "get mail whenever we could," the right "to go to church if we could get there" over the terrible roads, and the church itself, which was only a clearing in the woods. There was the right to go to school, to sit on "split logs," for a mere three months a year, while learning all there was to know from a "blue-backed Webster spelling book." He summed up by thanking the "newcomers" for railroads, trolley lines, cities and towns, churches and school houses, paved roads and markets.

4. Secession

As usual in Gulfport, political controversy arose once again when the issue of separation came back to the table. This time, though, there was considerably more calm and reason than was seen during the last fall's contretemps. In May a mass meeting had been called to discuss the splitting off of all territory east of 49th Street. The organizers claimed that the town was simply not able to afford to lay good roads in that area, and by returning to the County, they had a better chance at acquiring these improvements. A peaceful withdrawal, they said, would benefit everyone, and was in no way like the earlier attempt, which was based, all recognized, on "personal difficulties" among the aldermen.

There was some concern, however, about "adjustments to obligations" engendered by the $10,000 bond issue, so the question went to judicial proceedings in the summer, the secessionists promising to assume all costs of the hearings. The case was heard in September with no defense made by officials of the town, and the court ordered the eastern segment returned to the County. Property owners there were still held to be responsible for the 1913 taxes, though were in no way obligated regarding the $10,000 bond. New boundary limits were set, and names of the "secessionists" were removed from voting rolls. Among those were Jerry and Esther Wells, who operated the famous Ostrich Farm in Oak Park. This attraction, featuring bears, monkeys and of course the requisite alligator as well as trained ostriches, burned to the ground in the spring of 1913. Mayor Elmer said that it was the first and only serous fire within the town's jurisdiction since incorporation. Serious it was indeed, the Wellses only escaping with their babies, able to save no personal possessions. Though some of the animals survived, the birds unfortunately perished. After the secession, the Wells' property was no longer in Gulfport, though Mrs. Wells would have a voice in political matters, particularly those pertaining to the schools, for some years to come.

Gulfport's property valuations had risen to $149,630, an increase of about $45,000 over the previous year. The $10,000 bond issue had been approved with no dissent, so advertising and selling began at once, and encouragingly enough, a number of bids were received, "all good." By April the bonds had been purchased at par value with accrued interest by the Hatcheff Bond Company of Chicago.

The usual bureaucratic boggle then ensued, and it was July before the council announced that most of the hurdles had been met, and they would have the $10,000 in hand "within a few days." In fact the money did arrive early in August, greeted with much rejoicing that the town now actually had funds on deposit and could pay off every outstanding debt, as well as take on proposed new projects.

The sea wall was one of these, delayed not only by the lack of funding, but also by "red tape," apparently a fact of life even then, and "accidents to the dredge" (it was stranded on the beach when the tide ran out and did not become high enough to float it again for a week). Part of the red tape was a requirement for sanction by the federal War Department, but even more damaging was the aldermen's disapproval of the first plan submitted by Pinellas Estates. After a couple of meetings in April, an agreement was reached for the company to give the town possession and control of 1,510 of Bay frontage. They would erect 3 miles of sea wall to a height of 5 feet 6 inches high at low tide.

Three water lots were reserved for the town: number two, a sixty-foot width at the west end of the shoreline, near today's 58th Street, to be used for pleasure boats; number three, with twelve hundred feet of water frontage, running between 58th and 56th Streets; and number seven, approximately the east half of the area between Beach Boulevard and 54th Street. The council was working wisely to preserve, as they said, "Gulfport's magnificent waterfront," which Elmer Wintersgill called the finest on the coast. He went on to thank Pinellas Estates for having "maintained a splendid temperament" throughout these difficult negotiations, most of which they had lost.

The Wintersgills, of course, had a strong interest in improvement of the waterfront, with their Yacht Club and Mary Boat Company, now running four vessels: the *New York*, the *Indiana*, the *Maine*, and the *Florida*. To promote their ventures, they began a series of swimming races. Young men competed to see who could make it from Gulfport to Pass-a-Grille the fastest. The four or five miles were accomplished in just under two hours in one summer match.

Mayor Elmer, now in his third term, and Lester, President of Council, had just lost their father, Ralph Wintersgill, who had lived with Elmer and Mary since his arrival six years earlier. Old Ralph had just days before his death bought a new suit of clothes, with, it is said, his burial in mind, and one morning got up, put them on for the first time, then walked over to visit his daughter Elizabeth McRoberts. Returning home, he sat down on Elmer's porch and died. The funeral was held right there at the mayor's house.

Terms of the seawall contract provided for dredging 100,000 cubic yards of sand to fill in behind the wall, which, as they explained the process, would contain a 2-foot cavity in its base serving as a "suction channel." The final height agreed upon was 3 feet above high tide and 2 feet above extreme storm high tide. Two crews worked day and night in an attempt to complete the contract on time. Still, it was on and off, with constant "dredging difficulties," until Measey, representing Pinellas Estates, reassigned the contract to

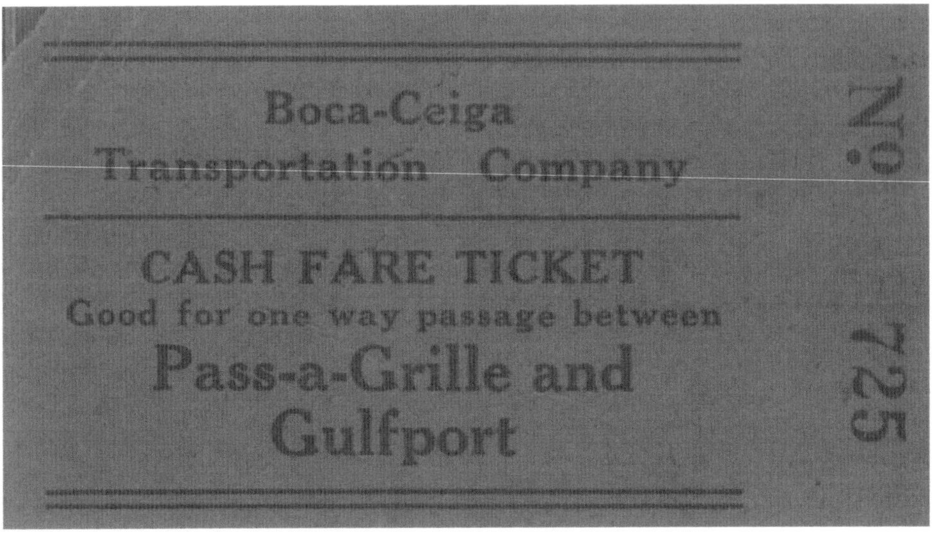

Ticket for passage on the Boca Ceiga Transportation Company's run to Pass-A-Grille.

another firm. All of 1913 passed in this manner, and by the end of the year, the forms for the seawall were finally being built.

With money from the bonds now in hand, council meetings had become busy sessions, pushing ahead more long-anticipated improvements, like the desperately needed drainage work. Sam Webb was quoted as saying, "Gulfport has been a little handicapped on account of the condition that prevails after heavy rains, but we will get dry and keep dry," a promise echoing down through the last century with terrible regularity.

Fourth Street (27th Avenue) was graded and drainage ditches dug. Council begged the streetcar company to ditch their roadbed and move some of the stations (obviously not very permanent structures) to "get them out of the drainage." The first serious road project began in late October, when a section running from the intersection at Disston (49th Street) and Lakeview (Gulfport Boulevard) west to Grant (54th Street) and south to the Bay was earmarked for grading, draining and possible "strawing, pending hard-surfacing."

Earlier in 1913, the aldermen had changed their minds about building a jail, when the bid price of $266 given by Henry Webb was deemed too high. Also, there wasn't much actual crime, for the Mayor's Court had convened only once, on May 26, when a case was heard against three of the town's boys who had been arrested for stealing a gun from Alexis Cusson's shed. These were Joe Steinwinder, Jr., then fifteen; Leander White, thirteen; and Willie Schludecker, eleven. As acting mayor, L.M. Wintersgill presided. "All the boys

The Wintersgill and Webb real estate office at the lower end of Davis (Beach) Boulevard. *Courtesy Webb family*

pleaded not guilty and after questioning . . . were given a good talk and were let out on probation."

A town hall was certainly needed. Meetings had been held in various places, the Casino, of course, the yacht club, and the Wintersgill and Webb real estate office on the corner of Davis (Beach) Boulevard and Dellett, which transformed itself into a city hall periodically by the simple expedient of hanging out a wooden sign. So the council decided to go ahead with the construction of a combined town hall/jail and in late August. Clerk Webb was directed to advertise for bids. The plan was to have one building, the town hall section frame and the jail brick, with a vault for municipal records to be set within a wall. Awarding the contract to Courtney Sawyer (who "started his construction business with the founding of the city") was the last official act of the outgoing council before the October election. The proposed complex would be located in what is today Chase Park, in the 5300 block of 28th Avenue South. In preparation for the building, young Irving Slauter, who was twelve years old, was given a little money to plow the newly cleared land, where pawpaws had grown wild since the earliest days of settlement.

W.E. Haynes had resigned and moved to Illinois, leaving a council seat vacant. Charles Thomes and J.L. Nash were proposed for that position when the fifty voters of the town met to nominate the official slate for the fall election. Elmer Wintersgill declined to run for mayor again, but said he would run for treasurer, so Benjamin Sands was named the official mayoral candidate. Elmer was off on a new tangent with his latest money making plan. This involved offering free trashcans to the City of St. Petersburg. He would take his profits from selling ads to appear on the cans. Elmer was always way ahead of the curve.

Ben Sands was living quietly in Gulfport, but he had another, former, life that was little known to his neighbors. He had once been the world famous "Bean King" with a story "like a romance of fiction," as the *Times* would say years later. Farmer Ben had married his wife Elizabeth in their hometown of Albion, New York, and in 1894 went into the bean business. He built a packinghouse and started traveling all over the country buying up bean crops, which he had shipped to his headquarters for eventual sale. In short, he created a sort of bean cartel. The business prospered and his profits rose accordingly. He built a substantial home for his wife and five children, two daughters and three sons, one of whom was crippled.

Then their affluent life was thrown into crisis when Ben Sands ran off with his stenographer. His son Lewis took over the business while Benjamin came to his senses during a year away in which he realized his "awful mistake." Elizabeth took him back, but directly thereafter, Lewis bought the tickets for his parents and crippled brother to come south for the boy's health—or just possibly to let the scandal die down.

The Sands arrived in Gulfport and built a bungalow in the Tangerine/Palmetto (51st Street) area. They liked the town, and Ben agreed to run for mayor, while Elizabeth became an ardent prohibitionist and active in the Women's Christian Temperance Union. All would be well for the next decade, until the great Sands Company failure would blow up to the tune of a million dollar fraud charge against Lewis. His subsequent life as a fugitive would end—of course—no place else but in Gulfport.

The council this year expanded to seven seats, and a considerable number of familiar names were announced as interested in the positions: Malcolm McRoberts, Guy Morrison, A.L. Nash, William Renney, poultry farmer James Ritchey, Walter Roberts, Joe Steinwinder, Courtney Sawyer and Henry Weathers. Roberts was also challenging Sam Webb for the clerk/assessor/tax collector job.

But the secession decision still had not satisfied a certain element of the town, and a new party arose to challenge the slate presented for the fall election. Surprisingly, Alex Leonardy ("one of the oldest settlers of Pinellas and pioneers of Gulfport") was nominated to run for mayor on what was being called the "Cracker Party," which had as part of its platform the splitting of the clerk/treasurer job into two positions.

The town election was scheduled for October 1, and inspectors were to be Elmer Wintersgill, John White, Albert Schludecker and E.E. Chandler. Ellsworth Chandler was new on the scene in 1913 but making up for it with activity; in the few months he had been in town, he had built and sold four houses and was working on a fifth, while renting out a cottage on Bon Air (30th Avenue) where he lived with his wife Louise and son Ed. He hit the news by catching the largest kingfish of the season, an event that excited him so much he went right out and bought his own boat. (Ed would also hit the news for various other reasons, none of them good, for years to come.) But most importantly, Chandler was working on another proposal for a hotel, this one to have twenty-eight rooms and twelve baths.

John White and his family may have just returned to Gulfport from Pine Key (today's Tierra Verde). While living there, at least three of the children had attended the little private school at Pass-a-Grille. These were fifteen-year old Rosa and the twins Ernest and Eva, ten; Leander, who was between them in age, seems never to have made the acquaintance of public education, preferring to spend his time on the water. Life did not go all too smoothly between John White and his wife Laura. Their quarrels were wild and loud. Still, speaking publicly about such things was not done—not done by most, that is. Rebecca's daughter let everyone know just what was going on, an action many did not find acceptable. She certainly had enough to complain about. John was a tall, strong, virile and handsome man, attractive to women and attracted to them. His romantic adventures were renowned. Their son Leander was growing up to be another of the same. Now in his teens, he was an extremely good-looking young man, ruggedly blond and handsome like his father. He may, even by then, have begun to earn the nickname "Ironhead," which would follow him the rest of his life.

The thirty-seven voters chose Sands for mayor, Thomes for the one-year seat and William Renney, Malcolm McRoberts and neighbors James Ritchey and Courtney Sawyer for the two-year terms. Elmer Wintersgill became treasurer; Sam Webb retained the clerk position. Newly elected marshal Lawrence Renney somehow got the tax collector position added to his own duties, and also took it upon himself to purchase two pair of purebred bloodhound puppies, after which he let it be known that he expected to use the dogs on "cases" in Gulfport and neighboring towns.

Once again his fellow aldermen named Lester Wintersgill president of council. Sawyer and Renney became the finance committee, Schludecker and McRoberts the street committee and Ritchey and Thomes took on auditing duties. Perhaps in response to the "Crackers'" concerns, the council voted to sit as an "equalization board" after each meeting, to hear in public complaints from the citizens. Many people were still voicing concern over the form of government itself. In just three years, the busy little town had outgrown its original charter (pieced together from several others) and now more "bunglesome" than useful. It was time to take a serious look at changing to the commission form, and council agreed to put the issue to a vote in the near future.

The tax rate for the next year was held at the same twenty mills (ten general, seven sinking fund, two roads and one sanitary), which would, with the latest assessments, provide some $3,000. The sinking fund (for the reduction of debts) was removed from a savings account generating 3percent and invested in certificates with an 8 percent return. Gulfport was in the black and moving ahead. There was now even a real city hall, for late in the year Courtney Sawyer had completed the simple building "in the early Orange Belt Railroad style." Built for $1,259.75 of the allotted $1,500, it was wired for electricity, originally painted yellow, and would stand there some fourteen years until 1927, when it was moved northward to the present city hall complex on 53rd Street. Even after the move, it lasted until 1953, at which time it was auctioned off for the materials, an obviously sturdy little building.

The annual financial report was duly filed, showing an income of $2,888.60, including proceeds from a tax sale, and expenditures of $2,885.07. Some $2,500 of the bond issue had been tapped, for general expenses, ditching, sidewalks and bridges. The town had even contemplated buying their own scraper, plow, grader and team, and set about shopping for a "fine span of mules," an idea they thought better of a few days later.

5. The School and the Church

The Gulfport Elementary School was now in full operation, its red brick shell faced with an imitation stone finish. The surrounding grounds were always in need of ditching, a chore that provided punishment for misbehaving boys. Once drained, the property was given over to gardening, and the children raised a great deal of their own food, though not always willingly. Sanitary facilities consisted of two small houses about two hundred yards from the main building.

The average teacher's salary at this time was between $35 and $50 a month, and the term was generally about six months. Margaret Wilder became principal in 1913 and held the position until 1915. A photo from this period shows Mrs. Wilder with the primary teacher, Miss Fannie Boswell, and their brood of about fifty children, some quite happily shoeless, arranged on the front steps of the school. Mrs. Wilder is credited with starting a kind of cafeteria, furnished primarily from the school's own garden and family

Gulfport Elementary as it originally appeared.

donations of vegetables and soup bones, but a first in the history of local school food services.

Mrs. Wilder was also recognized by the trustees and the town as a tremendously effective administrator. She took a "weak, uncontrolled school and immediately harmonized the pupils and enthused them to concentrate on their work." A visit from county Superintendent Dixie Hollins resulted in nothing but praise for her accomplishments and those of the trustees. Just two years ago, he found, the Gulfport school had been housed in a "rickety old shack" (Prop College?) with an enrollment of twenty-four, only about half of whom ever bothered to attend with any kind of regularity. And now the modern facility educated fifty-two local children through the eighth grade and did it so well that those, and they were perhaps few, who chose to continue their educations past the grammar-school level could go on to high school in St. Petersburg.

In 1913 the Camp Fire Girls' mock trial went into some kind of competition, in which it won third prize. Now, not only Prosecutor Webb and Defense Attorney Wintersgill were involved, but so was most of the rest of the town, the great majority of whom had never seen an actual trial and so must have put some real imagination into their roles. Alex Leonardy was the judge and Andrew Roberts the prisoner, while important parts went to Florence and Taylor Slauter, Rusha and Aurora Steinwinder, Principal Tranbarger, Elmer

Rousseau, Olga and John Sjustrom and a new girl in town, Mary Lou Faurot. The jurymen were Fred and Lawrence Renney, Laus and Willie Nash, Henry Weathers, Henry Slauter, Henry Sims, Fred Roberts, Harold Leonardy, Guy Morrison, Henry Webb and "Mr. Daniels" (the castle-builder or the reverend?). What a show that must have been.

Just east of where the town hall was going up in Chase Park, the First Methodist Church building came into being in 1913. The two were rather similar in appearance, square little wooden structures with small front porches and cupolas, though the church was the larger of the two, with its side wings giving it the shape of an even-armed cross. It stands today as the Historical Society Museum building, its heart pine shell as strong and solid as when it was built all those decades ago.

Right up until work actually began in the summer, a concrete block construction plan was still in place, and final cost estimates were running at about $2,000. But when the contract was let to Homer Lovelace, that plan had changed. It was now to be a 38- by 40-foot wood frame building with a seating capacity of 200, finished inside with plaster and wainscoting. Legend credits Malcolm McRoberts with the construction of this building; perhaps he did supervise the actual work under Lovelace, who had the distinction of being the "first regular contractor in Gulfport."

Announcement of the church's completion came early in August, though "painting, varnishing and placing of furniture" was still to be done. The final cost had come to $1,300, not counting the furnishings and incidentals. The Ladies Aid group was still working to raise funds, now for a piano, which was there, in place, on opening day, August 15. Services were set for 10:45 a.m. and 7:30 in the evening, with Sunday School at 3:00, times convenient to the trolley schedule. Those traveling out from St. Petersburg were advised that the church was in sight of the Gulfport station.

Reverend Daniel wouldn't be there to enjoy the results of his labors. He had graduated from Sutherland in June, married Miss Lida Miller, a stenographer from Kentucky, and took an assignment to a pastorate in East Fort Myers. Though "young in ministerial work and in years," he was much appreciated and credited by the town as the inspiration for both the development of the congregation and the building of its new home. His successor would be Reverend Oscar E. Rice, a fellow student in his last year at the seminary. Earlier in the year, he and Daniel had together entered an intercollegiate speaking contest on the subject of prohibition.

Pinellas County held a referendum on that very question in July 1913, but the close (778 to 668) vote of approval was contested. Gulfport went against the majority, favoring the wets twenty-one to thirteen. Many sources say Lester Wintersgill as Council President gave a fiery speech against the rum

The Methodist church, built 1913, and now located across 53rd street as the Gulfport Historical Society Museum.

traffic and asked that they pledge a "no" vote against liquor sales. However, what actually happened is that Lester took no part in the prohibition debate, stepping down in favor of another, unnamed, alderman. The reason for this no doubt had to do with the fact that Mayor Elmer was currently "organizing a club alleged to have the purpose of supplying members with drinks which could not be legally obtained in any other way." These private clubs were springing up all over the country in anticipation of the impending prohibition, and the Wintersgills were as usual on top of the trend.

Chapter VI
Boosting

1. The Bay View

A man named Frank J. Davenport took over Ellsworth Chandler's plans for a hotel after Chandler suffered a sudden stroke and died in March 1914. As a first move, Davenport requested electric light, gas and water franchises from the town government, promising them 2½ percent of the gross income after the first 3 years. While these options appeared to have no value at that moment, they were obviously going to be worth a considerable amount some day if Gulfport continued to grow at the presumed rate. Prices were holding up well and showed promise of doing even better. Some lots near the corner of Grant Avenue and 2nd Street (54th Street and 29th Avenue) that Herman Wendell had purchased with retired Michigan state senator John H. Parks had appreciated some 400 or 500 percent in a matter of months.

Davenport and his group put up a $1,000 bond and guaranteed to have light and water systems running within 6 months, though gas would take longer. The franchises were granted in May, on a 30-year term, with the town retaining the right to purchase them back after 3 years.

That settled, Davenport went to work on the hotel, breaking ground about the first of April at the corner of Davis (Beach) Boulevard and Bon Air (30th) Avenue. According to these new plans, the hotel building was specified to be three stories, "thoroughly modern," with first floor lobbies, parlors, dining rooms and kitchens and two floors of sleeping rooms and baths above." The contract was let to Beach and French Construction Company of "Bradentown."

In June the Bay View Hotel and Development Company was formed, with John Parks as president and Lester Wintersgill as treasurer. Davenport himself became secretary and general manager, with Malcolm McRoberts and a Davenport associate listed as "stockholder." Over time, the actual construction of the hotel, like that of the church, has often been credited to McRoberts, but the most probable assumption is that his contribution was limited to this part share, plus perhaps some engineering advice and expertise. Years later, his daughter Mary was described by her son Thompson C. Roberts, Jr., as a "fifth-part owner," which could mean that each of the officers had provided an equal amount of the original funding.

One innovation possibly correctly credited to McRoberts was a pumping station and water tower, built and operated for the guests of the hotel, and apparently not part of the town franchise. This plant provided the uncommon luxury of running water, unavailable to other residents of the community, who continued to hand pump their own water, tasting of sulfur and palmetto roots.

The pumping station and water tower at the Bay View Hotel.

Toward the end of the year the Bay View Development Company sold the electric franchise to the St. Petersburg Investment Company. This was a sensible move; Walter Fuller could run power down the trolley lines and have the town, or some parts of it, wired by the first of December, if, for once, all went according to plan. Fuller's expansion out along Central Avenue was in full swing, employing, among others, a young surveyor named Milton Smith, who in 1913 had married Florence Slaughter.

The Bay View was scheduled for completion in October, and advertisements now describing it as offering forty rooms and "fine fishing and bathing on the shores of Boca Ceiga Bay," began to run long before the building was finished. Meanwhile, the Development Company's plans continued to grow. They wanted to build six California-style bungalows on the property (was this the influence of Herman Wendell, who had designed such buildings before coming to town?). At $1,500 each, with four rooms and a bath, it was no doubt a good idea, but no more was ever heard of it.

There had been some thought at the time that the Tampa and Gulf Coast Railroad, which was in the process of running a line into Pinellas County, could be convinced to locate a terminal on the northeast corner of this very block. That eventuality did not come to pass, but the railroad company was persuaded to allow Gulfport a station at its far northeast corner, at Disston (49th Street) and 7th Avenue South. Some reports credited this achievement to a group of businessmen who raised a sum of money, perhaps as much as $5,000, to convince the railway of this necessity. Though the small depot, painted red, was used more as a repository for ice barrels and additional firewood than as a passenger station, it was a great excitement for the town to claim an actual stop on the line. The day it opened was a school holiday and all the children were given little flags to wave in celebration. Lorraine Gleaton, only four in 1914, remembered it well; in running along the tracks, she tripped and fell onto the flagstick, which pierced the top of her mouth.

Gulfport's own railroad station at 49th Street and 7th Avenue South.

Davenport and the Bay View Development Company had dreamed up yet another project, the most ambitious yet: an amusement park equal only to New York's Coney Island. Plans were to build a new casino, an 80- by 300-foot roller coaster and a "natatorium." This latter building, which he claimed was already started, would be made of concrete and offer various depths for swimmers and other bathing amenities in its 120-foot length. A subsidiary company was capitalized at $30,000 and disappeared like so many other grand plans.

The town's undertakings, particularly the granting of franchises and building of this new hotel, did begin to cause some attention to turn to Gulfport; "the little western suburb of St. Petersburg is putting on city airs," said the *Tampa Tribune*. Thus the town (or, in effect, the Wintersgills) decided it was time to form a Board of Trade, as St. Petersburg had done, to promote itself and its ventures, and above all its real estate. The founding group of twenty charter members elected Lester president, Sam Webb secretary and Alexis Cusson treasurer. Serving as governors were Mayor Sands, Senator Parks, Malcolm McRoberts, and two newcomers, Nathan B. McKinney and Walter Brooks. The Board, with its mission to promote Gulfport to tourists and new residents alike, began its work with a membership campaign. Buoyed up by enthusiasm, the organization divided itself into two teams and made the campaign a contest. The red team beat the blue team, and the membership surged to seventy, a considerable accomplishment given the current male population was not much more than that. Of course, for the sake of bolstering the numbers, it was even allowed that women could be admitted as "associate members."

The red team's prize for winning the membership contest would be a dinner at the "magnificent new $15,000 Bay View Hotel," the first event to be scheduled at that establishment. The banquet was set for November 12, 1914, and became the formal opening of the new hotel, though no guests would be registered for another week.

An oyster supper was served, along with plenty of speeches. Lester Wintersgill, Davenport, Parks, McKinney, Dr. Robbins, Judge Gray and Sam Webb all had something to say to the assembled guests. Mary McRoberts at the piano accompanied the singing of Alexis Cusson and Harry Webb. McKinney and Davenport gave recitations, and the evening ended with Walter Brooks' rendition of a "negro sermon." Apparently everyone contributed to the cost of the meal, but the losing team paid up for after-dinner candy and cigars. Thus the Bay View was launched at last.

Walter O. Brooks, who lived across the street from the hotel and was fast becoming one of the town's most prominent citizens, had arrived in Gulfport in 1912 with his wife Virginia and son Mack, eight. They had left their home

BOARD OF GOVERNORS
F. J. DAVENPORT, CHAIRMAN
B. SANDS
N. B. McKINNEY
M. McROBERTS
L. M. WINTERSGILL
A. L. CUSSON
S. J. WEBB
H. E. WENDELL
J. H. PARKS
W. F. WOODARD
W. O. BROOKS
JAMES RITCHEY

"THE EWAY TO THE GULF"
ULFPORT, FLORIDA
GULFPORT BOARD OF TRADE
L. M. WINTERSGILL, PRES. B. SANDS. VICE PRES. S. J. WEBB, SEC. A. L. CUSSON, TREAS.
A REAL ORGANIZATION
HEADQUARTERS: NEAR THE BEACH

Letterhead of the Gulfport Board of Trade, "A Real Organization."

in Columbia, Tennessee, for the usual reason, health. In an interview with Walter's daughter-in-law Sydney and his grandson and namesake, Walter, they said, "Every winter he (the elder Walter) used to get pneumonia and some winters he'd get pneumonia twice. The doctor finally said if you stay here another winter you won't live, so he sold out lock, stock, and barrel, and came . . . to Dade City and stayed there the first winter and then they came on down to St. Petersburg and stayed a little while . . . the winter and maybe into the spring and they bought this property in Gulfport and they lived there. He had been a farmer in Tennessee and he built a house and then he put a little store on it and that post office."

The Brooks' lot was on the southeast corner of Davis (Beach) Boulevard just down from Cusson's, and there they opened a grocery, making two such stores in the very same neighborhood. After Carrie Geiger's resignation as postmistress, Brooks took over the fourth-class mail franchise in October, 1913, continuing at first to operate from the Casino, where he got permission to cut through the pier floor so he could fish while on duty. He was the only applicant for the franchise, which paid $200 a year and was usually avidly contested. However, there was an examination involved, and that may have discouraged some of the other citizens from making the attempt. Before long Brooks arranged to lease out a portion of the Beach Boulevard store for use as the post office, and there it remained for several years. The general sentiment in town was that Walter might have the title, but it was Virginia who did the actual work involved in the postmaster's job.

Things weren't going quite so well over at the Bay View Hotel. The entire world had entered a new era, starting in the summer of 1914. That seemingly insignificant assassination of some comic-opera ruler in some fifth-rate Balkan country would soon begin to spread ramifications across continents. Everywhere it became obvious that war was inevitable. Within a month the New York Stock Exchange began a drastic fall, ending with an actual suspension of trading. Prices rose precipitously; sugar for example skyrocketed 75 percent almost overnight.

The 1911-1913 boomlet ended. We find Davenport commenting in the *Independent* that the "slump" was only a rumor and could be defeated if people would just stand by their city and continue to invest. He claimed the war would be "good" for Florida in general and Gulfport in particular. With Europe no longer a competitive destination, he foresaw not a decline but an increase in the tourist business. The experience of Disston City's first teacher, Arthur Norwood, and his second wife bore him out. They were on a honeymoon in England that unfortunately coincided with the onset of hostilities, and had an extremely difficult time getting home, having to wait over a month for a ticket on the crowded steamers.

Strangely enough, almost as soon as the hotel had become operational, it was also the subject of several liens, claims and lawsuits. Elmer Wintersgill sued for $405.73 and the Ideal Lumber Company had a *lis pedens* to foreclose a lien on the building, both in January 1915. In February Knight and Wall Company sued the "Bayview Hotel Development Corporation" for $445 plus $1,000 damages, and Davenport himself made a claim of $1,076.42. There were others, as well, indicating that some serious financial trouble was afoot somewhere.

Yet when the hotel inspector came early in the year to give the hotel its official rating, his score was an extremely rare "100 percent perfect." He went on to say this faultless rating was especially significant because the "hotel is out of reach of sewer, water, and fire systems of any city and has to provide these privately." He lauded Davenport's management, which was quite obviously by this time strictly by default. Davenport himself stated that he was continuing in the position "much against his wishes," until some person or firm could be found to take it over.

The hotel grounds, consisting at the time of most of the block on which it sits, were open to the public, with swings and playgrounds, picnic tables and croquet courts. Tennis courts were planned and parties were welcome, the hotel staff obligingly available to serve outdoor meals if requested. By midsummer the tennis court was in service and a club formed, the Davenports' son Vernon not surprisingly elected secretary/treasurer. Soon the members voted to admit girls, and some of the local young women such as Mary Lou Faurot joined the likes of Vern, the Ermatinger boys, Leon Cusson and Washington Wintersgill in the summer fun.

In August Davenport actually bought the hotel for the sum of one dollar, which may have served to liquidate the Bay View Hotel and Development Company for once and for all. He kept the rates throughout that fall and winter at two dollars a day or ten dollars a week and up, but the Davenports were more than ready to be done with Gulfport. Their elegant eighty-five-foot schooner, which they had expected to offer for guests' use that winter,

The Bay View Hotel, built 1914. *Courtesy Ernie Riske*

was wrecked in St. Augustine. The Boston-built boat had cost $25,000 new, and now lay in pieces, blown against the rocks by a northeaster. There was no insurance.

Whatever happened the previous year with the Bay View Hotel and Development Company had caused a yawning divide in the allegiances of those who mattered in Gulfport. When the Davenports were given a surprise party to celebrate their twenty-fifth wedding anniversary in November, the guest list reflected this new state of affairs. Present were the McKinneys, the Ferrises, the Brookses, the Lorenzo DeGrasses, Mayor (for the moment) Parks and Mrs. Johnson. Notably absent were any of the Wintersgill/ Webb contingent.

Only a couple of weeks later the Davenports pulled out of Gulfport for good. On December 11, 1916, the hotel title and the gas and water franchises were transferred to A.P. Avery of the Real Estate and Trust Department of the American Bank and Trust Co. The hotel management was taken over by J.R. McClane, "formerly of the Plaza hotel" (no clue given as to just which one), and his son-in-law R.B. Dubois. "Extensive improvements to the property" were planned.

Just before New Year's Eve, a final reception for the Davenports was held at the Bay View. Fifty residents attended, heard speeches by the two ex-mayors Sands and Parks (who had just lost re-election), and enjoyed ice cream, cake and coffee. After that the Davenport family left for their new home in Davista. In a year-end review of the town's situation, the hotel (a "high-class business property") was described as being mostly reserved for the season. Altogether, the report concluded, "Gulfport is looking forward to the most prosperous year of its existence."

McClane immediately snagged the current local celebrity Madame Stuart-Riching as an enticement to his guests. Just what Madame did seems to have varied with her audience. At the hotel, the parlors were opened to all who wished to observe her "interesting tests of character reading . . . seances, palmistry, and demonstrations in psychometry." But hardly had this event passed than there appeared a large ad in the *St. Petersburg Independent* offering the Bay View for sale. Illustrated by a photo, the ad touted this "safe investment" as being close to the finest fishing waters, on the carline, completely furnished and equipped and "overflowing with guests."

The McClane and Dubois families left abruptly; so suddenly were they "called away" that daughter Edna was forced to cancel on almost no notice an attempt to make the four-mile swim between Gulfport and Pass-a-Grille. (This was the latest fad for adventurous young women, eager to match what the boys had been doing for some time. In the spring of 1917, the first girl to go the distance made it in three hours and twelve minutes.) Some years later the McClanes could be found established at the Plaza Theater in St. Petersburg, where Edna played piano for the silent films and Mr. Dubois managed the theater when he wasn't leading tours to Cuba.

Lester Wintersgill was once again the man of the moment when, in May, he stepped in to keep the hotel open, "for the sake of the town." His management didn't extend to the dining room, but at least, he said, a stranger in town would be able to find a place to stay. No doubt to Wintersgill's relief, the Bay View Hotel was purchased in October by a Mr. and Mrs. W.F. Burgess of New York, the sale handled by Avery of the American Bank. The Burgesses promised, as usual, to make immediate improvements and to put the hotel in "first-class condition." However, within a week of this transaction, Mr. Burgess suddenly died, leaving the bank once more in search of a potential lessee.

One was soon found; Mr. and Mrs. H.B. Churchill of Boston signed on around Thanksgiving. Mr. Churchill claimed to have thirty-five years of hotel experience, including a stint at the Ritz-Carlton in Washington, D.C. His wife had her own resume of hotel management in New England resorts. Their plans were to specialize in "sea-food" dinners and dancing parties, but if they did so, their tenure was brief, and like McClane they soon moved on to more prepossessing establishments.

Who knows how many times the Bay View's management changed over these few years? There was a Captain Belmont and his wife in charge at some point, and they were succeeded in 1919 by Thomas and Beatrice Shirley, who were former operators of the St. Petersburg Country Club. Like all their predecessors, the Shirleys at once announced plans to renovate; the screened porch on the south side of the hotel would become a tearoom and the north side grounds were to be devoted to "amusements." By Thanksgiving, when a $1.25 dinner was offered, the dining room had been repainted yellow and adorned with arrangements of cosmos and ferns, and the delicious home-cooked turkey was prepared as, it was said, only Mrs. Shirley could do.

Rooms were now offered as singles or *en suite*, and the hotel finally was coming back to life. All the "holiday gaiety" of the decade's close centered around Christmas and New Year's parties at the Bay View.

2. Parks, McKinney and Politics

On January 20, 1914, the first council meeting was held in the new town hall. Gulfport's record books were audited and found to be "equal to those of St. Petersburg." Sam Webb had done an "exceptionally praiseworthy" job. He may have known nothing about bookkeeping, but he did know how to keep track of what came in and what went out, and after nearly four years there was a discrepancy of only three cents. Present assets were found to be $13,551.89 and liabilities $10,785.32. There was $1,748.68 cash in a bank account and $770.99 in realizable securities, drawing interest. This was an unusually solvent condition for a young town in an era when most municipalities had exhausted their tax revenues and were looking for ways to borrow more money.

The sea walling saga surged into 1914. In late January a storm washed away all the wooden forms, which had finally been ready for filling, actually scheduled for the next day. Nearly the whole breakwater would have to be rebuilt, the damages running to some $1,000. The work was now being handled by the Pinellas Dredging Company, the third or fourth but not the last to be employed in this ill-fated project. Resignedly, they promised to tear out all the shattered remains and "commence rebuilding." A few months later Pinellas Estates admitted the original plan had had some faults and abandoned the old design with V-shaped jetties that were supposed to collect sand from the natural action of waves and tide. Now a simple straight seawall was on the drawing board, one foot above high tide, with sand to be pumped behind it.

Philip Clausen had arrived in town and was working as captain of the barge that carried the new twelve-inch dredge, which belied its recalcitrance with a lovely name, "The Swan." He met and married Martha Lenora Renney, the

Gulfport's first town hall, originally located in Chase Park.

youngest child and only daughter in William Renney's family of nine. There was a pretty ceremony in the Renney home, decorated for Christmas and banked in profusions of ferns. Mattie, as she was called, wore messaline satin with a corsage of bridal roses, and the reception was held at the Casino. Florence Slaughter and Vera Leonardy were her attendants and Fred Renney and T.C. Blair (who would shortly marry Olga Sjustrom) stood up for Philip. When time came for the annual town election, a mass meeting was held as usual to nominate the slate. Elmer Wintersgill had apparently changed his decision of the previous year and once again would stand for mayor, this time opposed by the former state senator from Michigan, John H. Parks. Just as the Pennsylvania people had come a decade before, there was suddenly in the early teens a new influx of residents from Michigan, like the Sackriders, Dr. and Mrs. Jerome J. Robbins, the DeGrasses and Parks. He was a pioneer logger, mail carrier and retail storeowner in the Midwest before his election to the Michigan state senate, where he got the name "Working Parks" for his support of civil engineering projects.

On his arrival in Gulfport, he had taken out a permit for a "handsome $2,500 bungalow," duly built on what is today Dellett Avenue, and the elderly senator moved in with his niece Mrs. J.E. Johnson, also of retirement age, as

The sea wall about 1914, now in a straight-line formation.

a companion. People were extremely impressed that such a prominent man had come to live among them.

Lorenzo and Louise DeGrasse had come to town about 1912, at first tenting out on one of Senator Parks' lots, planning to build after a summer vacation back home. In 1914 Lorenzo wrote a letter to his hometown newspaper, enthusiastically praising his new life here. He extolled the virtues of Gulfport, its weather, birds, fish, government, school, church, hotel, car line, waterfront improvements, new roads and ease in producing three or four crops per year, not to mention how pleasant it felt to be working out in the sun. The temperature, he said, never rose above ninety-six degrees. A lot of people engaged in similar promotional activities about this time; there was even a name for it: "boosting," and it would only increase as boom times approached.

William and Mary Belle Sackrider had purchased a lot on West Davis Boulevard and built in the summer of 1913 a house called "Battle Creek," that still stands today at 2701 Beach Boulevard. Their neighbors to the north were Mr. and Mrs. Robert Kuder of Deal Beach, New Jersey, who had wintered in Pass-a-Grille before deciding on a permanent place in Gulfport. Their house, now a couple of years old, was already undergoing remodeling and fencing. The Kuders' daughter Bessie had recently married Paul Camp of Jonesboro,

"Battle Creek," The house at 2791 Beach Boulevard, built about 1913 by William and Mary Sackrider. *Courtesy Ernie Riske*

Georgia, the son of a banker and cotton broker, and the young couple returned to Jonesboro to reside for the time being. Dr. and Mrs. Robbins, retirees from Michigan, had acquired considerable Gulfport property, and built a home at 52nd Street and 27th Avenue, where they hosted boarders during their winter visits to the town.

The seven-member council format was still in place, so three two-year-term seats were up for grabs. The contenders were Albert Schludecker, local justice of the peace Leon Gray, Alexis Cusson and the current mayor, Benjamin Sands. Lorenzo DeGrasse and Alex Leonardy ran unopposed for treasurer and tax assessor, respectively, while Lawrence Renney and Cleveland LeNeave were vying for the marshal's job. Grover Cleveland LeNeave was an electrician, about thirty years old, his wife Eva a daughter of the "very French" Ralph Veillard, who helped write Pass-A-Grille's charter in 1911 and served on the St. Petersburg City Council for several years.

When the fall campaign for county elections began, Lester Wintersgill looked beyond Gulfport and entered the race for tax collector as an independent against the well-entrenched Democratic incumbent E.B. McMullen. He qualified after presenting a petition signed by forty "prominent citizens," and began campaigning in earnest on a platform of "competency and efficiency in return for responsibility." His greatest fear was that McMullen

The home of Robert and Eva Kuder, at 2629 Beach Boulevard.

would entice a third candidate into the race to split his opposition, and that is exactly what happened.

L.M. Wintersgill's campaign was not without its ups and downs; he alleged political trickery more than once. The job at stake was extremely desirable. The county tax collector got a percentage of the assessments, based upon a sliding scale. In Pinellas at that time the annual salary would have figured to be about $5,500, a handsome sum, particularly in comparison with Wintersgill's six-dollar-a-year pay as a Gulfport alderman. The election was held in early November, and the first count was so close—McMullen winning by a mere ten votes—that an official canvass was called for. In the process of this recount a few precincts were thrown out entirely for one or another questionable procedure, but the end result was not any better for Lester. McMullen won by seventy-one votes over the combined totals of his two opponents.

Back in Gulfport, Elmer Wintersgill suffered his first defeat; a twenty-three to thirteen loss to John Parks. The three winning councilmen were Gray with twenty-eight votes, Sands and Schludecker with twenty-four each. Alexis Cusson lost by a bare margin, receiving twenty-two votes. Wendell did in Davenport by twenty-four to twelve, and L.D. Renney defeated LeNeave twenty-two to ten for the position of marshal. These numbers indicate that about thirty-six citizens came to the polls, though Gulfport was now reputed to have eighty qualified voters, twice as many as two years previously. If so, they didn't bother to exercise the franchise.

Alex Leonardy's re-emergence as one of the town officials signaled the end of any bitterness left from the secession movement. The secessionists, now relegated to county status, began the year feeling disenfranchised. They were no longer welcome in their former precinct eight, and were not yet accepted into St. Petersburg's precinct eleven. Gulfport didn't care.

The hot issue in Gulfport this time was the question of changing the form of government from council to commission, and many folks took to spending the evenings hanging around the new town hall debating the relative merits of each. The vote came in on election day, November 17, in favor of retaining the "aldermanic" form, with a recommendation that a new charter be written to suit Gulfport's special needs.

The new council was sworn in the following week, promising that their very first business would be to begin drafting the new charter. Malcolm McRoberts was elected president, and the 1915 millage rate was set at twenty-five: twelve to the sinking fund, ten general, two for roads and one for parks.

The earliest minutes extant from a Gulfport Council meeting are dated December 15, 1914. This meeting marks the first political appearance of Nathan B. McKinney, who presented to council a bill for "figuring yardage on earth removed from Davis Boulevard." Nathan McKinney and his wife, the former Claudine Soule, a stepdaughter of the St. Petersburg Investment Company's Benjamin F. Measey, had arrived in town from Connecticut the previous year. With them were their daughter Ethel, then about twenty-five, and her husband Elbert Ferris. Nathan had worked in several northeastern locations (Ethel was born during a stay in New Jersey) in insurance, real estate and related fields. Here he became an agent for the Pinellas Estates Company, and Ethel shortly found work running the concession stand at the Casino. The McKinneys lived on the north side of Bon Air (30th Avenue), somewhere in back of the new Bay View Hotel, with Measey, his wife Amelia and daughter Marie as very near neighbors.

The charter committee was formed up and began functioning. Members were the aldermen and some Board of Trade representatives, but the actual work, of course, was done by Lester, Sam Webb, Judge Gray and the chairman, Nathan McKinney, who early in 1915 requested a special meeting of council to hear the preliminary report. The charter was read "in full" and approved by all councilmen with the exception of Sawyer, who had concerns over changing the clerk's and tax collector's offices to appointive positions. Otherwise, it was generally agreed to "put Gulfport ten years ahead of most similar towns," though the changes were, in fact, not extensive. One of these, for example, was to increase the allowance for bonded indebtedness from ten to 20 percent of the annual assessment.

Most of the 1915 meetings were, as always, concerned with the following big three problems of the day: drainage, sidewalks and roads. The town was beginning to move toward control over the old West Coast Realty (now Pinellas Estates) properties and the Veteran City parklands, when they "accepted jurisdiction over the streets of Boca Ceiga Park." But Fuller's interests still controlled the trolley right-of-way, and it was to Measey that the Street Committee turned to request some improvement in the condition of Davis (Beach) Boulevard. From 2nd Street (29th Avenue) south to the waterfront, this stretch was found to be "unsanitary and unsightly."

Also on early 1915 agendas was the matter of building a public dock. First the clerk was instructed to get prices on materials ("lumber, nails, etc."), "said materials not to cost in excess of ONE HUNDRED AND FIFTY DOLLARS ($150.00)." Then he was told to "procure a written agreement signed by a sufficient number of men who will agree to donate either labor or cash sufficient to erect complete the Pier herein described." That was all there was to it; get the cash, get the materials, get the men and "proceed with the work in accordance with the sketch submitted."

This sketch, prepared by Wendell, called for the pier to be 310 feet long with a 32- by 80-foot head, upon which would be located a pavilion with facilities for fishermen and boats. The site would be, as always, at the foot of Grant Avenue, now 54th Street. Since this was one of the periods in which the Casino was not much used, terminals for the boat passengers, a waiting room, and a freight warehouse were all proposed to be relocated here rather than on the old electric dock. A month or so later, Wendell revised his pier plan to a length of 283 feet and designed another structure to be built nearby, a commercial pier forty by 50 feet with 12-foot approaches. None of this, of course, would happen for a very long time.

Judge Gray resigned in April and Mayor Parks recommended that Nathan McKinney be nominated to serve the remainder of his term. McKinney took his oath at the very next meeting, and immediately plunged into the affairs of government. He joined a group of citizens, who, with the roadwork now officially approved, took off on an inspection tour, visiting other localities to view the various paving methods and materials. Along on the five-day auto trip were Mayor Parks, Lester Wintersgill, Ben Sands and the Reverend James MacLean.

They came back recommending "sand asphalt," an expensive process. This led, in late summer, to the raising of a petition by the citizens requesting the appointment of Davenport as supervisor of roads because of his support of simple shell paving. Shell was better, said Davenport, not only for its relative cheapness, but also because it could be laid with local labor, and should be used on all roads except Davis (Beach) Boulevard, which he agreed could be surfaced in sand asphalt.

Beach Boulevard south of the Bay View Hotel, showing the "unsightly" condition of the road.

When Malcolm McRoberts became seriously ill early in the summer, McKinney stepped right up to the position of Chairman of Council Pro Tem in his absence. In July McRoberts was sent home from the Augusta Memorial Hospital at await death, which came in August. During his eight years in residence he had become one of Gulfport's foremost citizens, and the entire town honored his passing by closing all stores and flying the flags at half mast the day of his funeral.

McKinney then assumed the council presidency almost as a matter of course, and soon was also serving as acting mayor while Parks was off touring. One of the measures he authorized was the requirement that building permits be issued to "all persons erecting structures of any description which are . . . intended to house human beings."

Council had ruled that the marshal be paid "when funds were available," which apparently they weren't at the moment, as Lawrence Renney went five months without a salary and finally resigned in disgust before he received any compensation for his services. His one big bust had been a surprise raid on a dance party of young St. Petersburg people at the Casino. His orders (or his own idea) were to prohibit any type of dancing except the two-step and the waltz. Reports don't say just what dance the partiers were enjoying, but do clearly describe a mass resistance to the threatened arrest. All the young men, and even the young ladies, proclaimed themselves willing to spend the night in Gulfport's new jail. In the end, better sense won out and they all returned to St. Petersburg to finish their dance in a freer atmosphere.

Jasper Mondon "Munn" Nash was hired as a replacement marshal until the November election, but he didn't last even that long; at some point he also resigned and was succeeded by Henry Slauter, which is interesting because that was just after Henry had been charged with assault and using obscene and abusive language while under the influence of liquor. After Henry was suspended "pending some charges," the job went back to his sons-in-law, Renney and Guy Morrison. The annual salary of $50 must have been apportioned in several fractions. Of course, the marshal also received a dollar for each animal caught "running at large" within the town limits, and this was still not an uncommon occurrence.

It would be yet another year, according to Jay Starkey, before the Lykes Company finally moved their herds out of the county, particularly out of Gulfport. A cattle drive, perhaps one of the last, through Davista (today's Park Street neighborhoods) wreaked total havoc, wrecking lawns, flowers and porches. Livestock would finally be completely removed in the fall of 1918 when ranchers were encouraged by the prospect of sales to the military, much as in the Civil War so long ago.

By the beginning of 1917 the identity of the official marshal is anybody's guess. Whoever he was, he immediately asked for and received a ten dollar advance on his salary, probably a smart move given the fluctuations in the position. A Renney ("Rainey") was still in office when a typical incident made the papers but not the Gulfport police logs. Three of the younger Nashes—William, Harvey and Barney—and Irving Slauter were arrested for stealing peaches from John Parks' property. The Nashes pled guilty and were fined accordingly, William and Barney ten dollars each and Harvey five dollars, but Irving insisted he hadn't done anything and was released with a warning. He also said there weren't any peaches there anyway, but the justice of the peace wasn't impressed. "Don't play in peachless peach orchards, then," he advised.

Will Nash, too, had been a deputy sometime during this period, a time in which he also had a look at the other side of the law. After cashing a forged check for $25, he was arrested and spent a brief time in the St. Petersburg jail before his plea of complete innocence was believed. Will's uncle Angus Nash and Lester Wintersgill had gotten into it during a meeting at the elementary school. Angus apparently held Lester responsible for the recent arrest of his son Jason on a charge of disturbing a religious meeting. Serving Angus with an arrest warrant for "starting trouble," Lester claimed he wanted to avoid confrontation, but was attacked and had to "defend himself," which resulted in Angus getting knocked down three times. Much later pictures of Lester Wintersgill show a small, slight little man with silver hair and blue eyes, not just the sort one imagines winning a round against one of the rough and ready Nashes.

The 1915 St. Petersburg and Beaches directory gives the first clear look at the population make-up of the period. There were about 140 adult residents, some 80 of whom were male, and therefore qualified to vote. Many of the men were employed in various trades, carpenters being the most heavily represented. A dozen or more gave no occupation, and were probably retirees. Another dozen were fishermen or boatmen. Seven had some sort of government position and 6 were farmers. There were a handful of professional men, perhaps 5, and as many again in the real estate field. A few merchants, teachers, students and 5 or 6 widows completed the entries. Of these, only 17 were freeholders, according to a new registration list of qualified voters, with information on whether they had paid their 1913 and 1914 poll taxes; many had not.

At the 1915 town meeting, an uncontested slate was presented: Parks for mayor, Ritchey, William Renney and Lester Wintersgill for the two-year council terms, Cusson as treasurer and Wendell as assessor. Cusson received a perfect vote of twenty, Ritchey and Wintersgill nineteen each, and Renney sixteen. Lester was once more chosen chairman of council, and McKinney became the new clerk on appointment from Parks. Alex Leonardy's final act as assessor was to present a report "as correct from careful calculation" that the total amount of taxes collected that year was $3,536.85. The treasurer's year-end report showed the balances in the various accounts perilously low, the sidewalk fund, for example, having only $1.99 left and the ditching fund a mere 8¢.

The only loser on the slate was Wendell, defeated by Sam Webb on a write-in vote. Sam's win had been reported in the *Independent* as nineteen to nine, occasioning a response from Wendell in the form of this "rather witty communication":

In your issue this evening you give a masterful and thrilling account of Mr. Webb's wonderful achievements in high politics, which the casual observer would sum up as a terrific landslide for the victor, and a deathblow for the regular candidate. As matters really stood, the vote cast was as follows: Wendell 9, Webb 11. I had repeatedly stated that I would under no conditions serve in any official capacity in the town's administration, as I have conscientious scruples against receiving the vast sums of filthy lucre which are thrust upon the politicians of this municipality. Just think of it; all that I have had to do as clerk-collector-supervisor of public works-building inspector-engineer, etc., etc., has been to devote about 25 hours per diem to those duties and all the rest of the time I had to myself and for this little trifle of service they forced upon me the vast sum total of 96 cents per week, with the privilege of spending my accumulated fortune in campaigning for the glorious title of assessor. Is it any wonder I am heart-broken over my terrible defeat? Ah, this is a cruel world.

Gulfport's council has had some contentious periods over the years, a pattern set as early as the secession efforts of 1912 and 1913. However, 1916 would see a new level of activity. The year began with Albert Schludecker and Benjamin Sands serving out the last of their terms; William Renney, James Ritchey, and Lester Wintersgill newly elected; and John H. Parks again mayor. But at the very first meeting of 1916, James Ritchey resigned, less than two months after winning the office. A controversy immediately arose over his replacement. At least two names were suggested (one of them may have been W.P. Woodworth) and subsequently voted down, at which time Alexander Milne was put forward and accepted. Milne was a fruit packer in his thirties from the Northeast. He and his wife Viola would soon buy property on 4th Street (27th Avenue) from Lester Wintersgill.

To make matters worse, Renney resigned in May. Woodworth was then nominated for that position, but the vote was tied, Sands and Schludecker supporting him and Milne and Wintersgill against. Alderman Milne then nominated Alex Leonardy and Sands again suggested Woodworth. The ensuing vote was split two to two in the same manner as before until Wintersgill came up with a compromise: Sam Webb. The vote was Milne and

Wintersgill for and Sands and Schludecker against. At that point Wintersgill resigned, and Schludecker, Milne and Sands presented a petition requesting a special meeting to vote "on the resignation of L.M. Wintersgill as President, the appointment of another member to fill the vacancy."

At the next meeting no business at all was conducted because while everyone, including Wintersgill, showed up, he refused to act as chairman and open the meeting. Whatever the hard feelings had been, they were seemingly overcome by the June 6 meeting, when all were in attendance and Wintersgill was once more elected chairman. Perhaps the problem had been solved by the return of William Renney, who had resumed his office, re-taken the oath, and immediately got back to work.

But a short time later Mayor Parks left for his usual summer hiatus, which really opened the floodgates. Wintersgill succeeded to the position of acting mayor, and Milne became acting chairman of the council. At the next meeting, Renney stepped in as acting clerk, making it three for three. The reason for this soon became apparent. "Charges were preferred against the Tax Collector and Town Clerk McKinney by the Mayor Pro Tem." A motion to re-instate McKinney was made by Sands and seconded by Schludecker, but again it was two to two with Renney and Milne against.

The first charge against McKinney was that he "promised your Hon. Board to give the Tax Payers of our Town as good service as they had had in the two years previous to his collectorship, and has failed to keep his promise." In this matter the vote stood, as usual, two to two. The second complaint was that he had failed to "read the Treasurer's Report in full." Apparently this didn't carry much weight, because Wintersgill withdrew this charge altogether.

Number three was his "Failure to turn over to the Street Committee all information and data which he had received as Clerk of the Road Committee when voted by Council to do so." Again, the vote was a tie. The fourth claimed that he was "short in his Tax Acct. at the time of his suspension from office." This charge, which was in plain language embezzlement, was tabled until an audit could be made. The council's attorney, Judge C.E. Speare, delayed the presentation of the auditor's report, saying, "it would only be the means of making much trouble." So the council met in private to discuss what to do, and agreed to have it read at a July meeting. The books were now balanced, but L.M. Wintersgill insisted there had been shortages.

On July 11, Nathan McKinney, accompanied by an attorney of his own, tendered his resignation. Schludecker didn't want to accept it, but his co-voter Sands was on leave of absence, and so it passed, two to one. Mayor Pro Tem Wintersgill suggested Sam Webb to be McKinney's replacement. The vote in favor of this move was unanimous, and Webb immediately took the oath of office, becoming clerk if not council member.

All this trouble had brought about one procedural change. An ordinance was passed allowing that the mayor or acting mayor would now be empowered to vote on all questions "in an effort to break the deadlock that has prevailed in many instances," a considerable understatement.

Not long after that it was suggested that a supervisor of public works really was needed, and while Lester, as Mayor Pro Tem, wanted Sam for that job, too, there were objections, primarily from Lawrence Renney, and the motion was tabled. Mayor Parks finally returned from his long summer absence, so Wintersgill dropped back to his position of council president, and it looked like things could return to normal, but of course that did not happen. Ben Sands was the next to resign. Alex Leonardy was appointed to replace him, receiving, for once, a unanimous favorable vote, and things did finally calm down.

When election time came around again, the town was probably very ready for it. There were now officially forty-three voters in Gulfport's precinct eight, and most had participated in the hotly contested presidential election. Woodrow Wilson swept Gulfport twenty-nine to six, a much greater margin than in the nationwide results, which were so close they took a couple of days to sort out before the president was declared re-elected.

The incoming council represented a clean slate, and Clarence Brantley (twenty-one votes) became the new chairman. Clarence and his wife Lula lived on the waterfront east of Davis Boulevard. He was presently working as a boatman, making three trips a week from "Petersburg" to Gulfport, bringing ice from the downtown plant and picking up fish to sell.

The aldermen were F.L. Coppins (thirty-one votes), Joe Steinwinder (twenty-six), boat captain William Johnstone (twenty-one) and James Ritchey (twenty). The field of candidates had been twice as large, and the five losers were Lester Wintersgill, Albert Schludecker, Nathan McKinney, Alex Milne and Walter Roberts. Elmer Wintersgill regained the mayor's seat, prevailing against John Parks by a mere two votes. Frank Coppins, then about forty-five, had a wife Olive and five sons, and had just bought a home here. A brick mason by trade, he had other local family, including three sisters who had married prominent St. Petersburg men.

William Renney defeated Davenport for the office of tax assessor by three votes, and Alexis Cusson was re-elected town treasurer against a write-in campaign for Alonzo Hoyt. Fred Roberts became the new marshal, the position now being appointed by the mayor. In his spare time, Fred had formed an "alligator club" and appointed himself head hunter, taking groups to the "lairs" three times a week while the tourists were in town. There were still plenty of these around, and deer and panther could still be seen in the wilds of Bear Creek.

"After the hunt" people gather near to admire a trophy. *Courtesy Webb family*

The election, which was mildly contested, required that ballots be recounted and "a few errors were found but not changing the result of members being elected." This year's valuation was $133,140, and the budget was worked out to thirty mills, the same as the previous year. The general fund would get ten; sinking fund, eight; dock, five; road, three; street cleaning, two; sanitary, one; park, one. Revenue was expected to be about $4,000. At the end of the year, the town had assets of $3,177 over liabilities and the total debt was less than $11,000. Salaries for the coming year were set as follows: councilmen, fifty cents per meeting; tax assessor, $50; town marshal, $50; town treasurer, $50. John Parks had loaned the town $200 in 1915 and the note was still outstanding; funds were "not available," but Elsie Wintersgill, Lester's daughter, was given a total of $15.25 for typing work she had done, including specifications for the road proposals and preparing some ordinances.

"The officials and people of Gulfport are showing a progressiveness which is certain to bring that charming little place right up to the front," reported the *Independent,* adding that the fresh group of councilors were "live hustling men . . . in complete harmony" with the mayor of the "pretty little town." The newspaper generously declined to comment on the novelty of that situation.

The political dust had by no means settled. A petition was circulated requesting the council appoint W.P. Woodworth town clerk and tax collector, "believing it to be for the best interests of the town, and that he is well fitted for the position." It was signed by twenty-five people, or just about everyone in town, though no action was taken and Sam Webb, praised for his "careful attention to details," held onto the job. William Woodworth did get an official position, that of assessor, in 1918. It was about this time that he sold his house and twenty acres of waterfront property to the Reverend MacLean for $1,000 and moved up to Lakeview. Alderman Coppins resigned in June and was replaced a few weeks later by Lawrence Renney, who had been proposed by Johnstone and Ritchey.

Councilmen got a raise to one dollar per meeting, with a $1.50 fine for absence and "no excuses allowed." Ex-mayor Parks was still asking for repayment of his loan, and still being told to wait for the "first available money." Millage was continued at thirty. The town went ahead and borrowed $800 against the next year's taxes ("being less than one-half the taxes levied") through an issue of $100 revenue bonds.

In 1917 Elmer defeated Clarence Brantley for the mayor's seat, and Lawrence Renney, Charles Whitbeck and old Mr. Henderson (of the "Henderson forty") were elected to join Johnstone and Steinwinder on the council. Charles Whitbeck, forty, and his wife Sarah arrived on the local scene in 1916 when they bought the Ermatingers' house at 49th Street and 26th Avenue. They had moved south from Pennsylvania hoping to find a better climate for Mrs. Whitbeck, who suffered from tuberculosis. This plan apparently worked, because they immediately launched into local society, entertaining at the house (whose name they had changed from "Shady Dell" to "Shadylawn") with meals and musical programs.

John Parks took a run at bigger and better things when he launched a campaign for County Commission. Unfortunately what he failed to do was become a registered voter on the primary books. It seems he had registered in the "general election books," but forgot the other, which disqualified him as a candidate. He immediately asked the public to write in his name, but the County Clerk put an end to that, too, saying Parks would have been disqualified anyway, because he had failed to file his campaign statement on time. So the June primary went on without him. It was reported that there was "absolutely no interest" in it anyway, "except by the candidates themselves."

Though this usually stirred more interest than county affairs, only eighteen voters turned out for the 1918 town election. Nathan McKinney ran a "poor race" against Elmer Wintersgill, losing by twelve votes to five, with one write-in for Mrs. Julia Lucky. The candidates for council stood without opposition and were automatically elected. These were the current council: president, Henderson, John Dobler and "M.D. Forest," the first appearance of a future figure of importance, M. DeForest Yates. Martin (possibly Marlin) DeForest Yates and his wife Anna, a couple in their sixties who had arrived from Schenectady, New York, quickly began acquiring real estate and prominence in town affairs. Yates had been an auditor and comptroller for a municipal public works department in New York State. Dobler, thirty-nine, had bought land from Dolly White and built a waterfront home for his wife Rhea and her mother Clara Burgess.

One of the most important, or at least officious, winter residents ever to claim a connection to Gulfport also arrived here about this time. After more than twenty years wintering near Little Bayou, Julia Lucky bought six lots from John Chase's widow Maria and built an imposing home on the water near today's 50th Street and 31st Avenue. With her lived a woman servant, almost certainly the only one in town. Mrs. Lucky, in her sixties, daughter of one wealthy Tennessee judge and wife of another, was aunt to the local teacher, Miss Fannie Boswell. Julia Lucky was "prominently identified with every program of civic movement . . . deeply interested in botany and contributed many interesting papers on this subject to publications as well as frequent communications to the press on local topics." She was also actively interested in Republican politics, and often "visited by political candidates for opinions and advice." Not surprisingly then, no sooner had she settled into her Gulfport home than she began to take on a semi-public role in town affairs. (Women, of course, had not yet achieved the right to vote.)

The final election of the decade, though described as "quiet," was also extremely close. Elmer Wintersgill had stepped down after six terms as mayor, and the race was between John Dobler and Nathan McKinney. "Not until the final ballot was tabulated by adding machine" was the result known, and Dobler had become the new mayor, beating McKinney by fifteen to thirteen votes. Interestingly enough, Dobler was described as "of Girard, Pennsylvania," rather than as a resident of the town whose administration he was about to take over.

Charles Whitbeck was elected to another term on council, as was L.D. Renney. New members were William Swift and John Griffin. Courtney Sawyer won office as the tax assessor and F. B. Lamb, an elderly gentleman from Connecticut, as the town treasurer. Griffin and his wife Elizabeth came here from New York; he was in his early eighties. William Swift, a partner to Walter Brooks in the real estate business, was originally from Illinois. He and his wife Olivia were forty-three and thirty-nine at the end of the teens. They had two daughters; Mary, fourteen; and Olivia, eleven; and a baby son, William.

The 1920 census showed 110 households and a population of 350. Women's suffrage had slowly been gaining ground when first Clearwater then Pass-a-Grille had granted female property owners the right to vote in the late 1910s.

Now with the passage of the 19th Amendment, women were enfranchised throughout the country. In Gulfport there were fifty-four qualified electors before women were allowed to begin registering in September. In an effort to encourage potential female voters to exercise their new right, they were exempted from paying poll tax, and the seventy-two votes cast in the fall election indicates that some did participate.

A new bond issue for public improvements, particularly waterfront amenities and street lighting, was proposed by council, though there was considerable public sentiment that any money so raised should be used for much-needed water and sewer construction. The official response was that the town was so large and the population so scattered that the cost of laying piping would be prohibitive. The aldermen hoped that an upgraded waterfront would stimulate an increase in property values that would eventually become so great the town would be able to reconsider the water and sewer situation.

Courtney Sawyer and Fred Blair ran for mayor against the incumbent Dobler. William Swift was challenged for the one-year council term by none other than the late mayor Parks' long-suffering niece, Jennie Johnson, who continued to live in Gulfport after her employer's death in January. She became one of the first Gulfport women to run for public office, along with Mrs. Clarence Helmick, who ran for council that year with five other candidates: George Lewis, Charles Thomes, Fred Roberts, the incumbent Yates and her own husband. Lewis, a carpenter, and his wife Clara were winter visitors who decided in the fall to make Gulfport their permanent home and settled on Pinellas Avenue (52nd Street). Sam Webb's wife Abbie ran for assessor against Alex Leonardy, and Alex Milne stood apparently uncontested for treasurer. Thus, in this first election since women's enfranchisement, three of the 14 candidates were female. While none would win, it is commendable that some would put themselves forth in the attempt.

Alexander Milne was a partner with a man named O'Berry in a large St. Petersburg fruit packing enterprise. Milne-O'Berry celebrated its second year of success in shipping the "Golden Sunset" brand of fruit by enlarging the business, now said to the the biggest such plant in the county. They acquired an old grapefruit grove on Bear Creek, some twenty acres, in May 1921.

Dobler easily took the November 16 election, garnering thirty-six votes to Blair's nineteen and Sawyer's seventeen. Swift defeated Mrs. Johnson forty-six to twenty, and Lewis and Yates took the two-year seats with twenty-seven and twenty-six votes respectively. Leonardy reclaimed the assessor's job with forty-two votes, and Milne, though no competition was ever mentioned, got forty-nine. As if it weren't enough that both Mr. and Mrs. Helmick lost, their son Almer was a member of the board that oversaw the election.

3. "Boosting"

The tourist business was definitely on the rise. In Gulfport it took the form of seasonal cottage rentals rather than hotel visitors, and a list of departing tourists published in April was surprisingly extensive; the town must have gone all out indeed to provide winter rentals for such a large group. Dobler, Webb and Yates had merged to form yet another real estate company. These gentlemen were, of course, the mayor, the town clerk and the president of council, so it is not surprising that they found business extremely satisfactory.

Sam Webb was becoming a master at the art of "boosting." He even took time out from boosting Gulfport to boost the efficiency of advertising in the *Independent* with this story. One of his favorite dogs disappeared one day in the summer, and Sam advertised at once in the lost and found column. Within three days the dog turned up, and Sam insisted that was because the dog, like everyone else in town, read the *Independent* ads. Even with war looming on the horizon, Sam had faith that Gulfport was finally coming into its own. Post office receipts were up 45 percent in the fourth quarter, and more prospective buyers than ever were looking at the little town on the Bay. "There are great times ahead," Sam concluded optimistically.

Webb and the other members of the school board had not stopped complaining to the county that St. Petersburg was wrong in allowing Gulfport children to attend their schools. They knew that a dozen or more students had taken that option, eliminating the need for one teacher and leaving two of the Gulfport school's four rooms vacant. The outside authorities wouldn't listen to them, responding that any such ruling could interfere with the tourism business. The Gulfport trustees said they didn't care what the tourists did, they just wanted their own kids back in their own school. As usual in such dealings, the protest was futile.

The school itself was doing well, when students in 1914 posted the highest average rating in the county, and graduated five youngsters, including Albert Ermatinger and Otto Schludecker. Every grade in the school sent flowers to the graduates, and the trustees gave candy to the girls and a comb and brush set to the boys, indicating that this was, indeed, a major event in the lives of these children and the town. Gulfport Elementary was proclaimed a "real model," for its gardens, the high level of public interest, the active mothers' club, the P.T.A., and a very involved school board. This community interest was particularly exceptional, because absolutely everyone attended school functions, and the school was the center of the town socially financially, and "in every wholesome way."

Mrs. Wilder was readily re-hired for the 1914 to 1915 school year. Joining her were two new teachers, Miss Ola Allen and Miss Ethel Daum (whose name was given in one report as Miss Dumb, and, oh, how the children must have enjoyed that). They, with the school board's help, were campaigning hard to get a telephone installed at the school, for there was none anywhere in the vicinity and no way of summoning help in case of accident or emergency.

The woman who would become the school's longest serving and most beloved teacher had arrived in town. This was Mary Lou Faurot, whose parents, Ebenezer and Mary (or Marie; she was born in Austria in 1858), had arrived from Kissimmee. They stayed in one of Hoyt's cottages before building a house, the first, on the southern end of Palm Avenue, today's 50th Street. Mary Lou was a 1915 graduate of St. Petersburg High School, along with Elsie Wintersgill and Carrie Brantley (Clarence's daughter). Mary Lou and Carrie, who was hired to teach at Pinellas Park, would spend many summers to come furthering their educations at the University of Florida Normal School, but right now Mary Lou was presiding over the Methodist Sunday School, with its "splintery homemade benches, best described as rickety. In cool weather, they threw 'fat lighter' pine splinters into a pot bellied stove," according to the church history. Mary Lou would begin her teaching career in the fall at Glen Oak School.

Again in 1916 the superintendent's report had found Gulfport Elementary School superior and "thoroughly equipped . . . with modern teaching apparatus," its two acres "beautified and planted," its three teachers now presenting both domestic science and manual training. The report concluded with applause for the great improvements over a mere four years ago, when "this district had a one-room leaning shanty which served as a school building." But when school resumed in the fall, the domestic science program had disappeared. In its absence, the girls would be provided the opportunity to join a "canning club," offered in all schools lacking domestic science training. Under this program they would be taught to be "good housewives," who knew all about preserving guavas, making jelly, and planting, cultivating and canning tomatoes.

Gulfport Elementary was one of the features in the Board of Trade's 1915 boosting brochure. None of the reported 5000 copies has been found to be extant, but this text seems to have come from that publication.

Gulfport claims a right to more than your passing interest for it holds out to you the opportunity of making it your STEPPING STONE to health, wealth, happiness, and prosperity . . . Gulfport is provided with up-to-date stores, schools, churches, post office, amusement pavilions, fish docks, a magnificent hotel, good roads, good water, good soil, good neighbors and an unsurpassable climate.

THE GULFPORT SCHOOL is one of the many things we are proud of. It is housed in an artistic stone building consisting of four large airy light rooms and with extensive playgrounds and gardens. It had an average attendance last year of eighty scholars. The building was designed to accommodate 160 pupils and there are indications of this proving inadequate if the present rate of increase in our population continues. The high commendation for the Gulfport School is given by the County Superintendent of Schools, who, in his personal examination of all schools of the county, given semi-annually, places the Gulfport School at the top of the list. This speaks well for the efficiency of the teachers and directorate. The courses of study are thorough and practical, covering all grades through to the High School.

The brochure also played up the new building and the fabulous climate.

The waterfront at Gulfport is being extensively developed by the construction of sea walls, numerous public parks, drives and avenues, and the setting out of tropical and ornamental trees and shrubbery. Gulfport is a town of marvelous sunsets, a town of exceptional health, and offering numerous inducements to the man of moderate means to make his home. By proper manipulation you may have on your table luscious fruits and fresh green vegetables every day in the year, from your own garden. The soil is for the most part a light, sandy loam, very easily cultivated with occasional tracts of rich black muck land which is especially adapted to the rapid production of the finest garden truck. In this unique climate we grow to perfection plants and trees of the temperate zone as well as those of the tropics. Mangoes and avocado pears, guavas, paw-paws, bananas and pineapples mingle with the citrus fruits such as the orange, grapefruit, lime and lemon.

Albert Schludecker might have disagreed with some of that, as he and Emma were still struggling to keep the farm going, even as their children one by one left home. In November Albert killed an enormous rattlesnake, four and half feet long and in the process of digesting a full-grown rabbit that it had swallowed whole. On Christmas Eve the hard-working mule had "got sick" and by the next morning had to be removed from his stall by tearing out a partition. "i don't expect him to live. Emma and i picked 86 pounds of beans in the afternoon," wrote Albert. Sure enough, the mule died the next day, and that was the Schludeckers' Christmas. To replace it, having not too long ago spent $75 on a cow, calf and bull, he was forced to seek a loan from the Central Bank. With a borrowed $100 in hand, he went out and bought a horse.

But the real estate market actually was increasing in activity here, as everywhere. In 1915 Wendell advertised an eight-room house on three corner lots, on the car line, with electric lights and a sidewalk, for the amazing sum of $3,000. Corner lots along Davis (Beach) Boulevard had been going for about $400 and "inside" ones $350.

The Wintersgills were involved in the usual number of new schemes. The latest was an attempt to secure a Western Union office for Gulfport. Even the *Independent*, which always treated the town more politely than did the *Times*, found this idea a bit grandiose. But if Elmer's cause failed, Lester had been granted a permit to build a real passenger station at the old 4th Street (27th Avenue) site, and his Gulfport Realty had just sold 26 lots between the pier and Disston Avenue (49th St.), with a combined total of 220 feet of waterfront, for $10,000. He promised the properties would be sea walled and improved for the building of "fine new homes."

In 1916 there was a movement toward building another church, spearheaded by the Reverend James T. MacLean, a fifty-seven-year-old Princeton graduate, who had become a Gulfport property owner when he bought Woodworth's lots. His plans involved constructing a 200-seat concrete block building, which would be an advance over the smaller "frame" Methodist Church. Construction began in the summer at Grant and 4th (54th Street and 27th Avenue), and the walls of "artificial stone" were raised by September 1. The interior was "exquisitely" finished in oiled natural woods and featured stained glass windows, and the promised tower rose above the church building when it opened in February 1917. MacLean and his wife had donated the lot and raised most of the money to support the erection of the building, boasting that not one dollar had been solicited for the construction. Even in the future, there would never be collections, but voluntary offerings only, they said.

The Reverend became the pastor of his own little kingdom, for in denomination, the church was "independent," not officially Presbyterian until 1947. In 1947 the church became Presbyterian. As one citizen remarked, "He bought it, he built, it, and he ran it." Mrs. MacLean, it was said, would bring an alarm clock to her husband's services, and when he had spoken long enough, let it ring out. She took over the Sunday school, while Mrs. Charles Whitbeck became the organist and head of the Missionary Society. The wedding of John and Laura White's daughter Rose and Richard Surber was the first major event, held on July 25th.

Just at this time there was a new craze afoot involving crafting small items from pine needles. In St. Petersburg a busy little Pine Needle Club had sprung up, where "any woman wishing to support herself may do so, by learning how to make baskets and trays." This was an era when women were at last beginning to think of themselves and their rights to a political voice and a measure of independence. Arts and crafts were emerging as one possible avenue to these ends.

Mrs. Lucky was inspired to bring this idea to Gulfport. There was a tiny building, not much more than a shed, which had been located on the rail

The Reverend James Maclean's church, built 1916.

spur near the Tangerine sawmill and used for storage of ice barrels, which she seems to have had moved down to Bon Air, behind the Cusson store nad across from the Brooks' post office, perhaps not exactly where it stands today at 5461 30th Avenue, but certainly nearby.

The shed was pressed into service as a kind of clubhouse for teaching crafts to the local girls, and there the teenagers happily made shell purses and pine needle baskets until Mrs. Lucky got another idea; what they really needed was a library. She had some shelves installed in the little building and began the collection with a donation of her own books. The girls apparently found this a worthy project, too, for everyone growing up in the town for the next decade or so held happy memories of working in "Mrs. Lucky's Library." The collection grew steadily, financed by their benefactor's gifts and a rental fee of two cents a day per book.

Gulfport's greatest promoter, the now ex-mayor Elmer Wintersgill and his wife Mary took a four-months auto tour in their National "machine" in 1915. They carried camping gear and planned to make it through Washington, D.C., New York City, Pennsylvania and Ohio, traveling part way at least with a caravan of other brave souls. Mary Wintersgill must have been the bravest of these, for Elmer was making this a "boosting" trip for Gulfport; he had painted a two-foot high pelican on each side of the "bonnet" over the motor and stretched Gulfport pennants from the front of the car to the windshield. Mounted on the roof was a St. Petersburg pennant, to which he planned to add a new one from each city visited. They returned, unscathed, in late September, having covered four thousand miles with no car trouble, so they said. Elmer then launched another new business, this involving renting a large vacuum cleaner to households. In the early fall he took off on a statewide tour with Noel A. Mitchell of St. Petersburg, who was running for governor. The Mitchell/Wintersgill trip came to a dramatic end in Jacksonville where the candidate was arrested on a bad check charge. He left Elmer and his car there, took a train home, and complained loudly that the accusation was totally false, just another political smear. In Elmer's absence, one of his lady clients complained, "I will be delayed in my house cleaning because Mr. Wintersgill has gone off with the vacuum cleaner."

Early 1921 brought the biggest news in some time when John Dobler announced plans to build a "fine 41-room hotel" east of Grant Avenue (54th Street) between the Bay and today's 31st Avenue. The design of the first floor called for a large lobby ("almost all windows") with a side entrance, a dining room backed by a kitchen and serving rooms, plus sixteen "outside" bedrooms. The second floor would have twenty-five more guest rooms, and each pair of these would have a bathroom between, allowing, if desired, for an *en suite* arrangement. Every room would be equipped with a lavatory and hot and cold running water. There would be a basement on the bay side, to contain a heating plant storerooms, and a bakery to furnish fresh breads and pastries for the guests.

The attic would be reserved for servants' accommodations. Garages were also planned to house guests' cars. Shortly after this announcement came the further news that a Tampa well driller had struck on the property, at 147 feet, "one of the largest and finest artesian wells . . . from a big stream free from sulfur and fine to drink." Although the well still exists, it is not considered potable today.

In addition to this project, Dobler continued to serve as mayor and judge of the municipal court, where cases of drunk and disorderly conduct, as usual, predominated. But this minor rowdiness didn't distract from the fact that things were going pretty well in greater Gulfport. When the mullet season opened in January, the Hibbs Company reported shipping one hundred thousand pounds of fish the first month. Boats were now beginning to be motorized. Conversion from sail to gasoline engine was an expensive proposition for the subsistence-level fishermen, who could sail at no cost, albeit not as efficiently. T.C. "Church" Gleaton was one of the first locals to use a motorized fishing boat, created by mounting an old automobile engine in a sailboat, creating a power-driven skiff.

Hauling in the mullet.

The auto engine conversions did not always have the capability to do things like go in reverse and were dangerous to the crews more used to sail. Al Renney nearly lost a hand when a sudden lurch threw him off balance, catching his fingers in the engine cogs and crushing several of them. And Louis Roberts ("one of the well-known boys of Gulfport") lost a large part of his left foot when he slipped in his boat and became entangled with the engine. Alone and well out into the Gulf, his distress signal was answered by Lee Allen, who rescued him and got him back to shore and medical assistance. Louis was "suffering fearfully and bleeding dangerously," the engine having "literally chewed off toes and bone." The mangled parts were successfully removed and no further amputations were anticipated.

Albert Whitted flew over one day in February 1921, to visit with the pilots of a big naval seaplane that had dropped anchor on the Gulfport waterfront. The plane, which had a 78-foot wingspan, a 400-horsepower Liberty motor capable of 80 knots, was stopping on its way from Key West to Galveston, Texas, to make some minor repairs. Whitted was at this time running a profitable business, taking tourists for sightseeing flights in his "Bluebird."

When the Michigan Society met in "Gulfport Park" in January, Mayor Dobler and Mrs. Lucky were guests of honor. Mrs. Dobler had continued to move up in society as her husband's career progressed, now presiding over the

Admiring Albert Whitted's *Bluebird*.

A picnic of the Michigan Society on the grounds of the town hall. *Courtesy Ernie Riske*

town's most prestigious ladies' group, the Late Book Club. But in the early summer of 1921, just before leaving on his usual vacation, John Dobler suddenly resigned his office, claiming the "business necessitated" by the building of the new hotel would keep him much too occupied to carry out his duties. Council President Yates became acting mayor and Al Milne assumed Yates' office.

By summer's end, Walter Brooks reported that the post office had made great gains in 1921, posting in July and August a 95 percent gain over the same period in 1920. He said the office was open every day, even for an hour on holidays and Sundays, and offered free "containers suitable for parcels" for all his customers. He was planning enough improvements to warrant a raise to third class status. These included new lock boxes and parcel post cabinets "to prepare for the winter rush."

Lester Wintersgill ended the year as guest speaker at the "Nut Club," an organization in which, it was said, he had led some "spirited debates." This time, during a meeting at Pass-a-Grille, Lester brought a telescope and planned to demonstrate—by focusing it on a buoy 12 miles out—that we are living not on the outside but on the inside of the earth.

Chapter VII
The Storm

1. Tragedies

In the last years of the 1910s and the beginning of the 1920s everything seemed to move into a higher gear. Women could vote and liquor was illegal; it was indeed a different world. Even as they reveled at successes with real estate and roads, the townsfolk found themselves at the mercy of war and weather. Accidents, tragedies and disasters both local and worldwide shadowed the families of Gulfport. The Webbs were just one of the families affected, though by a particularly heartrending series of events.

One daughter of Sam and Abbie (Thomes) Webb, Lillian Ethel, had died at the age of nine in an especially unusual and sad event in 1912, one that has never been fully explained, though it seems that she was shot accidentally by another child. In the 1980s her sister Elsie wrote this about it: "The trauma evidently was so painful to Mother, it was not spoken of very often. But I remember when I started school that I used to sneak up to the attic and open the old trunk to see the red plaid dress, bullet hole and all. The gun was stacked away behind the chimney up there. Ethel had no headstone, and since I have read of one unmarked grave there [Glen Oak Cemetery], I am concerned it might be Ethel's, the sister I never knew."

Another Webb daughter, Gwen, also suffered a terrible accident, this in her mother's own kitchen. Abbie Webb was making up the fire with damp wood just before New Year's Eve, 1914, and thought to add some coal oil to help it ignite. However, one of the Webb brothers had been working about the house and left a bottle of gasoline where the coal oil should have been, and Abbie picked it up by mistake and poured some on the fire. With flames everywhere and the bottle alight in her hands, she turned and threw it out the kitchen door, unaware that three-year-old Gwen was standing there.

The child suffered serious burns about her face and damage to her eyes, and for a while there was concern that she might lose her sight completely. Abbie Webb, as might be expected, was described as "heartbroken," but her

Above: The Sam Webb home at 2519 Beach Boulevard, built 1914. *Courtesy Webb family*

Left: Abbie Gwendolyn "Gwen" Webb (1911–1964) *Courtesy Webb family*

little girl survived and went on to do well. (In 1920 she won a five dollar gold piece from the Audubon Society for a charming letter reporting four pairs of nesting martins; Ted Girard took first place, but Gwen's second-place victory was the highest ever for a girl.)

Sam Webb's brother Henry, better known as Harry, had been widowed in 1912 when his beautiful young wife Lucy died of blood poisoning following the birth of her seventh child, Harry Jr., who was subsequently adopted by the Lawrence Renneys and raised along with their two little sons, Rufus and Russell. Still, Harry was left with six children, the oldest, May, only twelve. He supported them by taking out fishing parties on his boat the *Lucy Y*, and working in construction (one such job was for Tangerine Avenue farmer Charles Perrington, who, by the paucity of his tax assessment—four cents—must have needed some improvements).

One of the strangest of Gulfport's many mysteries occurred one morning in 1916 when Harry's motherless daughters were going about their usual chores. The eldest, May, then sixteen, had some sewing to finish; and Lillian, almost fourteen, was out scalloping; so the task of preparing batter cakes for lunch fell to nine-year-old Florence. This she did, using baking powder from one of two cans of "sodarine" she found in the kitchen cupboard. She was puzzling over why the cakes didn't rise properly when Lillian came in and corrected the situation by adding more powder, this time from the other can.

After eating, the entire family with the exception of Lillian, who had apparently gone back out, fell into "the throes of a violent disorder." A doctor was called and immediately saw that they had somehow been poisoned. He suspected one of the boxes of "cheap baking powder" had contained too much alum, so after administering remedies for poisoning, he poured the contents of the sodarine cans down the sink.

Gradually the others recovered, leaving only seven-year-old Evelyn still suffering the effects. Her condition grew worse instead of better, and after lingering for six long days she died. Even in those times, an incident like this triggered some questions, and it was announced that "legal steps would be taken to ascertain the cause of death." Evelyn's body was autopsied, and Prosecuting Attorney McMullen ordered a chemical analysis of her organs, which were forwarded to the state laboratory. The suspect sodarine cans and their contents were, of course, long gone.

In the meantime, Magistrate J.M. Endicott began an investigation, questioning all members of the family regarding the "powerful corrosive poison" that had claimed Evelyn's life. Lester Wintersgill and the town attorney, Judge Speare, supported Harry at this interview, during which he admitted to having kept arsenic about the house, "for use in the process of curing some hides." It further came to light that he had kept the arsenic in an old sodarine can, though he insisted that was stored in a locked closet, nowhere near the kitchen. However, when he went to look for this can, he couldn't find it.

Then they heard that May had cleaned out the kitchen cupboard just a day or two before, bent on exterminating some of the roach population, and put like cans together when replacing the food stores. The assumption was made that somehow the arsenic had ended up there disguised as sodarine, and Florence had used it in her original batter, which of course did not rise. When Lillian came in, she had added the true ingredient from the other can, causing the cakes to appear as usual. They concluded that perhaps the arsenic didn't diffuse fully through the batter, and little Evelyn got a concentrated amount of it in her portion.

Harry and the other children were now fine (though he complained of still feeling "a little giddy"), and the family was congratulated on "controlling themselves extremely well under the black shadow of the tragedy." Neither did the investigators find any "enmities among neighbors or family," and so the conclusion was reached that there was "no evidence of a crime" and no reason to hold an inquest. A month or so later, the toxicologist's report came in. There was no trace, not one sign, of arsenic in the child's remains. The mystery deepened, seemingly insoluble. Life went on in Gulfport, though not Evelyn Webb's.

But perhaps the most mysterious tragedy of all occurred at the home of a man named Charles E. Brown who had arrived from Highlands, New York, and taken up residence just north of Clam Bayou, buying some land adjacent to the old Puig property. He planned to start a chicken ranch with the help of his sister and her husband, Mr. and Mrs. William C. Richter. With them came Mrs. Richter's son from a previous marriage, four-year-old Robert Allen Striker.

One winter day in 1914 just four weeks after his arrival, the little boy disappeared, completely and utterly, in what would become one of the most baffling and long-standing local enigmas. Robert had gone outside to play, and when the adults went to call him in for lunch, there was no sign of the child anywhere. There was a small dock at the rear of their property where Robert had frequently played, and his favorite toy, a little broom, was found in a boat floating nearby in about two feet of water. A frantic but thorough search began immediately. In those days, the Bayou was extremely shallow, nowhere more than three feet deep, and crystal clear. At once the men of the town came to aid in the search, experienced fishermen all and so familiar with the Bayou and the Bay that they knew and explored every possible path a small body might have taken.

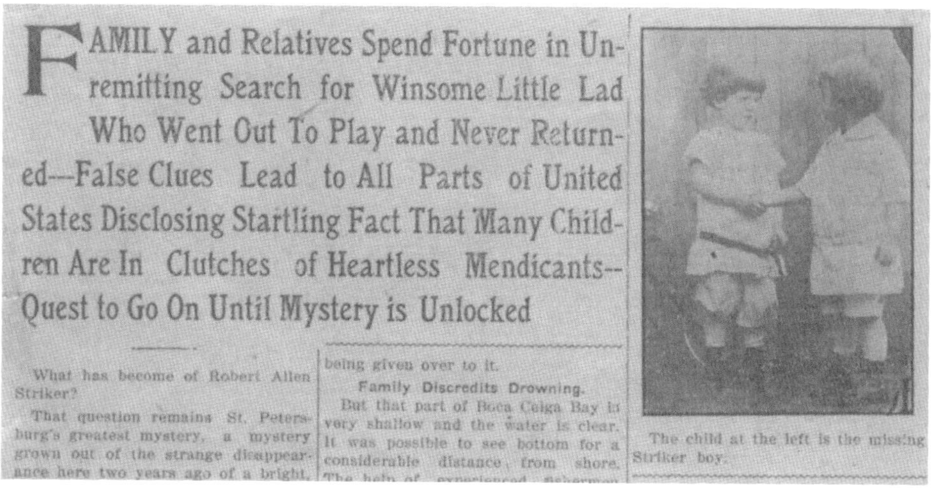

FAMILY and Relatives Spend Fortune in Unremitting Search for Winsome Little Lad Who Went Out To Play and Never Returned—False Clues Lead to All Parts of United States Disclosing Startling Fact That Many Children Are In Clutches of Heartless Mendicants—Quest to Go On Until Mystery is Unlocked

What has become of Robert Allen Striker?

That question remains St. Petersburg's greatest mystery, a mystery grown out of the strange disappearance here two years ago of a bright,

being given over to it.

Family Discredits Drowning.

But that part of Boca Ceiga Bay is very shallow and the water is clear. It was possible to see bottom for a considerable distance from shore.

The child at the left is the missing Striker boy.

Front page of *The St. Petersburg Times*, April 23, 1916, reviewing the mysterious disappearance of little Robert Striker.

Some felt that such a little child, weighing forty or forty-five pounds, might have floated far out into the Bay before sinking to the bottom in deep water, but the family was convinced that the search had been so complete this did not happen. Next they scoured the jungle surrounding the home, and there also produced not a hint of a clue.

Thoughts then turned to kidnapping. Robert's father, Burt Striker, had also remarried and was known to want custody of his son. Telegrams were sent to New York and soon ascertained that Striker was there and had no idea of the tragedy in Florida. This would have been the end of the story, had not Brown felt so responsible for the disappearance he offered a reward for information and launched a national search that produced some surprising results.

There is perhaps no clearer indication that even Gulfport had entered the modern age of communication than is shown by the way in which this case was pursued. The story was published and the child's description broadcast nationally, something that would have been unimaginable only a few years previously. Associated Press and the Hearst News Services were up and functioning and helped to publicize the search in response to the pleas of Brown and the New York City Police, who were officially in charge of the investigation, which would continue into the next year and for some time afterward. Sightings came in from all over the country and were tirelessly—and fruitlessly—followed up by the family, who traveled as far as San Francisco to look at small children put forth by those with both honest concerns and money-raising schemes.

Five years later, in December 1919, word was sent to St. Petersburg of an ad in an Ohio newspaper seeking the parents of a boy found at Allentown, Pennsylvania, and believed to be Robert Striker. A photo and a detailed description, including moles and scars, were sent to Uncle Brown, as the Richters' whereabouts were no longer known. Charles Brown knew, and forwarded the information to Mrs. Richter, who had returned to Brooklyn. She went immediately to Allentown and sadly discovered once again that the child was not Robert. Mrs. Richter wrote to Brown and the newspaper that the bogus claim had been made by a "notorious" woman for her own personal gain. She remained convinced that her son was still alive and would one day be found. But Brown's $500 reward was never claimed and nothing more was ever seen of Robert Allen Striker.

Accidents were far from uncommon among the town's residents, particularly the children. Jason Leonardy injured his hip, and the displacement was left so long untreated that it could not be reset. Little Russell Renney, only four, stuck his finger into the exhaust port of an engine that was awaiting repair on the family porch. He told his brother to "turn her over," and when the engine did just that, it severed the end of his finger at the first joint. Arthur and Mary Mann's two-year-old son James drowned by the Gulfport pier when each parent thought he was with the other until he was discovered to be missing.

Every family lost at least one youngster, usually before their second birthday, from a variety of ailments. One of Fred and Nelly (Leonardy) Roberts' children contracted typhoid during the 1913 epidemic. Walter and Maggie (Slaughter) Roberts lost a son and daughter in successive years, both under the age of two. Chester and Ruth (Roberts) Sawyer lost a two-month old son, one of a set of twins, in January 1914. Just a few months later the survivor was nearly taken as well, when lightning struck their Lakeview home. Ruth was lying down with the baby, Herman, when the bedroom took a direct hit. The bolt came in through the phone wire, ripped out the door casing and one wall, then split in half, one fork coursing across mother and child. Though Ruth was "shocked," it was the baby who was far more affected, the lightning running up his arm, over his neck, and singeing his hair.

She thought the only thing that had saved her life and that of her son was the felt mattress they were lying upon, and the fact that they were not touching any part of the metal bedstead.

The other fork of the lightning found their little girl Ophelia, about six, who was sitting on the floor in another room. It stunned her, demolished the back end of the room, blew four holes in the roof, and exited by the porch, killing the family cat.

2. Merriment

The late teens saw a series of giant parties featuring games and music, tales of the early days, and lots of food, often old-fashioned clam chowder or chicken pilau. There was always music, for everybody played and sang, sometimes entertainment by "postcard projection," the affairs went on until "very late." Some were held at the Casino, where all the surrounding porches were filled with sleeping children awaiting the finish of their parents' revelry. The Wintersgills alone hosted three or four parties a year, celebrating birthdays or anniversaries—or elections. They needed little in the way of an excuse to socialize.

One form of entertainment was a "tacky party," an event familiar to the locals but a complete mystery to northerners. The idea was to appear "as grotesque or old-fashioned as possible." At one such shindig given by the C.C. Sawyers (Courtney and Inez), some eighty guests caroused until "a late hour," the old settlers among them in antique costume and regaling the audience with their wonderful stories. Clarence Brantley told jokes and "used the bones to good advantage," and the Renneys played for dancing. Alex Leonardy's niece Bertha Wells won the prize for the oldest costume and Fred Roberts for the most comical. Fred was a party favorite for his cooking, his fiddling and this time his get-up, a combination "fisherman, cowboy and Chinaman."

There was good reason for the merriment; the beginning of 1917 heralded perhaps the best times thus far in Gulfport's short history. When the tourist influx got underway in January, it was reported that only two cottages and a furnished apartment were vacant. The Bay View Hotel, under its new management, was nearly always filled, and a passenger record was set one day when 10,466 people took a ride on the trolley. Six new cars were ordered to meet the demand, and there were renewed promises that the Davista trolley line would connect to the local one somewhere west of Davis Boulevard, since Fuller for the moment still controlled both of them. Fuller's son once told Sam Renney's son Bill this story about those days:

Every so often [my father] hired operators from out of town to come in, ride the car line and boat line, and attempt to catch cashiers and conductors stealing receipts. There was a group working in town and Sam came up to the front office and asked to see 'The Old Man,' who was, of course my father. He appeared completely at ease and undisturbed. He said, 'Mr. Fuller, all the boys have spotted your spotters, and you are wasting your money. The next time you have a bunch come in, tell them not to wear derby hats or coats, because we immediately know what they are here for.'

Despite this prosperity, or maybe as part of it, the cost of simple food staples was rising alarmingly. In 1917 prices were 25 percent higher than the previous year and 50 percent higher than they had been at the beginning of the war in 1914. As the year wore on, the mini-boom occasioned by Walter Fuller's activities earlier in the decade began to collapse, and eventually a receiver was appointed to take over the St. Petersburg Investment Company and its thirteen related businesses. Among those Fuller was forced to sell were the Favorite Line of steamers, the Boca Ceiga Boat Company, and the Pass-a-Grille Hotel; he would soon lose his entire empire, land, boats, and the streetcar line. Actually the townspeople were pleased that this would mean an opportunity for a new party to come in and redevelop the neglected services.

The faithful old Gulfport fleet came up for auction in the spring of 1920. The 75-passenger *Spray* was first on the block and brought $1,100, followed by the slightly larger *New York*, which went for $1,300. Both carried engines of about 25 horsepower. Finally came the *Gypsy*, the largest of the 3. Made of oak and copper bottomed, she had carried a 3-cylinder, 2-cycle 75 horsepower Kahlenberg engine, 2 lifeboats, and 160 life preservers. Still, the going price was only $1,000. When Fuller finally finished paying off his debts, the boat company managed to give 87¢ on the dollar, but claimants on the Investment Company did not fare as well. They got 3¢ on the dollar.

Davenport's optimism to the contrary, the European war did have a devastating effect on the infant tourist economy. The Casino saw only a few events during this period, when it was under the stewardship of Elbert and Ethel Ferris until Elbert's death in June 1917 at a sanatorium where he was being treated for an unspecified disease. Nathan McKinney then took over as Casino manager, no doubt helping Ethel, until they found a replacement in the summer, when Thompson C. Roberts accepted the job. He was a newcomer to town, unrelated to the local Roberts clan, but soon gained a connection when he married the Wintersgills' niece Mary McRoberts. Thompson continued to serve as a streetcar conductor, and most of the work of managing the Casino fell to Mary.

Their stewardship was not long, for the Casino was shortly put up for sale, described in ads as a large dancing pavilion, with a restaurant, lunch counter, cigar and refreshment stands; in all, a "cool and pleasant resort for dancing and other amusements." A year later it was still on the market, along with two boats, as "a good paying proposition," and $600 would take it all (the business, not the building, which was still the property of the St. Petersburg and Gulf Railway).

Elmer Wintersgill temporarily turned his attention to promoting a war economy by trying to get people to eat a weed called "poke," which, he said, made a very good salad green and grew just everywhere. He wrote to the newspaper with thorough instructions on how to plant, how to cook and how to season this new food. This followed another amusing letter in response to an article bemoaning the difficulty of raising cows in this climate. He said he'd kept three cows for years with no problems. Just pay attention to what you're doing, he advised.

But as usual that was not his only project. He had invented a new type of dredge that would separate the shell from sand to speed up the process of the eternal and ongoing dredging. Another most important maritime improvement was made in 1916 when a channel was staked out through Boca Ceiga Bay, clearly showing for the first time a navigable path through the sandbars from Davista to Gulfport to Pinellas Point.

Second Street (29th Avenue) in need of improvement. The Thomes home is on the left.
Courtesy Webb family

Some advances had been made in the paving projects. Pinellas Avenue (52nd Street) had been hardsurfaced all the way from the water up to Tangerine. This was considered the most important road in the community because it ran past the school and near the town hall and the church. New roads were being laid along Disston Avenue from 2nd Street (29th Avenue) to the Bay, from 1st Street down on Grant (54th Street) Avenue, and from Grant to Davis (Beach) Boulevard along the waterfront. Six inches deep and sixteen feet wide, they were finished by rolling and oiling. Parts of Lakeview and Pinellas within the town's borders were scheduled for an upgrade, the idea being to connect the shell roads with the brick pavement further north on Disston and the newly tarred St. Petersburg end of Lakeview. This was completed in the summer and now motorists could finally get through to the town's waterfront on something other than Gulfport's occasionally (or frequently) impassible and infamous sand roads. At last, the town fathers bragged, you can get to Gulfport by auto!

In fact there were two ways to get here; Lakeview, which in those days ended in a southward curve at what is now 59th Street, and Central, both of which were paved to Disston, though Central was much the better. Gulfport was now placed to be something new, a destination for "pleasure runs in the auto." Everyone celebrated the "dustless, mudless, waterproof and automobile proof" roads, at least until the final coating with "tarvia," which apparently was a real hazard while in its molten state. Mayor Elmer promised that while one way into town would always be open, it was really best to keep off the tarvia until it had fully hardened.

Walter Brooks invested in a Model T and soon started meeting the incoming trains and carrying people's trunks to their destinations. Visitors in those days, of course, came for the entire winter and brought with them an enormous amount of luggage. His son Mack recalled many years later the joy his father felt at seeing the completion of the road paving out to Gulfport. Between Maximo and Disston, Lakeview had been "deeply rutted in the dry weather and a quagmire in the wet, and the intersection at Lakeview and Disston a particular mess, completely impassible most of the time, but once the job was finished, as Mack said, "This put us at the end of a free-way!"

As many as 200 "machines" were now parked along the waterfront on a Sunday afternoon, their owners off to the beaches on boat excursions. Ironically enough, no sooner had this burst of traffic reached the town than the authorities found cause to rail against it ("Speeders fined by Wintersgill"). Mayor Elmer had erected a large sign at the entrance to the town proclaiming that the 12-mile-per-hour speed limit would be strictly enforced and violators would be fined $10. He claimed there was "utter disregard" for this regulation, and the penalty would increase "severely" until the nuisance stopped. Sure

Cars filling all the beach parking spaces.

enough, in the next session of the mayor's court, the first violator was found guilty. From then forward, speeders enriched Gulfport's treasury.

Even Walter Brooks fell afoul of the new law, when an officer arrested him for getting from Disston to Davis in one minute. His wife stood up as a witness for him, testifying that the "distance . . . was traveled in 1-1/2 minutes which was a difference of one half minute." The mayor didn't quibble; he discharged the case "on condition that the cost of witnesses be paid by the defendant."

3. The War Comes to Gulfport

At Gulfport Elementary, the students were made to grow Victory Gardens supposedly to help in the war effort, but much more likely to simply feed themselves. The home economics class certainly cooked from it. World War I, which had seemed little more than a distant diversion to that point, was coming closer to home every week. For some years there had been a rule against married women teaching, on the assumption that they would be taking away a means of support from more needy single women. However, with so many men going into the draft, this rule was modified to allow wives of serving soldiers to resume teaching careers.

In January 1917, the United States had broken off diplomatic relations with Germany, and a few months later began a program of draft registration for all men ages twenty-one to thirty-one. In Gulfport's precinct eight, eleven answered the call. John Guy Morrison, Grace Slaughter's husband, was the oldest at thirty-one and in descending order of age the following others were: Philip Clausen (Mattie Renney's husband) and Thomas Elmer Rousseau (Mabel White's husband), both twenty-nine; Clarence Stefanski (Carrie Roberts' husband), twenty-eight; Almeron Morris Renney (Clara Sjustrom's husband), twenty-seven; Harold Alexander Leonardy (married to Mazie Ray), twenty-six; William A. Nash, twenty-five; Joseph Roberts (who had just married Ida Wells), Percy Roberts (also newly wed to Ruth Stiles), and Robert Taylor Slauter, all twenty-three. Harry Scott, Nita Cusson's husband, was another local who registered on the appointed day, June 5.

Elementary students working in their Victory Garden.

Despite this draft call, the War was still more of an occasion for patriotic fervor than worry. Registration day was a grand holiday, with parades and speeches. "Slackers" who failed to register were condemned and actually, in many places, hunted down. The generation of men too old for the draft signed themselves up for the Home Guard, some familiar names among them: Norwood, Ermatinger, Singlehurst, Hibbs and Girard.

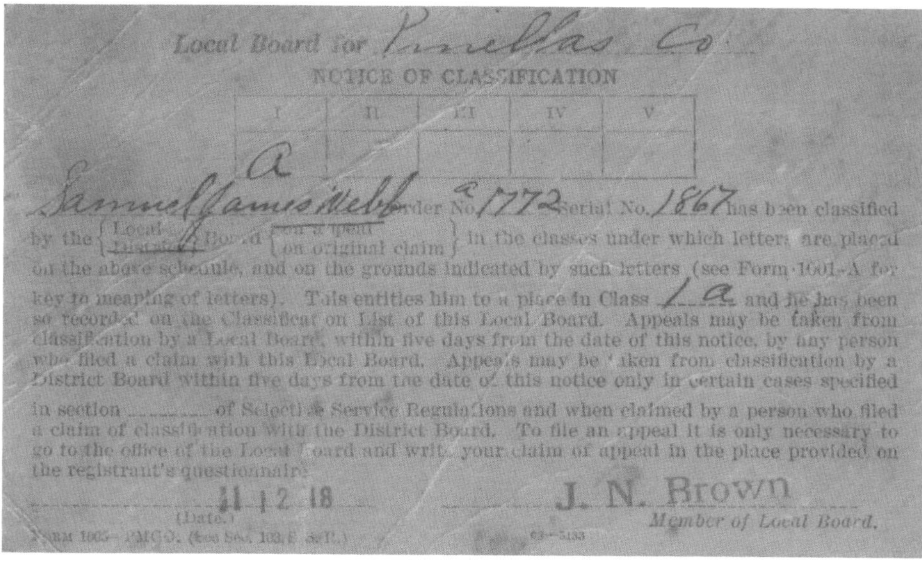

Local Board for Pinellas Co.

NOTICE OF CLASSIFICATION

I	II	III	IV	V
A				

Samuel James Webb Order No. 1772 Serial No. 1867 has been classified by the Local Board on original claim in the classes under which letters are placed on the above schedule, and on the grounds indicated by such letters (see Form 1001-A for key to meaning of letters). This entitles him to a place in Class 1 A and he has been so recorded on the Classification List of this Local Board. Appeals may be taken from classification by a Local Board, within five days from the date of this notice, by any person who filed a claim with this Local Board. Appeals may be taken from classification by a District Board within five days from the date of this notice only in certain cases specified in section .... of Selective Service Regulations and when claimed by a person who filed a claim of classification with the District Board. To file an appeal it is only necessary to go to the office of the Local Board and write your claim of appeal in the place provided on the registrant's questionnaire.

11 12 18
(Date.)

J. N. Brown
Member of Local Board.

Sam Webb's draft card. *Courtesy Webb family*

Others enlisted before the draft caught up to them. For example, Albert Whitted, in the air arm, of course, and Casey Ingram, a future Gulfport businessman, in the Army. Frank Davenport was another of these, joining the Navy although he must have been well past the age of required service. Ed Brantley, now twenty-four and a first mate on the Favorite Line until its demise, joined the Merchant Marine. The MacLeans's adopted son Joe was in Chicago taking an aviation mechanics course. Alec Stefanski, though well past seventy, was one of a party of eighteen carpenters who signed up to go north to help build camps for the Army. The pay was good: $33 a week and all expenses. Herman Wendell sold out his property and went north to design housing accommodations for workers pouring into the eastern industrial centers.

The ladies got into the war mode by helping to form local Red Cross units. That organization suddenly became everyone's charity of choice. One list of donors, published in late June, included the following Gulfport people: Dr. J.J. Robbins and John H. Parks each gave ten dollars; William A. Renney, Walter O. Brooks, the Ritcheys, the DeGrasses and both McKinneys all gave five dollars (Mrs. McKinney was the local captain of the drive); Mr. and Mrs. Whitbeck each gave three dollars, as did Parks' niece Mrs. Johnson; the Reverend MacLean, Sam Webb and Elmer Wintersgill each gave two dollars; while one dollar was donated by Mrs. William Johnstone, W.W. Swift, Harold Leonardy, Albert Schludecker and Lester Wintersgill. This is a pretty good indication of the social elite in the Gulfport of that era.

Local ladies organizing a War Bond Drive.
Courtesy Cloe Dance

Dr. Robbins' wife Harriet had just died, and, after fifty-two years of marriage, left the old Civil War surgeon alone in their large home, as their children had remained in Michigan. That summer he went back to visit and returned with a "considerable surprise" for his friends and neighbors in the form of a new wife, a lady named Elizabeth Tabor. He would enjoy this partnership only briefly, dying himself within the year. Elizabeth would also soon remarry, to a man named Walter Brooks, though not the postmaster or any of his relations. When yet a third, and again unrelated Walter Brooks would shortly come on the scene, town records become hopelessly confused. It was said that mail could be delivered to the respective families only by looking at the letters' postmarks.

In late spring the Red Cross women held a social and card party for the benefit of their wool fund (used to make sweaters for soldiers) and raised $50. "Pretty little flower girls decorated the guests." Next came a Liberty Bond drive, and Gulfport contributed an amazing $4,250. The "Drives" came one right after another. In June there was a War Savings Stamps Drive, and the Gulfport captain of that project was Mrs. Dobler, assisted by Ethel Ferris and Mabel White Rousseau. Mrs. Whitbeck hit the headlines with a pledge of $1,000, an astronomical amount in 1918 Gulfport. Postmaster Walter Brooks summed up all the campaigns in a July letter, stressing these accomplishments: the Liberty Loan quota had been $2,250, which the committee of Parks, McKinney and Dobler had exceeded by $1,800; the Red Cross Drive with the same committee had also gone over the top, as had the Savings Stamps Drive, even without Mrs. Whitbeck's whopping donation. The ladies of the latter committee had visited every house in town and got pledges from even "laboring people." Only three men, Brooks concluded, had refused to contribute. One can imagine their popularity over the next few months.

A further draft call came in July, and on this list were Chester Sawyer (Ruth Roberts' husband), twenty-eight; Andrew Roberts, twenty-seven; and Oscar Sjustrom, just twenty-one. So also was Raymond Cusson, twenty-nine, who was first denied and then granted an exemption, which allowed him to return to his work as an interior decorator. Exemptions based upon the inability of the draftee's wife to support herself and any dependent children, were claimed and won by Sawyer and Almeron Renney. Not many women, of course, were able to meet the criteria of independence.

Also on the July roll were the names of Alderman William Johnstone and Claude Coppins, son of his fellow council member, F.L. Coppins. Coppins joined the Navy, and Johnstone went off to the Merchant Marine. Of the rest, however, it seems few if any were called to active duty. The town's one fatality was Joe MacLean, who died as a result of the gassing he had endured while serving.

Philip Clausen failed the physical, Clarence Stefanski left the area, moving to Akron, Ohio, to work in the Goodyear plant there and take up residence with the Lovelace family, who had relocated the previous year. Elmer Ermatinger was sent to Indiana as an instructor in a "gas school," training recruits how to use their gas masks. William A. Nash failed to show up for his physical and was supposedly automatically drafted, although that doesn't appear to have happened.

The Schludeckers' son-in-law Jack Potts had in 1917 a severe incident of hallucination, in which he claimed to have killed two "chinamen" who were threatening the security of the country. The press reports described Jack as "normally bright and capable," but having obviously "slipped a cog somewhere." Joe Steinwinder, Jr. suffered something similar and died at the sad young age of twenty-one.

Taylor Slauter chose to join the coast artillery company, and his departure for the service was a community-wide gala event. First there was a party at the Casino, with dancing and refreshments. Then the next day Henry Slauter drove his son and a bunch of friends to Clearwater to meet the train that would take Taylor to his assigned camp in Mississippi. Accompanying the draftee were Lawrence Renney, one of the Brantleys (probably Ed), Guy Morrison and Courtney Sawyer. Some of them returned at once to Gulfport, and some stayed overnight to see him off the following day.

The Manns and the Wilsons visiting their relatives at Ft. Benning in 1918. Kneeling: second from left, Claude Wilson; fourth from left, Clayton Fulford; sixth from left, Arthur Mann. Standing: second from left (in bow tie) Harry Mann; fourth from left, Peter Wilson, followed by Luther Wilson, William Thomas Fulford and Tom Easters. *Courtesy Mann/Wilson family*

A remarkable photograph taken at Fort Benning in Georgia in 1918 shows enlisted man Luther Wilson receiving a visit from his father Jasper and brother Claude, his brother-in-law Harry Mann and Harry's brother Albert, who would marry Henry Weathers' daughter Sally. Though the Manns and the Wilsons would move here the following year and become important Gulfport citizens, they were at this time still living in the fishing village of Cortez in Manatee County.

The war had become a more serious matter, even here so far removed from its reality. Trains were commandeered to haul freight, not tourists. Shortages of necessary commodities forced the creation of heatless days, lightless nights, then wheatless breakfasts and meatless dinners. One day in February the *Independent* was astonished to report that there was absolutely nothing to do in all of St. Petersburg that evening, for the theaters and restaurants were forced to close and even the multitude of social clubs, civic organizations and church groups had cancelled their usual meetings. Gulfport's old teacher Arthur Norwood, now a prominent businessman in St. Petersburg, was appointed the food administrator of Pinellas County and took as his first project an inquiry into the high cost of fish. All this obviously did not bode well for the tourist industry, and things got a little tenser as the year wore on. Shortages increased, and pressure was exerted on everyone to be "patriotic." In one of the most chilling of local historic events, an Inquisition-like "Committee of Twelve" was established in St. Petersburg to test the loyalties of certain questionable citizens, people who may have made ill-considered remarks in public.

Mrs. Lucky voiced her opinion in a scathing letter to the *Independent* protesting the "comforts and entitlements" of German prisoners-of-war, who, she claimed, were "getting fat in criminal idleness" while good American citizens went "meatless, wheatless, and sugarless."

With such dramatic events on the world and national stage, the local political situation had simmered down, and everyone got behind an interesting opportunity for national glory. Federal investigators came to survey the Gulfport waterfront for the site of a coastal air station. The government had approved the construction of eighteen "airplane and balloon" stations along the nation's shores, primarily on the Atlantic and Gulf coasts. These would serve as defenses against aerial and submarine attacks, which were becoming a cause of great fear with the discovery of enemy subs not far off the eastern shore.

Gulfport was site number 6, and the investigators found the proposed location "a tract of land about 30 acres on the south side of the town." They recorded a good expanse of water facing the beach, with a general depth of 7 feet, and a shoal sandspit directly in front of the property. This sandbar extended out about 500 feet, and was exposed at very low water, but they felt it "could be removed with a moderate expenditure, and the water made suitable for seaplane operations."

The filled area was described as having a low irregularly shaped concrete wall and a dock immediately to the east. Houses abutted the property on the north, the actual town of Gulfport, which they called "very small." The report concluded that this was the best site in all of the Tampa Bay area for the following reasons:

1) It was located on the mainland.
2) It was near to possible "scenes of operations" (attacks?)
3) With a "good hard road" and an electric railway, accessibility was excellent.
4) There was proximity to centers of labor and supplies.
5) Very good drinking water and plenty of electric power were available.
6) Its exposure was on a well-protected body of water.

The negatives were enumerated as well, and they were all concerned with cost, which was found to be greater than at some other sites because:

1) Acquiring the property, located right in the town, would be expensive.
2) Further filling and sea walling would be another, considerable cost.
3) Additional dredging would be required to eliminate the sandbar.

As may well be imagined, this exciting possibility raised a lot of support locally. Even Mayor Al Lang of St. Petersburg got behind Gulfport's efforts, as did the entire County Commission. Nathan McKinney had been the official guide for the federal investigators and was unanimously chosen as the proper person to put forward the cause, so the very morning after council gave him authorization, he went to Washington to lobby the issue.

Not much time passed before Mayor Elmer Wintersgill joined him there to add another voice to the campaign. For Elmer it was a stop-off on the way to a New Jersey shipyard where he would volunteer his services as a caulker, which, he said, was his "former trade." In his absence, William Henderson, the current chairman of council, would fill in as acting mayor. Sam Webb would handle Elmer's real estate interests.

Nathan McKinney returned from Washington early in July and regaled everyone in earshot with tales of his travails in that "seething metropolis." Only a year or so ago, he said, one could still see horse-drawn carriages with elderly coachmen in rustic livery. Now it was all a wild blur of hurrying people and feverish activity. There were no hotel rooms, no waiters in restaurants and sky-high prices everywhere.

Of course, as it turned out, the airplane "landing station" did not come to Gulfport, no matter how hard McKinney and Wintersgill lobbied. A final decision was made in favor of Fort Dade, on the west side of Egmont Key, because the seaplanes, which ran to some ten thousand pounds, needed more depth of water in which to land safely.

The War brought with it one more trouble, the 1918 influenza pandemic. Early that year some vague reports began to be heard of a rapidly spreading "pneumatic plague." Up to that point illnesses in the crowded army camps had been restricted to measles and pneumonia, with the occasional case of meningitis, but by July the world began to recognize the "Spanish grippe" as a separate and dangerous malady. Though its origin was actually Oriental, it had first been noticed in Spain, where the effects of war were less, and soon spread throughout Europe. "Will it come here?" was the question of the day, rapidly followed by, "What will we do if it does?" Quinine was thought to be an antidote; that and rest were about all the medical community had to offer.

By October, with eighty thousand cases reported, even the national draft call was cancelled. Tampa and Miami were seriously affected and closed all public venues, including schools and sports events. St. Petersburg and the rest of Pinellas County were far better off. "SPIF," as it was called, claimed many relatives of local citizens, all living in other parts of the country, but here, no deaths were recorded by the time the epidemic began to wane in November. Irving Slaughter recalled 1918 first as the year of his marriage to eighteen-year-old Lillian Webb, and second as "a real bad time," when he spent three weeks in bed with the flu. Joe Roberts, then twenty-four and exempt from service owing to his class four status as a commercial fisherman, remembered that the epidemic was less devastating here than in many other places. It took the worst toll among young women, he said, especially the pregnant ones. In this his memory was correct, as the flu did rather mysteriously have a more serious effect on people under forty. It was this younger generation who contracted the illness in the few cases reported around here, all of which were relatively mild.

Promoters of course credited this to the fact that "air and sunshine are fatal to the disease," and there was speculation that residents had some kind of immunity.

When the armistice finally came in November, this town like so many others was the scene of shouting and shooting. Walter Brooks, for one, found a new way to make money when he started selling surplus goods, a business actually handled through the post office. His daughter-in-law Sydney said, "He'd get a carload and truck it down on the siding about where Webb City is now [she was speaking in 1984] and he would sell out of that car—people would go there—they'd sell army blankets, army shirts, those heavy shirts they wore in the First World War, khaki shirts, they were wool and scratchy. I think {Mack} wore those kind of clothes to school when he was a young boy—they were cheap. And they sold a million cans of army corned beef." The canned meat was particularly popular; people knew when Walter was off to lay in a new supply and tied a white cloth on their mailboxes to alert him to stop and make a delivery.

4. The Bridge

Gulfport had yet a final problem to deal with before entering the 1920s, and that was the coming of a bridge to the beaches, which would reroute a lot of the tourist traffic away from the town and its waterfront.

William D. McAdoo, said to be from Greensboro, North Carolina, had been around Pass-a-Grille for some time, living on his boat and buying up land, including some of the old Sawyer holdings. By 1918, he owned the north half of Long Key, about 500 acres (a good part of it swamp land), which he had bought from Fuller and company, whose plans to build a bridge across to the mainland had collapsed along with the rest of their empire.

To make his land holdings worth anything, McAdoo knew they had to be accessible by auto, and so he started his campaign to build a bridge over from Davista. As an opening move, he revealed the "discovery" of two mysterious wooden boxes in a shallow lake on one of the keys. The key got the name Treasure Island as a result of this stunt.

He refused to discuss their contents when he brought them into St. Petersburg, accompanied by armed guards, and deposited them overnight in a local bank. The next day they were shipped off to an unknown destination, and speculation grew that they were filled with the great lost pirate treasure old Zephaniah Phillips had sought all his life.

Ed Brantley, who was in charge of McAdoo's yacht at the time, said years later he had helped his employer set up the stunt, loading old chests with pig iron and burying them somewhere around today's Blind Pass. They then carefully staged the "discovery" and let rumors fly. Albert Miller, for example, told this version of the tale decades after the event. He said that once McAdoo was walking along the beach after a storm that had exposed shoals all over the Bay and the bottom of an old boat as well. "He saw a chest there. Well, he got in there some way and the chest was too heavy to do anything with," until he got some help. He never showed or told anyone what was in them, but "shortly after that, Mr. Macadou {sic} made considerable investments around town. Most people thought that he had probably come into quite a lot of money."

He received county permission to build a privately financed toll bridge, some five thousand feet in length, across water of an average three-foot depth, using the argument that it brought supplies closer to the soldiers stationed at forts on Egmont and Mullet Keys. Opened in February 1919, it cost twenty-five cents to get over and nothing to get back, and the beaches were now little more than a half hour's drive from the center of St. Petersburg.

The Casino struggled along, offering dances most weekend nights, but Gulfport was no longer necessarily the way station for excursions and consequently much less of an attraction. To make matters worse, by June 1919, there was a very serious threat that the streetcar system itself would cease to be unless someone came up with a plan to save it. Wrecking companies were already bidding on it for salvage when St. Pete voters came through, purchased it, and put a new economy schedule in effect. The Gulfport run would now be every two hours, from 6:15 a.m. to 10:15 p.m. outward and from 6:40 a.m. to 8:40 p.m. back. The fare was set at a flat ten cents, no deals or multiple ticket purchases allowed, and a pay-as-you-go system was initiated, eliminating the need for a conductor.

Though John Campaign White had bought the Mary Boat Company from the Wintersgills and moved it to Pass-a-Grille, the town still went ahead with plans for a new dock. It would be in its usual place, just in front of the Doblers' recently-acquired property, neighboring the old White homestead where the little nameless general store continued to serve the locals until the patriarch of that family died on February 13, 1918. Captain Joshua White left his widow Louisa, and five surviving children, two sons and three daughters. When John White took over the homestead, he closed the store and made it into a barn. Local lore suggests there was a hierarchy to the title of "captain." It was not uncommon for a man to be called "Captain Jim" or "Captain John," using his first name, but only a few were granted the honor of being "Captain White," last name only, as was Joshua. Captain White had been, of course, one of the legendary ones who had sailed far and wide back in the days of the schooners and sharpies.

In all, 1918 was a very bad year for the entire White family. John's sister Dolly, then about thirty-six, became a young widow when her husband Richard Bozeman died from Bright's Disease. Dolly was forced to open a boarding house in her St. Petersburg home in order to support her four boys. She received no help from the Bozemans. Dolly's mother Louisa and her mother-in-law Bozeman presented the most dramatic contrast possible in two women of similar age. While Louisa White, grossly fat and clad in laceless loafers, was strong enough to slaughter and hang a hog on her own, Esther Bozeman was an aristocratic lady who wore high-buttoned shoes half way to her knees, weighed sixty-eight pounds, and maintained that the blacks who had accompanied her family down from Georgia were still "her people." After Mary Elizabeth Barnett's death in 1916, Dolly's sister-in-law Mary Bozeman would become Tom Sawyer's third wife and mother of six more Sawyer children.

John and Laura's oldest daughter Rose Surber died in November, just a day after the death of her newborn infant.

Then there was Barney, John's younger brother, who while still a teenager had developed a reputation for "persistent drunkenness" and vagrancy. After one of his frequent arrests in St. Petersburg, he was sentenced to six months on a chain gang and remained in jail for several weeks without any apparent major change in attitude. Immediately upon his return he got drunk again, threatened the chief of police, and was not heard of for some time after that.

With the bridge now open, the new pier would see more use by tourists and fishermen than excursionists, and to increase its attractiveness, the recently formed Town Beautiful Society undertook to build a "rest house" there. Like so much else, this organization was run by Mrs. Julia Lucky, who assumed half the $11 cost of this undertaking. In addition to her work with the "Society Beautiful," she found personal philanthropic projects, like buying some of the old White property, a section known as "the wild orange grove," perhaps one of the original Barnett plantings along the bluff. This she promised to improve and donate to the city as a playground and park, which didn't happen, though the small wooded area a bit north of her home came to be known as Lucky's Park.

5. The Hurricane

The defining event of the early 1920s was the hurricane that destroyed the first Casino, which brought the town's most flamboyant developer since Hamilton Disston himself into the picture.

The great hurricane of 1921 originated in the western Caribbean on Tuesday, October 21, started a course north-northeast then veered north across the western end of Cuba. After that it took a "recurving" path, turning back eastward, and made landfall in Florida just south of Tarpon Springs. Southward from there to Fort Myers, tides rose seven to ten feet above sea level, taking with them beaches, bridges and seawalls. Without official measurements, the general consensus is that winds reached over one hundred miles per hour, and seven inches of rain fell, most of it between three and nine p.m. on that Tuesday afternoon.

The day before it hit, the *St. Petersburg Times* proclaimed the hurricane would not affect Pinellas County. "The storm failed to reach any force

Monday night, though there were stiff winds." Also dismissed was a remarkable barometric reading Monday at noon, 28.81 degrees, the lowest ever recorded locally.

"At that time," remembered Irving Slaughter, "there was no system of any kind to forewarn the people of an approaching storm. They had to use their own judgment and instinct, so it was only by the grace of God that no one was killed or even injured." In this, Irving was not quite right, for the papers had printed hurricane warnings from Key West to Apalachicola, but perhaps few took them seriously. There had not, after all, been a serious storm since the shore-shifting hurricane of 1848, long before any living memories. The people went about their business as usual.

Unbelievably, that very evening the citizens of Gulfport met to choose a slate for the November election. The caucus must have taken place at the town hall, because by that time the Casino had been reduced to kindling. Irving Slaughter: "The first Casino and docks were destroyed along with the streetcar tracks. All boats, fishhouses, net spreads were wiped out. The original shoreline came to within 100 feet of Beach Boulevard on the west side and to within two hundred feet of 30th Avenue. The entire area was filled by dredging and raised about 11 feet. The storm washed away much of this fill along the car track bed, and the tracks themselves up to Dellett Avenue. Large trees were scattered everywhere . . . the hardest wind came from the southwest."

"One house [Captain Sweat's] on Shore Boulevard west of Beach Boulevard was washed about 100 yards north and had to be relocated by house movers." Reverend MacLean's place, at 52nd Street and 31st Avenue, was damaged by waves surging 500 feet inland. Reports also stated, without specifying their locations, that the "Johnson, Dietrich, and Heller houses" were gone. Heller was the new owner of the boat line, and James Deidrick was an Ohio developer who had bought a house from McKinney on Shore Boulevard. In later years he and his wife Irma lived at 5619 31st Avenue South, which may have been the location of this building. A member of the Huckins family described the Deidrick house as not exactly gone, but "completely turned around."

In addition to having his house "blown flat," Jesse Sweat, currently a captain with the Boca Ceiga Boat Company, lost two boats. He managed to save the *New York* by taking it out to sea, then spent the next day or so ferrying supplies back and forth to Pass-a-Grille, which had been hit hardest of all.

With power and phone lines down, communication was knocked out for about thirty-six hours. Boats and bridges were gone as well, so residents in one city didn't know the extent of damage in the next. Barney White, always around somewhere, was said to be the last eyewitness to the sight of Pass-a-Grille before it disappeared into the storm. That town was thought to be literally wiped off the map. The next day boatloads of coffins were dispatched, only to discover that while the island was almost completely under water, there had been no actual fatalities.

In order to get out a special extra edition the following morning (printed by power generated from a motorcycle engine hooked up to the linotype machine), the *Times* sent reporters to Gulfport through the damaged roads, valiantly swerving between downed power and phone lines. There they woke Walter Brooks, who reported other heavy losses in addition to those of the docks and Casino, houses swept away and scores of roofs blown off. The sea wall was smashed into a "crumbly mess," and debris washed up as far as the Bay View Hotel. The entire shoreline was a jumble of trees, shingles and broken glass. While the waterfront was virtually demolished, inland parts of town were little affected, partly because early builders like the Whites had had the sense to elevate their homes in the time-honored way to avoid flooding.

Others were not so lucky. A vacationing "author and explorer" named Langdon Gibson, brother of famed artist Charles Dana Gibson, had just arrived at a rented cottage on the waterfront. His wife said something to the effect that she wished she could see what a tropical storm was like, well that wish came true. The house was "blown over and collapsed." The Gibsons were unhurt, but lost some valuable books and records and rapidly removed themselves to St. Petersburg's Poinsettia Hotel.

The Girard family was at that time living in the jungle area of St. Petersburg, in a two-story house that survived the storm though several others in the immediate vicinity did not. Jerome Girard recalled, "we had 32 people in our house and ran out of food." Among these were some neighbors who had recently arrived from the north with a supply of canned goods. Though the water was above the windows of the neighbors' house, there was a foot or so of air space in the rooms. "So my brother and I took our boat and a sack and dove under and got the food," which included a cherry pie. This they wrapped in oilcloth and carried out to the hungry group. "It didn't go very far with 32 people, but everybody had a bite."

Walter Brooks' first estimate of the damage, $100,000, was shortly reduced to $75,000, and a couple of days later, Council President Al Milne announced that the figure would not exceed $30,000. Total damage in Pinellas County was estimated all over the board, but was finally determined to be about one million dollars, perhaps eight million in today's money. However, were such a storm to hit now, it could destroy as much as fifty billion dollars worth of property, due to the excessive building in beach communities. This, of course, did not include the misfortune to the "complete fishing outfits" of so many residents. For these people, the desolation ran far deeper than simple material loss.

"The fishermen were the hardest hit by the storm because their boats, net spreads, everything was destroyed [that] they had used for their livelihood," said Irving Slaughter. This was the most serious of all the disasters, for to these men the loss of the means to make a living was more harmful than the loss of a house to a wealthier person.

Not many large vessels were sunk; the *Favorite* was the only such boat that went down, and it was later raised, though not in very good shape. The *Favorite* was ferrying tourists to the Statue of Liberty as late as 1970. But the smaller, working craft were completely wrecked, along with their nets and other valuable equipment. Some twenty-five were destroyed in Gulfport alone, most of them washed up in front of the Dobler Hotel, which had lost its roof and garages to the high winds. The Mann brothers' fleet was obliterated. They, like the Gleatons and other fishing families, had traditionally kept very much to themselves, and no doubt this crashing loss did little to lighten that natural reserve.

The fishermen would have to find other ways to feed their families that winter, and so while the authorities rebuilt roads and docks, they constructed stills and brewed moonshine.

Chapter VIII
Still Going

1. Shine On

If Gulfport had in earlier days a reputation for being a disorderly community, that reputation was nothing compared to the one that developed in the early 1920s. This was due in great part to the natural inclination of the fishing fraternity to adapt itself to the business of providing illegal liquor, which was accomplished in two ways, bootlegging and brewing.

Though it seems unlikely at first consideration, Gulfport's fishermen were among the strongest proponents of Prohibition. Violating this nearly unenforceable law provided them with rewards far greater than the small risks and smaller punishments and brought much-needed money to their destitute families. While simple transport of illegal liquor was the more lucrative activity, until the fishermen could get their boats back in action many of them concentrated on making moonshine.

At this distant remove from that era, most of us are unfamiliar with the complexities of the distillation process, which called for some rather sophisticated skills and materials. A cooker was required, preferably of copper. This had a cap over the open end, which acted as a primitive pressure relief valve, loosely sealed to keep the cooker from blowing up if the fire got too hot. A small copper tube or "arm," tapering down to only an inch, projected from the top of the cooker, with a coil called the "worm" attached to its narrow end, which, once in place, ran through a water barrel to the collection jug. Near the bottom there was a large hole fitted with a copper tube to drain off the spent mash.

The locals became experts at fabricating this machinery. The worm, for instance, was made from a length of copper tubing, filled with sand to prevent kinking and wrapped around a fence post to create the spiral.

A 1992 issue of *The Old Pinellas Press* gave a typical recipe. First the mash had to be made, by letting grain sit for a few days in warm water until it sprouted. Then, dried and ground to a meal, it was mixed with boiling water, and yeast was added. After "working" for perhaps four days, the bubbles subsided and the resultant reeking substance became sour mash, mostly carbonic acid and alcohol.

A fire of dry wood was built, hopefully as smokeless as possible not to cause undue attention, and the cooker heated up. The sour mash then went into the cooker so that the heat could vaporize the alcohol, which rose to the top as steam and escaped through the arm to the coil, where passage through the cold water in the barrel caused the steam to re-liquefy. The first run through this process produced a rather noxious brew that could be drunk, if purified somewhat by another run through hickory charcoal. The better brewers, though, would clean the cooker and make a second run at a lower temperature to clarify the liquor and improve the taste.

It was not necessarily, though, always this technical a process. One of the old ladies of the Wells family was renowned for her home brew, which she claimed to make in her teakettle by the simple method of holding a plate over it to distill the steam. Every few days she came into town with her horse and buggy and delivered "a load of wood" to her faithful customers.

A still was discovered in the area just about every week, for though home brew was not very profitable, given that no one had much money, it provided locals with something to do and something to drink. In February 1922, Taylor Slaughter and Sam Renney were arrested by a deputy sheriff after a raiding squad located a whiskey still on a beaten path just "200 yards from where they were working on their automobile." A tip had led the authorities to the still, found in a clump of ragweed about a half mile south of Central Avenue near Bear Creek. This was a serious professional rig of fifty-gallon capacity, and all copper including the worms.

A month later Church Gleaton and one of his sons were discovered operating a still on an island in Papy's Bayou. The sheriff's department "destroyed many barrels of mash," took the two Gleatons into custody and saw them fined $100 and sentenced to sixty days on a chain gang, though the latter judgment was later suspended.

A few days after that Joe Roberts was arrested for a similar offense, compounded by the fact that the gasoline engine he was using to power the still had been stolen from Captain Sweat. Roberts denied knowing anything about it at the time, though in an interview sixty years later he chuckled over once "finding" a catch of shine floating in the Bay in burlap sacks. Boca Ciega Bay was, of course, the ideal shallow repository for stashing illegal cargo during transfer between rumrunners and bootleggers. This is one reason, possibly, that caused Al Capone to buy a large section of land running north from Clam Bayou to Lakeview Avenue.

Gulfport law enforcement never dealt with such crimes. It was the sheriff's department that maintained the search-and-destroy effort against violators of prohibition, many of them from this town. One such was found dead drunk in a car full of moonshine on a St. Petersburg street. His penalty was a $25 fine for the illegal liquor and $5 for being drunk.

Guy Morrison's arrest was most unusual. The sheriff had discovered a still operating very near to the Morrison house and had his suspicions, but no proof of Guy's involvement. So he merely shut it down and took away the seven gallons of shine. The next day Guy went to St. Petersburg to report the theft, which must have truly made the sheriff's day. No record remains of Guy's punishment, if any, but it didn't stop his chosen trade, for in May of 1923, the "most elaborate" still yet seen was discovered at his home, along with a large quantity of fresh shine. This thirty-gallon all-copper device had an extensive coil, which the federal officers said would have "cost a large sum." Despite its location on his property, Guy said he had no idea what it was or how it got there. He spent the summer of 1923 in jail.

2. Recovery

Irving Slaughter said he thought that the newspapers made such "a notorious affair" of the storm that it stopped a lot of new people from moving to Gulfport. But while the hurricane frightened and amazed newcomers, it did not have the terminal effect on development that might have been expected. By the time curiosity seekers flocked to view the damage, golden fall days of breathtakingly clean and shiny air had returned to promise paradise again.

Towns everywhere hurried to patch up their images by making the most rapid repairs possible. Electricity and the streetcar line were both back functioning by Saturday, just four days after the storm. The track bed was rebuilt on the same lower level existing today, though the cars now stopped at Shore Boulevard, which, forever forward, would be the end of the line. Even the McAdoo Bridge to Pass-a-Grille was reopened before Christmas.

Plans were immediately put in motion for a new Casino and pier, though the latter was deemed the priority. (Reconstruction of the Casino would have to wait another three years, and then it would be a private, not municipal, venture.) The town seized the opportunity to rebuild a wharf that would serve both commercial and recreational purposes.

The Hotel Dobler, having survived the hurricane, was open when 1922 began. Unlike the Bay View, which was silent at the moment, it was advertised in the *Times*, claiming to have "everything new." The Dobler was described as being six miles from St. Petersburg, one half-hour by streetcar, with rates of

The Dobler Hotel opened 1922 after surviving the hurricane.

A successful fishing excursion.

three dollars a day (four dollars with bath), meals seventy-five cents. Other perks included hot and cold running water in all rooms and "fine flowing sulphur water" for health treatments. And of course, the famous fishing excursions. The Manns now owned the *Florida* and had it back in action by late winter, when Dobler guests reported one successful day aboard in which they landed 900 pounds of snapper and grouper. Another time the catch included a 3,000-pound devilfish. So they said.

The old *Gypsy* was now completely out of service, having been converted into a combination houseboat/floating restaurant anchored beside the Gandy bridge-building project. During the Gasparilla celebrations, it was made into a pirate ship, and when the Smithsonian sent a team to excavate at Weedon Island, the *Gypsy* was moved there as a café boat catering to visitors.

3. Principal Phillips' War

Almost all of 1922 and much of 1923 was devoted to an endless fight over a seemingly innocent matter: the position of principal of the elementary school. It all began in the spring, when the current principal, Edwin Dew, was "severely beaten" by the parents of a student he had whipped. Warrants were issued for the arrest of both mother and father, although no names were ever released in newspaper reports. Given the extreme partisanship of the events that followed, it can be assumed one of the more widely connected families was involved; the Nashes come to mind.

At any rate, to avoid further exacerbating this situation, the county school board announced toward the end of the school year that Dew would be transferred to North Ward Elementary. Parents at that school, aware of Dew's being "tangled up in a row" in Gulfport, protested strongly that they didn't want any part of him either. As usual, the complaint had little effect on the school board's decision, and off Dew went. Assistant Principal "Professor" Cecil R. Phillips was promoted on a temporary basis.

At the same time there was a crisis of another sort; the school was out of money. Gulfport's sub-district ran short of funds in the spring, as did many others throughout the county. About $675 was needed to stay open until the summer break, and the town at once gathered forces to raise this amount. A committee of Fred Roberts, Mrs. Ruth Sawyer and Cecil Phillips himself was appointed to see to the fundraising.

At a mass meeting held to deal with this situation, about $250 was raised, with pledges of $450 more, enough to cover the estimated costs for the final five weeks of the semester. A few days later a box supper—Henry Weathers serving as auctioneer—brought in another $64.15. By mid-April "vigorous efforts" were being employed to raise the $300 still needed, some of the pledges apparently having failed to materialize.

Despite all their work, the school supporters didn't quite make their goal, Gulfport Elementary was shut down, and Phillips was reassigned to Pinellas Park until the end of the school year. Before he left, he made a public statement disclaiming any responsibility for the deficit and the early closure. The locals then asked the school board for permission to re-open on August 21, to make up for the five weeks lost by the spring's financial problems.

The Mothers Club, the Social Club and the Mayor and Council stood firmly behind this request, and promised to work to raise the necessary funds.

There was an element of the local population that very much wanted Cecil Phillips to take over the school. The "professor" had appeared out of nowhere and would soon become the most forceful—and controversial—personality on the Gulfport scene. Phillips, now in his late thirties, was a graduate of Emory University, where he had been an outstanding athlete, setting records in track events and captaining the football team. He was a member of the Phi Gamma literary society, a star debater and ranked third of forty-seven in the class of 1908. What he had done with these outstanding credentials before his Gulfport assignment, and in fact why he had even accepted such a job remains unknown. But in the spring of 1922, with Edwin Dew as good as gone, Phillips was more than ready to become the new principal of Gulfport Elementary.

It should have been a simple matter of a county school board appointment, but that body refused to make the decision, stating that the Gulfport sub-board was coming up for re-election in June, and a change in personnel there might affect the prevailing sentiment. As Davista and Pass-a-Grille now fell within the Gulfport district, it was thought that perhaps a representative from one or both of these might stand a chance at gaining office. Obviously this portended an interesting campaign, or, as the *St. Petersburg Independent* put it, in Gulfport, "where there have been so many factional fights in the last few years, it is not unlikely this will be the warmest contest yet."

The current Gulfport board was composed of Alex Leonardy, W.W. Swift and A.L. Thayer, Sr. of Pass-a-Grille (an old seaman and collector of marine specimens). When the town put forth the same slate, opposition factions proposed Walter P. Fuller (representing Davista) and Sam Webb to replace Swift and Leonardy, Thayer seemingly meeting with everyone's approval. Then began an acrimonious bureaucratic hassle over election details. First it was announced that the town candidates failed to qualify because their nomination petition was signed by only seventeen voters, not the requisite twenty-five. Then the challengers were disqualified also, as they missed the filing date. Consequently the ballots delivered for the election were completely blank, forcing voters to write in the names of their choices.

As expected, there was a "deal of wrangling" on election morning. Each voter was made to present proof of his or her qualification, and failure to do so resulted in denial of the right to vote. The *Independent* filed its story at noon, claiming that feelings were growing so intense that trouble was "not unlikely." "Watchers" at the polls (and there were probably a goodly number of these) predicted that the opposition board was ahead.

This prediction proved to be right. Thayer took the lead with forty-seven votes, closely followed by Fuller at forty-two. Swift and Webb tied at thirty-five, Leonardy received only twenty-two and Pass-a-Grille's old settler George Lizotte garnered a surprising twenty-five. With a tie for the third seat, the county board announced it would decide and simply make the appointment, which, as current sentiments lay, all knew would go to Webb.

The incumbent town clerk (Swift) and his predecessor (Webb) were apparently at odds over this matter—and perhaps others. Factions were, as usual in Gulfport, developing, both for and against Cecil Phillips. Arrayed in his favor were Swift and Mayor McKinney, while Webb was aligned against him and supported by Mrs. Lucky and her minions.

A simple resolution was, of course, not to be. Before the county board got to rule on the matter, on the very morning following the election in fact, another ballot for Swift was found, throwing the whole outcome into dispute. Although this put his side ahead, Phillips complained to the press regarding the lost vote. The next day's headline read: "Corruption in School Election at Gulfport Charged." Judge Speare was called in to explain to the county authorities what had happened, for lo and behold, now two Swift ballots had turned up.

Someone had noticed that while seventy-five people had cast votes, only seventy-three of these were tallied. Henry Weathers, acting as clerk of the election, was asked to account for the two missing votes. This he did. One, he said, had blown out the window, been retrieved by M. DeForest Yates and brought to his, Henry's, house. The other was found still in the ballot box, which had been in a locked room at city hall. Speare certified the two as perfectly legitimate ballots, and the county had no choice but to accept Swift's election. They did, however, choose to renege on their decision to appoint a principal, and an alternative plan was set forth. "Let the parents pick," was the final word out of the county before they threw up their hands and tried not to think again about the electoral process as practiced in Gulfport.

This of course only opened the way to full-blown mayhem. To recover, perhaps, from the messy election that his supporters had won, Phillips left on an auto tour. Interestingly enough, his companion on this trip was St. Petersburg school superintendent George Lynch. Upon their return, things were really heating up in anticipation of the parental "straw vote" to decide the position of principal.

But before that could happen, new players entered the drama. The citizens who had met that fateful October night of the great storm had chosen Nathan McKinney and George Lewis to run for mayor and six nominees for council, from whom three would be chosen. McKinney easily beat Lewis, fifty-two to thirty-seven, who stayed on council to serve out the second year of his term, as did M. DeForest Yates. Charles Whitbeck was re-elected, and new members were Norman Fowler, a boatman who lived on Shore Boulevard with his wife Stella, a daughter of Captain Jesse Sweat; and John Cronkhite, son-in-law to the Sackriders. John and Kate Cronkhite had come to town with their daughters a few years earlier, returning briefly to Battle Creek for the birth of their son, John Jr., in 1919 (so he wouldn't be born a Cracker, said Kate). This election was noteworthy for the victories of Elsie Roberts and Abbie Webb, who ran for treasurer and assessor, respectively, and were the first women to win office. With one or two brief exceptions, a half-century had yet to pass before the town would elect a female council member.

Lewis resigned his seat in May and a man named John A. Brown was appointed to succeed him. Fowler also resigned, in July, and was replaced by Charles May, who, with his wife Martha was proprietor of the Florida Nook Tea Room on Shore Boulevard (where on Tuesday and Friday afternoons, classes in pine needle basketry were taught—Mrs. Lucky at work again?). When the whole Phillips issue came to a violent head the second week of July 1922, much of it revolved around this "young man of one year's residence," Alderman John Brown.

One summer evening, he said, he went to the home of Clerk Swift to pay his taxes. Hearing voices within, he paused outside the door, not wishing to disturb the family if they had company. The voices inside belonged to Swift and Phillips, who were talking about the list of names of parents eligible to vote in the upcoming election. Swift was taking the position that the list was not complete, as some wives had been included and some had been left out, and he felt that it should include all the mothers or none.

During this conversation, the Swift daughter, Olivia, heard noises outside and went to investigate. There she found council member Brown "hiding in a bush" near the window, and Phillips and Swift came racing out to see what was going on. Brown jumped up and tried to get away, but Phillips hit him, breaking the skin on Brown's forehead. In return Brown swung but missed, and all the while, accusations flew back and forth, the other two calling Brown a spy and worse.

The Florida Nook Tea Room on Gulfport Beach.

As Brown then tried to run away, a crowd appeared "out of nowhere," threatening some serious violence. Brown later claimed they "held him prisoner," while he was forced to admit that he had been sent by "two residents" opposed to Phillips taking over as principal. Swift stepped in and told him to get out quickly, which he did, jumping in his car and driving off.

The press loved incidents like this, so illustrative of Gulfport's rough and ready nature, and the next day's report was headlined, "Row Over School Causes Near Riot in Gulfport." When the mayor's court convened a few days later, McKinney heard charges against Brown, including "trespassing in a suspicious manner and disorderly conduct." The council member pled guilty and was fined $35 and costs of the court, which he immediately paid. He also publicly apologized for attacking Phillips, calling the action a mistake, a "boner."

All this, however, did little but whet appetites for further confrontations. One of the ever-popular mass meetings was called to consider the current messy situation, during which Brown and his fellow councilmen May and Yates were asked to resign. The other two serving members were not involved; John Cronkhite was away on a summer vacation, and Charles Whitbeck was either ignored by the irate citizens or on the right (Phillips) side of the issue. May and Brown resigned, but Yates refused to do so and was immediately set upon by the crowd, who held the sentiment that Yates and "his supporters" were behind the anti-Phillips movement. After his speech in protest, he was "smashed on the nose, kicked, etc."

Resistance was a futile gesture. Even if Yates remained on council, there would be only he and Whitbeck sitting for the couple of months until Cronkhite returned, and the two would not constitute a quorum and could not conduct any business or even appoint replacements for Brown and May. In all this, by the way, Mayor McKinney hardly figured; he had either lost control entirely or simply decided to stay out of the battleground, hoping that the Phillips forces were strong enough to carry the day on their own. Fred Roberts, currently serving as marshal, was no help either. He was busy preparing for a "big season," which involved seeing to the repairs of roads and sidewalks. Fred actually resigned from his police position in June when the situation heated up and was reinstated in September, neatly avoiding much trouble.

The *Independent* happily pointed out the promise of further mayhem: "Danger of a Riot Prevents Further Election in Gulfport; Further Fights Expected." The town, urged on by Mrs. Lucky, objected to this and sent a strong letter of protest to the paper, asking that "Gulfport" and "bloodshed" not be used in the same article in the future.

Yates held out just one day and then resigned, sinking the situation in Gulfport even further into "peculiarity," as it was euphemistically described. Nobody knew how to go about getting a new election without the authority of council to call one, so they put it aside for the moment to concentrate on getting through the parent straw vote, now scheduled for just a week later. Maybe after that, the newspaper editorialized, "Peace will reign in Gulfport—for a few days, anyway."

The election for principal was actually rather anti-climactic; with sixty-seven of the eighty eligible parents participating, Cecil Phillips won forty-five to twenty-two.

Hard on the heels of this vote, there was held another of the famous mass meetings to nominate a slate—somebody—to replace the three missing council members. The Swift/McKinney faction, holding the upper hand at the moment, were expected to put forth Otto Schludecker, Leander White and Roy Mann. While Mann was a thirty-five-year-old father of three, Otto was twenty-four and Leander just twenty-two. All were members of fishing/farming families, and extremely surprising choices for the more recently arrived elite personified by McKinney and Swift. Actually there may have been a good reason for Leander's selection; within little more than a year he would be married to McKinney's daughter Ethel Ferris and father of the mayor's first grandchild. When the meeting was held at the town hall on

August 8, the names that actually made the ballot were Leander's and Roy's. Old William P. Woodworth replaced Otto Schludecker, possibly because Otto's arrest record would not bear infinitely close examination.

The events of this summer had left the town's reputation in tatters. When Irving Slaughter came before a St. Petersburg court over a knife fight with a man named Hunter, the judge sitting on this case had by now had enough of Gulfport. "Conditions there, especially among the younger citizens," he said, "are not of the best, and a number of young men there have been arraigned on previous occasions on charges of assault." He promised to give future offenders "as much punishment as the law allows," in an effort to reign in the "trouble that exists there."

Embarrassed by this public scolding, a group of townspeople got together to form a Law and Order Society "for the purpose of assuring proper conduct on the part of some of its citizens." The men and women who met at the town hall began by recognizing Gulfport as "a rather lawless town," which, and here is the crux of the issue, "makes it practically impossible to induce anyone to buy property here."

With Sam Webb as secretary, Alex Milne took the chair of the new organization and opened his remarks by pointing out a sadly obvious fact: the municipal court wasn't working very well. When the rare case of an arrest by a Gulfport marshal came before the mayor, it was usually not prosecuted. Too often the miscreants would be released and later arrested in St. Petersburg for another crime.

One example was the kidnapping of the Brantleys' adopted son by his birth mother and a couple of accomplices, of which there was no local record. The four-year-old child, Walter, "struggling and crying from fright," was taken from his home just at dusk by two strangers who had gotten in by asking to use the phone, a deed the sheriff's office called "one of the most daring kidnapping plots ever to come to [our] attention." As the two strangers dashed from the house, Brantley grabbed his shotgun and fired at their automobile, which was rapidly getting under way. "A volley of shots from a revolver in the hands of one of the kidnappers was the reply."

The child was found in Tampa the next day thanks to Brantley's son-in-law Lloyd Rhodes, who trailed the kidnappers across the Bay. Thelma Freer, Walter's mother, had tried to steal him previously, although the Brantleys had legally adopted the child. One of the men was seriously injured by Clarence's buckshot, having taken four large wounds in the back and legs, which were left untreated during the escape and became infected. Later in the year, all three would be indicted by a grand jury.

The Law and Order Society appointed Mrs. Lucky and Lawrence Renney to go before the mayor and demand action, particularly to institute a new system of hiring lawmen. Proposed was a full-time marshal to be paid not the ridiculous pittance now allotted, but a real salary of $90 a month. They wanted to employ an "outside" man, they suggested, a novelty indeed in a community where officials and offenders, when not one and the same, were almost always closely connected.

With Mrs. Lucky and Sam Webb in prominent positions, it is fairly obvious that the Law and Order Society was more a further means of protest against the Phillips-McKinney faction than a serious attempt at constructive reform, because what effect, if any, these resolutions had on the local legal system is hard to discern.

Lawlessness by no means ceased in the town. There was a big brawl between a lady named Georgia DeBarry and much of the populace, when Mrs. DeBarry had her children fire off a few rounds to "show" certain people who were annoying her. What the police logs never mentioned in this case was that just after this occurrence, the DeBarry house burned to the ground. One evening a group of men and boys gathered outside her home, yelling and threatening to "tar and feather" her. Sometime after midnight they left and she slept for awhile, awakening at two in the morning to a loud crash. The place was ablaze, and she was lucky to get her children out, saving nothing but some clothes and a few small possessions. Thinking better of life in Gulfport, the DeBarrys immediately moved away.

By now it was fall, time for school to resume, and Mary Lou Faurot was considering a reassignment to Gulfport to teach in her hometown. Superintendent Lynch counseled against it, saying the situation there was pretty rough. Mary Lou said she had lived in Gulfport some years and knew the townsfolk, knew that they were really good people at heart and she would be just fine. However, she continued teaching third grade at Glen Oak for at least another year, as she appeared on the roster there in the fall of 1923, after her marriage to Richard Gray and the birth of their son Donald. Dick Gray, born in 1888, had come to Pinellas in the wake of his brother Miller, a real estate agent interested in the burgeoning Florida market. Gray had been apprenticed to a German painter in Pennsylvania and done some theater work, so he was exploring possible careers in the arts at the time of their marriage, when he was thirty-four to Mary Lou's twenty-eight.

The faculty, minus Mary Lou, met at the home of Principal Phillips to make plans for the coming year. Among the new teachers was Mary Mann Easters, wife of Tom and mother of Mildred, Virginia, Frances and Donald, a ten-year-old who would not live out the school year.

Things started off well, but just before Christmas the peace was shattered again when Principal Phillips became embroiled in another, more serious, matter. This time he was charged by Mrs. Henry Jarvis with "assault upon her person"

Richard Gray painting, one of many found about Gulfport, even today.

(and, of course, disorderly conduct). She swore out a warrant but failed to appear at the hearing, so the case was dismissed with a fine of ten dollars and costs. Five days later Phillips was arrested again, and a hearing set for early in 1923.

As usual the Gulfport police logs are extremely vague on the circumstances surrounding this brawl. The trouble had begun at a general store, where Mr. Jarvis, the proprietor, had entered into a name-calling match with Principal Phillips. After not only proclaiming him a liar but also threatening to cut his throat, Jarvis came to blows with Phillips. The principal hit back "several times, flooring him [Jarvis] each time." Mrs. Jarvis then interfered, attempting to break up the fight. There was some pushing, shoving and threatening between the principal and the lady, but the row itself came to an end.

After the Jarvises' non-appearance in court, Phillips counter-sued, charging Henry Jarvis with "threatening his life by sticking a knife at the throat," and "otherwise attacking the said Cecil R. Phillips." He also claimed a case of slander against Mrs. Jarvis for her use of "profane and abusive language while fighting complainant, thereby causing disorder and confusion." When the Phillips-Jarvis case was heard, a "large crowd" was, not surprisingly, present. The principal was accused of hitting Mrs. Jarvis, and she with "striking him with a pickle bottle while he was pounding her husband." Both sides were represented by legal counsel, but Mayor McKinney dismissed everything anyway, fined Phillips another ten dollars and sent them all home.

4. Truce in the Town

As the town came out of the chaotic summer of 1922 and into "the season," the council tried to accomplish some actual business, and they did at least manage to get some forty-one new streetlights installed. Mayor McKinney was elated to announce the sale of fifteen lots, most for "winter abodes." Construction had begun on ten new homes and cottages within a mere thirty-day period, with seventy-five or eighty more expected to be built during the winter.

An ad promoting an auction of Gulfport real estate stated the following: "There is no reason why ordinary cottages [elsewhere] . . . should sell for $4,000-$5,000 when better cottages on cement sidewalks on hard streets at Gulfport should go begging at $2,000 and $3,000. Gulfport has the Bay, the transportation on the streetcars, the brick road, the shell road and everything else that goes to make realty values. Still Gulfport values are lagging away behind everything else in the vicinity of St. Petersburg." Whether for the great buys or not, people were arriving daily, settling down and taking on leadership roles in the town.

As happened periodically in Gulfport, a different set of people were moving into prominence. There was Herman Berls, who had just come from New Jersey with his wife Lily and son Herman Jr. to take up residence on the water near the foot of 51st street. He and another new citizen, John Hucknall, were both also building on Davis (Beach) Boulevard. Etta Wilbur's brothers, the Yawgers of Battle Creek, put up a house on Dellett. Wirt Billings moved here with his mother Gertrude, an elderly lady who had been one of the pioneer settlers of Denver. Also arriving in 1922 were a couple who would become extremely prominent in the years to come. Harry and Kathryn Thorne, then in their thirties, came to Gulfport from Belmar, New Jersey, with their two young children, Robert and Barbara, and Harry's elderly

Harry Thorne's studio on 31st Avenue, drawing by Frank Mills.

father. Harry Thorne was a photographer, the official photographer in fact of several professional sports teams, and his images would define the look of the town long into the future. They set up a home and studio on 31st Avenue, just north of the Boca Ceiga Inn.

Still very much on the scene were the Yateses (who would soon build the grand "Twelve Oaks" on 27th Avenue), the Brookses, Reverend and Mrs. MacLean, the Cronkhites, the Bay View's Shirleys, Captain and Mrs. Griffin, the Wintersgills, the McKinneys and of course Mrs. Lucky. Mrs. Lucky's husband, Major Cornelius E. Lucky, died in 1922, at eighty-two, in his Knoxville home. She announced that now she would give up the Tennessee residence and live permanently in Gulfport in what was generally recognized to be the finest house in town.

The mayor felt that it was now absolutely necessary to do some permanent paving, particularly on the lower ends of Davis and Grant Boulevards and all of Shore Boulevard, roads notorious for frequent washouts during heavy rains. McKinney circulated a petition supporting these improvements plus the construction (or re-construction) of the old seawall, now almost totally in ruins. The cost for the paving would be assumed by adjacent property owners rather than by bond issue, and McKinney said he had their complete support.

When the town election came up in November, the slate was returned unopposed—or almost. Nathan McKinney won re-election with forty votes against one write-in for Mrs. Julia Lucky (could she have been doing this

Grant Avenue (54th Street) before paving.

herself?) Leander White and William Woodworth were elected to two-year terms in the seats they had assumed during the summer, and Roy Mann won the one-year seat under the same conditions. Elsie Roberts continued as town treasurer, but Abbie Webb lost her position as assessor to the controversial principal himself, Cecil Phillips.

When the 1923 season began, the Bay View Hotel was advertising on the front page of the *Independent*, the Shirleys still in charge. It was quite another story for the Dobler, whose first incarnation was nearly over. It never opened for business this year, and therein lies one of the oldest and most pervasive of Gulfport legends. The story has been recounted for these many decades that John Dobler once allowed a black worker to remain overnight in one of the hotel's attic rooms. When certain people got wind of this act, which went counter to the unwritten law that no colored persons could remain in town after dark, they attacked and injured Dobler, pistol whipped him, some say, so badly that he never regained his strength or spirit. Whether this event occurred now or at the Dobler's second closing in 1925 is not clear, for other perhaps more diffident sources claim that he simply wasn't a very good manager, and the hotel was poorly promoted and not well run, with never more than a few guests.

Whatever the case, it was announced in March that the hotel had been sold to a Mrs. Jane Baker and her daughter Gladys. For a price rumored to be $75,000, they acquired the 2-story stucco building with its 41 guest rooms, 19 baths and 91-seat dining room. It was described as fully furnished, with electric heat, a private bathhouse and a 5-car garage on a 120- by 600-foot lot, with riparian rights. The Baker women took over at once and renamed the establishment the Gulfport Inn.

The infrastructure and amenities of the town were just beginning to take shape during this period. Firefighting had been extremely primitive and not at all effective, as has been seen when the well-water-and-bucket methods were employed. The Jesse Easters home, located on Pinellas Way between Tangerine and Lakeview, was lost in a 1922 fire, the third to go down in the same spot in just three years. Although several fire companies responded, there was simply no water in the area and only an adjacent chicken coop and its contents were saved.

Firemen practicing in an undeveloped area of Gulfport.

The first improvement in this department was the acquisition of a hand-pulled two-wheel cart, on which was mounted a soda-acid tank and a hose reel. Now fires could be fought wherever this cart could be hauled, or, if close by the waterfront, as far as the hose could reach. Still, one of the Gulfport Roberts families were unable to save their home in a March 1923 fire. The father was away fishing at the time, but the wife and ten-year-old son escaped unharmed. Soon after this the town acquired a motorized fire vehicle when a Studebaker truck was donated for public use. After parts of its body were removed, air and water tanks were mounted. The pressurized air served to expel the water.

There was some kind of privately owned water system functioning in the early 1920s, for in January, 1922, the council had ordered this company to stop pumping on nights and Sundays and to find some way to quiet the noise the pumps were making. The waste removal systems were still very basic. Outhouses contaminated the nearby ground water, which was all too often pumped up for drinking. Indoor plumbing was beginning to make headway also, along with septic tanks, which, especially in low-lying areas, were prone to overflow.

Gas lines were installed by the summer of 1923, and the telephone system was coming along, too, as the Peninsula Telephone Company took over the Gulfport franchise and began the conversion to dial operation. The town dump was still located on Fiddlers' Flats.

The spring of 1923 was a period of relative peace. Fred Roberts again resigned as marshal and Irving Slaughter took over. He lasted about three months, until John Campaign White regained the position during the next Phillips adventures, which began at the end of the school year when the principal's position again came up for renewal. The old animosities had not disappeared. Trustees Fuller and Thayer recommended that he be returned to the job, while Swift ("formerly a close personal and political friend") changed his mind and stood against the re-appointment. It's all politics, said Phillips publicly, claiming that the heart of the matter was a "lively fight" for mayor looming on the horizon.

Mrs. Jerry Wells, still living in the Oak Park area, took an active role in the new debate. She scorned the idea of politicians becoming involved in what she felt should be the concern of parents only. Julia Lucky had a few things to say, also. As a "close, personal friend of Swift," she was working against Phillips primarily to defeat McKinney, to whom, for some reason, she had taken an aversion (the forty to one loss?). This only exacerbated the situation, for Mrs. Lucky was not in a good position to say much about the elementary school, having no children therein and still spending a great deal of her time in her Tennessee home. Phillips made sure these facts were known in a paid advertisement in the *Independent*.

In a surprise move, though certainly not one without precedent, Mayor McKinney left for a long vacation toward the end of June 1923, claiming ill health. While his opponents felt his condition was more a matter of sure knowledge that his political career was on the decline because of his association with Phillips, McKinney and his family did indeed have considerable chaos on their personal plates. In March their daughter Ethel had suddenly married young Leander White, eleven years her junior. No announcement of the wedding appeared, though there was a party held for the "recent bride and groom" by a friend of Mrs. McKinney. Guests received favors in the form of boutonnieres of orange blossoms and snapper novelties containing party hats, which they were requested to wear. (Did "Ironhead" White comply?) The McKinneys had a house built for Ethel, Leander and their new daughter Bertelee, using reclaimed lumber from the recently destroyed waterfront buildings, particularly the Casino.

5. The School Brawl Returns

Gulfport, the papers said, was "now on the verge of another political row." But by leaving town, the mayor chose not to become involved in the "stiff political fight in the offing," and left affairs in the hands of the strong and steady John Cronkhite, who became acting mayor by virtue of his position as President of Council.

Of course, that was not the end of the inflammatory situation, not in Gulfport. The county school board was willing to go along with another year of Phillips, but his support in town was slipping. While the board claimed that sixty-two of the seventy-five concerned families supported Phillips as principal, his influential enemies, Clerk Swift and Mrs. Lucky among them, were apparently gaining strength, and protesters were regularly showing up at board meetings in Clearwater.

No matter; the county gave him a contract for the 1923 to 1924 school year and an 11 percent raise. Peaceful means having been unsuccessful, the town turned to its preferred alternative: violence. As Phillips was walking home (wherever this was) from school one evening, he encountered "two strange men loitering about the school house." At least one of them followed him and shot at him. An interesting sidelight on this unusual educator is shown when he "returned fire."

When he arrived home, amazingly unharmed, his wife reported more suspicious loiterers, so Phillips crept into the dark backyard and on a signal, his wife switched on the lights, revealing a stranger with a pistol aimed at the house. Phillips fired four more shots, and two came back at him. Lawrence

Renney and Irving Slaughter heard the gunfire and arrived to investigate. All they saw was an automobile speeding off eastward. Phillips claimed the occurrence had been a deliberate attempt on his life and swore he could identify the gunman.

For a couple more nights gunshots were not rare in the evening air, occasioning the newspapers to report more "manifestations of bad blood in Gulfport politics." That it was politically motivated, indeed, remained Phillips' feeling as well; he attributed the attacks to irregularities in the "village finances," which he had encountered in his position as tax assessor for the town.

Acting Mayor Cronkhite had foregone his usual summer away to see to town business, and at once asked for the resignation of Marshal Irving Slaughter and appointed in his place John Campaign White. White, the town's first marshal and now a manager for the Hibbs Fish Company, was also now the father-in-law of Ethel McKinney. This meant he was most likely aligned to the Phillips side in the never-ending battle. Ironically, Irving Slaughter, looking back at this time from the distance of more than sixty years, called his days as marshal the best of his life and said if there were any time to which he could return it would be this.

The rest of the summer was spent in speculation over what course Cecil Phillips would choose, if he did indeed not return to Gulfport Elementary. First he considered becoming a candidate for the state legislature, then sharply on the heels of that possibility came the offer of an office within the Boy Scouts organization. He had been active in Scouting, helping with summer camps, and was particularly noted as a great storyteller. Though newspaper articles always pointed out that Phillips had "made a decided success" of his term as principal, there were now a considerable number of parents in the town who wanted no more part of him.

A group of these sent a delegation to the county school board, asking permission to enroll their children in other schools if Phillips returned to Gulfport. Speculation grew that he would withdraw "in favor of politics" from both the school and his position as town assessor. This latter was now being questioned as well, and the council called a hearing to investigate charges that his assessments were unjust and that he had failed to turn over the tax books on time. Phillips refused to attend the hearing, but sent a response. His job, he said, was complicated by the fact that he couldn't get tax books from the previous year, so he had to rely on figures from the county appraiser's office. And the assessments weren't due in July, anyway, but September. If council refused to pay him for his work, he concluded, he would sue. Council removed him from the assessor's office.

Swift, now firmly on the other side, immediately announced that he would resign from the Gulfport school board if Phillips was retained. Walter Brooks, another of the anti-Phillips coalition, explained that Swift's resignation was conditional, and that if Phillips went Swift would stay.

Phillips' next move was decidedly the least popular of all. Finding himself one day on a streetcar with old William P. Woodworth, he got into an argument with the venerable gentleman. To the principal, Woodworth's remarks were nothing but lies, and he was forced to respond with a "long and impassioned speech." When even this did not do to change the old settler's opinion, Phillips hit him.

For this offense Phillips found himself in the local court, where he pleaded not guilty to the charge of assault and battery on the grounds that the offense did not occur within the town limits. This didn't carry much weight with Cronkhite, who fined him $40 and costs and ordered him bound over to the next term of the circuit court. Striking a man "aged and crippled, with a twisted hand," one who had lived in Gulfport for over a quarter century, was considered irredeemable.

Marshal White had his hands full for the next few days, as fights broke out all over the village, due to the citizens expressing "differences of opinion."

Just a few days after the Woodworth incident, Phillips went to an executive session of the county school board, which was also attended by some fifty Gulfport parents, who represented over one hundred students, about two-thirds of the total enrollment. They presented a petition accusing the principal of inefficiency and misconduct and finished by stating unequivocally that they would not permit their children to attend if Phillips continued in his position. To put the lid on the situation, a letter from Gulfport school board member Thayer was read, in which he, too, rescinded his approval of the principal's appointment.

Facing the inevitable, Cecil Phillips officially withdrew. His friends saw this as an altruistic move, the only way to end the row, which had now become, they insisted, entirely political. This may have been true, but the town didn't want to leave the public with that impression. Walter Brooks was chosen as spokesman to write an open letter, claiming that the situation was due to conduct by Phillips "such as would mitigate against his remaining in the school," and not politics at all. Of course not.

School opened, minus a principal, a teacher, and forty children whose parents were still holding out for Phillips' return, or, failing that, his agreement to teach the pupils privately.

The protesters were now also demanding that another teacher be dismissed. This was Miss Ernestine Wilbur, daughter of Ernest and Etta, who lived on Sunset Avenue (56th Street) and were friends of the McKinneys. Nothing apparently came of this movement, as Miss Wilbur taught for some years into the future. But Phillips said he had told the school board that his removal would not end the unpleasantness in Gulfport.

County Superintendent Blanton had tried to ignore the situation but was now forced to visit the school and name a new principal. At the moment Mrs. Lily Berls was acting in the position. She was a graduate of Columbia University, a rather outstanding credential for a woman of the time, and soon received official sanction to assume the office. The school now had dwindled to only sixty pupils, a bare third of its proper enrollment. Phillips had set up a private school in the Sunset Avenue house of Mrs. Catherine Lowe, despite rumors that he would be visited at night by those who still wanted to run him out of town. The little school had attracted some forty or forty-five students, and the remainder had disappeared into a variety of school and non-school settings.

Phillips in the meantime had accepted a position as field agent for the Florida Game and Fish Protective Association, a job in which he would organize county units of the agency throughout the state. And so he left Gulfport and took up this new work, at least until his 1926 arrest for illegally killing deer on an island near Fort Myers. When Cecil Phillips died in Deland in 1930, his obituary remarked with massive understatement that he was "very well known here."

Thus the "hot wrangle" was dying down as some of the parents began to give in, and Gulfport Elementary's enrollment crawled up to ninety-seven. It was hoped these new options for the dissenters would perhaps end the endless row for once and for all.

And strangely enough, it did. Mrs. Berls' administration lasted only the one year, 1923 to 1924, after which she became principal at the new Childs Park Elementary. She was succeeded in Gulfport by another Phillips, this gentleman a very different type from his predecessor. Charles M. Phillips held an agricultural degree from Cornell University as well as a master's in education from the University of Florida, and gave up "agricultural work" to begin his teaching career that year. He would put the little school on a firm foundation before moving on to become the first principal of the new Disston Junior High School. Then Mary Lou Gray would begin her long reign as the town's foremost educator.

Elmer Wintersgill, who always had one or two extra careers in the wings, became a deputy sheriff, and it was in that capacity that he was credited with "solving" a bizarre mystery involving gunshots and screams in the middle of the night. Alerted by a neighbor frightened by an unholy noise, Elmer raised a posse and set out to investigate. What he discovered was not a victim and perpetrator of a crime, but a party of five men hunting skunks, or, as they would have said, polecats. The men had decided to quit about 1:30 a.m. in the morning and called in their dogs by firing shots in the air. The howling dogs were on the scent of skunk and didn't want to give up the chase. So much for the shots and screams.

But Elmer Wintersgill's career in Gulfport politics was finally at an end, when in 1923 he lost to John Cronkhite fifty-eight to twenty-three in a bid to become mayor for the seventh time. There was some speculation that the vote would be contested, due to "balloting irregularities," but with no close races at stake, nothing much ever came of the idea.

The new council took office without him. When the town books were audited, it was officially reported that there was a cash bank balance of $7,221.22. Postmaster Walter Brooks announced his office's year-end income as $919.69, and compared it with the $402.57 he had taken in at the beginning of his tenure in 1915. He said there had been twenty new houses built in Gulfport just during the previous year. To what did the town owe its success? "The climate," he said, "is just a little better here than anywhere else."

Afterword

THOSE PEOPLE WHO HAD ARRIVED in the desolate Point Pinellas so many years ago now seemed as remote as characters from an ancient book, but when Florida moved into the bizarre period of speculative mania known as "boom times" some were actually still around: Jacob Disston, Will McPherson, the Norwood brothers, John Francis Girard and old "Tzar Bennett" among them. Tim Kimball was still living just where he had settled upon arrival from New Orleans a half century earlier. William Neeld and George Meares were on their original homesteads, too.

Alex Leonardy had died in 1924 at seventy-two, just days past the golden anniversary of his wedding to Martha Jane Slaughter, who was now the senior member of her clan. Their three sons and four daughters were Flint (now living in Ft. Myers), Henry and Harold, Viola (Mrs. Henry Weathers), Lorena (Mrs. Angus Nash), Nelly (Mrs. Frederick Roberts) and Vera (Mrs. Joseph Johnson). The funeral was attended by 200 people, and a line of cars over a mile long proceeded from the Leonardy home to Glen Oak Cemetery. His pallbearers were all grandsons: Clyde Leonardy; Harry Weathers; and Barney, Harvey, Jason and Glen Nash.

Leonardi's Elixir for the Blood was still going strong, even though Alex wasn't, now claiming to keep the user young eternally. Leonardi's Liver Aid had turned into Leonardi's Cough Syrup, and promised to cure as many if not more ills, creating some speculation that it might have been one of those alcohol-filled remedies so popular during Prohibition. Leonardi grapefruit were still on the market, at twenty cents a dozen.

Henry and Mary Nash Slaughter were both living. Their children were Minnie Clara Nobles, Margaret Aurelia "Maggie" Roberts, Grace Louise Morrison, Christine Rebecca Renney (who would outlive them all, dying in 1988 at the age of one hundred), Inez Lucy Sawyer, Florence Smith, Robert Taylor Slaughter, Henrietta Slaughter (born mentally disabled, she never married, living with her mother until Mary's death in 1937 and after that with one or another sister) and Willis Irving Slaughter. Christian Nash, the little grandmother of the vast Nash clan, had died in 1920 at the age of eighty after fifty years local residence. She left eight children, sixty-five grandchildren, fifty-four great-grandchildren and a great-great-grandchild.

Mary Elizabeth Barnett Sawyer Quinn had died in 1916. Jack Quinn died in April 1922, at fifty-three, drowned just offshore in front of the Dobler Hotel, where some small children found his body. He had been hauling wood from the end of the pier to the shore in a heavily loaded boat when he suffered some kind of fatal attack. Raymond Quinn and his sisters Lily, Julia and Ella were now complete orphans, though Mary Elizabeth's Sawyer children, Chester and Gladys, would have their father Tom around for some years to come. He lived to eighty-two.

James Barnett, Jr. was a familiar and beloved figure about town. "Uncle Jim" (for he was that to most of the Gulfport population) stayed with various relatives, did odd jobs, ate whatever people gave him, and always had a piece of candy for the kids.

Laura Barnett White was hanging onto her marriage to John Campaign, though it would very shortly take the severest of all possible blows, when she would defend him from an incest charge by their sixteen-year-old daughter Lucille. They did eventually divorce, and he would marry Bennie Roberts' ex-wife Amanda and move to Panama City, where he died at the age of seventy-six. Laura did not remarry, and made it almost as long as Christine Renney, dying just before her ninety-forth birthday.

Three of the White children were gone at unreasonably early ages: Rose in childbirth at twenty, Vernon from appendicitis at eighteen, and Dolly at only fifteen. The other seven were Leander (husband for now of Ethel McKinney), the twins Eva (who married Barney Nash) and Ernest, Lucille, Charles, Clarabelle and Dorothy (who married Arthur Benn). Ethel McKinney White's step-grandfather, the old Investment Company's B.F. Measey, died at seventy-six in 1923, and the E.E. Wilburs took over the old Measey house.

Malcolm and Elizabeth Wintersgill McRoberts were gone, but Lester and Elmer lived on. Lester would for years be a Gulfport fixture—night watchman for the police, volunteer fireman, goat farmer. But Elmer would die just before Christmas 1926 in the most appropriate place possible—the town hall.

Jane Daniels, in-law to the many Thomeses and Webbs, died in June 1922, at the age of sixty-seven. Her husband John remained in "Castle Chalon" until his own death just a couple years later. His obituary described the "aged man" living in the "ruins of the old chateau on Disston Boulevard," a "hodgepodge" of building materials in the middle of which he sat every day, alone, with never a visitor. The strange structure was destroyed by a fire of unknown origin shortly afterward.

The young flying hero Albert Whitted, son of early Gulfport settlers T.A. and Julia (Phillips) Whitted, died in August 1923, downed in the Gulf off Pensacola when a propeller on his plane came loose and damaged the machine. The St. Petersburg municipal airport now bears his name.

Sam Renney's old nemesis Queen the alligator finally came to the end of her long and cantankerous life. Renamed Juliet, she was killed by her mate, Romeo, while fighting him.

Old Alonzo Hoyt had died in Tampa in 1918; William Woodworth lived on, as did Alexis Cusson, William Renney and Joe Steinwinder. The Webbs, the Renneys, the Gleatons, the Manns, the Schludeckers, the Robertses and the Brookses all continued to live in Gulfport. But they were oh so soon to be surrounded by a type of wildlife unlike any they had encountered in the olden days: "binder boys" in straw hats and white buck shoes pushing lots in nonexistent subdivisons with glamorous Mediterranean names.

It all began at an auction of some land Fuller held at the intersection of Disston and Central Avenue. It was a last desperate move, he said, "to save a sinking ship," to unload the lots he had acquired, burdened under a "maze of interlocking mortgages . . . and liens." The prices were going fairly well, and Fuller was beginning to think he might be able to pay off some debts, when two fashionably dressed gentlemen arrived in "an enormous old (but expensive) Pierce Arrow." These men never bid, mingled with the crowd or spoke to anyone, so speculation ran wildly through the community of brokers and buyers.

The tall, blond and reportedly handsome one then approached Fuller and offered him a half million dollars for some twenty-one hundred acres of land along four miles of unbroken waterfront, most of the southwest part of the peninsula. This was the mysterious Jack Taylor, who would bring into the midst of this raucous, clannish, tight-knit little town one of the most glamorous resorts in the country. Instead of alligators, scrub palmetto and moonshine stills, there would be opera singers, golf champions, silent movie starlets, socialites, Monganthaus, Zigfelds and Babe Ruth.

And life in Gulfport would keep on going south.

Selected Bibliography

Books

Allen, Frederick Lewis. *Only Yesterday: An Informal History of the 1920s*. New York: Harper & Row. 1931.

Arsenault, Raymond. *St Petersburg and the Florida Dream, 1888-1950*. Virginia: The Donning Company, 1988.

Baker, Rick. *Mangroves to Major League: A Timeline of St. Petersburg, Florida (Prehistory to 2000 A.D.)*. Southern Heritage Press, St. Petersburg, FL, 2000.

Bethell, John A. *Point Pinellas*. St. Petersburg, FL: Great Outdoors Publishing Company 1914, reprinted 1962.

Board of State Institutions. *Soldiers of Florida in the Seminole Indian, Civil, and Spanish American Wars*. Florida: Privately printed, 1903.

Breen, T.H. *Imagining the Past*. Wesley, MA: Addison-Wesley Publishing Company, 1989.

Craven, Robert H. *F.A. Davis Company, 1879-1979*. Privately printed,1979.

Dowling, Julia Jane Howell. *Stories Told by Julia*. Printed by Pasco County Historical Society, 1987.

Federal Writers Project of the WPA for the State of Florida. *Florida: A Guide to the Southernmost State*. New York: Oxford University Press, 1939.

Frantzis, George T. *Strangers at Ithaca*. St. Petersburg, FL: Great Outdoors Publishing Company, 1962.

Fuller, Walter P. *St. Petersburg and its People*. St. Petersburg, FL: Great Outdoors Publishing Company, 1972.

Fuller, Walter P. *This Was Florida's Boom*. St. Petersburg, FL: *St. Petersburg Times*, Florida, 1954.

Gould, Rita S. *Pioneer St. Petersburg*. St. Petersburg, FL: Page Creations, 1987.

Greer, Thomas H. *A Brief History of Western Man*. Harcourt, Brace, and World, 1968.

Grismer, Karl H. *History of St. Petersburg*. St. Petersburg, FL: Tourist News Publishing Compnay, 1924.

Gulfport Historical Society. *Our Story of Gulfport*. Privately Printed by the society, 1985.

Hurley, Frank T., Jr. *Surf, Sand, and Post Card Sunsets*. Privately printed, 1977, reprinted 1989.

Jackson, Page S. *An Informal History of St. Petersburg*. St. Petersburg, FL: Great Outdoors Publishing Company, 1962.

Kennedy, Margery and Doris Waltz, eds. *Pass-A-Grille: A Patchwork Collection of Memories*. Printed by Women's Fellowship of Pass-A-Grille Beach Community Church, 1981.

Meares, Herbert A. *Lovingly Yours, Athel*. Privately printed, 1997

Parry, Albert. *Full Steam Ahead! The Story of Peter Demens*. St. Petersburg, FL: Great Outdoors Publishing Compnay, 1987.

Perry, I. Mac. *Indian Mounds You Can Visit*. St. Petersburg, FL: Great Outdoors Publishing Company, 1993.

Pinellas County Planning Department. *Pinellas County Historical Background*. Pinellas, FL: Pinellas County Planning Council, FL, 1986.

Starkey, Jay. *Things I Remember, 1899-1979*. Brooksville, FL: Southwest Florida Water Management District, 1980.

Stoughton, Gertrude K. *Tarpon Springs, Florida: The Early Years*. New Port Richey, FL: Privately printed, 1975.

Tebeau, Charlton, W. *A History of Florida*. Miami, FL: University of Miami Press, 1971.

White, Louise V. and Nora K. Smiley. *History of Key West*. St. Petersburg, FL: Great Outdoors Publishing Company, 1959.

Young, June Hurley. *Florida's Pinellas Peninsula*. St. Petersburg, FL: Southern Heritage Press, 1996.

MAPS

Coast Guard Chart No.177, Tampa Bay, Florida, 1879, corr. 1885.

Map of Hillsborough County, Florida, compiled from U.S. Land Office, U.S. Coast Survey and Special Surveys, Florida Land & Improvement Co., November, 1882.

Map of St. Petersburg and Vicinity included in Townships 31 and 32 South of Ranges 15,16, & 17 East, Florida. J.P. Titcomb, C.E., 1902.

Map of the Terminus of St. Petersburg & Gulf Ry. on Boca Ceiga Bay, Hillsborough County, Florida, 1905.

Street map of St. Petersburg, St. Petersburg Chamber of Commerce, 1925.

Periodicals, Articles and Newspapers

Dean, Claudette Renney. "Our Man on the Tightrope." *Gulfport Gabber*, December 31, 1992.

Kaczor, Bill. "Forgotten Industry Kept Alive." *Miami Herald*, March 12, 2000.

Lizotte, George, diary excerpt published in "Spotlight".

Pittman, Craig and Julie Hauserman. "Uprooting Fallen History." *St. Petersburg Times*, December 13, 1999.

"A Biographical Sketch of Mrs. Mary E. Brown, pioneer of Tampa and descendant of illustrious Italian ancestors." 1925 clipping, publication unknown.

"Making Hats from Palmetto Buds is Odd Hobby of Gulfport Woman," 1943? clipping, publication unknown.

Pasadena Progress, Volume I, Number 1 and Number 2; Volume III, Number 1

St. Petersburg Times, 1901-

St. Petersburg Independent 1907-

Old Pinellas Press, Vol. I Issue 2, 1992

Gulfport Tribune, selected articles

Gulfport Citizen, selected articles

Audio Tapes

Harold Anderson, 5/13/83

R.E. Bozeman interview with Helen Ross, 10/5/83, 6 sides

Sydney Brooks and her son Walter, 7/7/83

Jerome Girard interview with Helen Ross, 1/29/83, 4 sides

Wessie Gleaton and her son Jesse, 6/25/83

Walter Lange and J.D. Girard, 6/29/83

Marion Evans McCullough, 9/22/83

Cecil Slaughter, 7/7/83

Cecil Slaughter, 4/14/83, with Thompson C. Roberts, Jr., Flo Fussell, and John Sjustrom

Willis Irving Slaughter and his son Cecil, 10/21/84

Lorraine Gleaton Watson, undated

Nathan White, 8/17/83

Albertus Miller tape, transcribed excerpt

Video Tapes

Kimball interview with Catherine Hickman and Claudette R. Dean, 3/2/96

Unpublished Sources

Fuller, Walter P., letter to William S. Renney dated September 22, 1971.
Kautsky, F.H., "The First United Methodist Church of Gulfport: A History of the Church, Its People, Area, and Events", 2000.
The Diary of Albert Schludecker, 1910-1913.
Bertha Strauss Wells, "Some Joys of my Family History, 1868-1966".
Enrollment Records of the Gulfport Chapter of American War Mothers.
Historic Property Associates, Inc., Historic Buildings Survey of Gulfport, Florida, St. Augustine, 1992.
Piper Consulting, History of the Glen Oaks Cemetery Site, Planning Department, City of St. Petersburg, 1993.
Minutes of the Council of the Town of Gulfport, December 15, 1914 to December 18, 1917.
Municipal Court Log of the Town of Gulfport, June 15, 1912 to July 12, 1926.
Ordinances, Letters, Statements of the Town of Gulfport, 1910 – 1916.
Tax Rolls, Town of Gulfport, 1920 – Present

Index

A

B

C

D

E

F

G

H

I

J

K

L

M

W

Y